FROM
Da TO Yes

Understanding the
East Europeans

YALE RICHMOND

The InterAct Series

GEORGE W. RENWICK, Series Editor

FROM
Da TO Yes

Understanding the East Europeans

YALE RICHMOND

INTERCULTURAL PRESS, INC.

For information, contact:
Intercultural Press, Inc.
P.O. Box 700
Yarmouth, Maine 04096, USA

Book design and production by Patty J. Topel
Cover design and chapter graphic by Lois Leonard Stock

Printed in the United States of America

00 99 98 97 96 95   1 2 3 4 5 6

Library of Congress Cataloging-in-Publication Data
Richmond, Yale.
From Da to Yes : understanding the East Europeans / Yale Richmond.
p. cm. — (InterAct)
Includes bibliographical references and index.
ISBN 1-877864-30-7
1. Europe. Eastern—Description and travel. 2. Business travel—Europe, Eastern. I. Title. II. Series: InterAct series.
DJK19.R53 1995
940'.09717—dc20   95-3679
CIP

Table of Contents

vi

Nations have their own identities—spiritual, intellectual, cultural, and political—which they reveal to the world each day through their actions....

—Vaclav Havel

What is sometimes called the national "psyche" was formed by a variety of factors and circumstances through the centuries. An exploration of the nature of those factors, make it possible to gain some insight into the "spirit" of a nation.

—Oleksander Kulchytsky

When nations have existed for a long and glorious time, they cannot break with their past, whatever they do; they are influenced by it at the very moment when they work to destroy it; in the midst of the most glaring transformation, they remain fundamentally in character and destiny such as their history has formed them.

—François Guizot

To all Americans—advisers, volunteers, and other private citizens—who are giving so generously of their time to assist in the democratic transition in Eastern Europe.

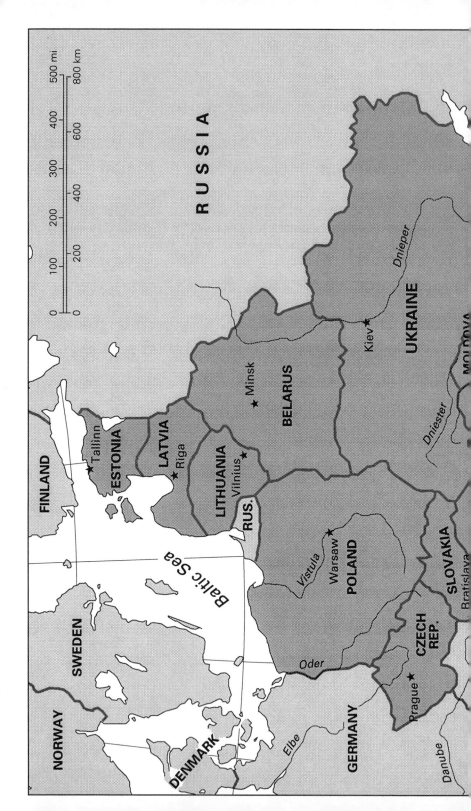

Preface

The factor of national character is often eschewed by historians and social thinkers in our times; nonetheless, it is wrong and foolish to ignore, let alone, deny, its existence.

—John Lukacs, *Budapest 1900*

With the collapse of communism, Americans are finding increased opportunities in Eastern Europe for joint ventures in business, cultural affairs, scholarly activities, science, and humanitarian and technical assistance. Other Americans are seeking ancestral roots in a part of Europe from which many millions can claim descent.

My purpose in writing this book is to provide a concise and readable introduction to the nations of Eastern Europe that lie between Western Europe and Russia so that readers may understand how these nations, in a part of the world little known and less understood in the United States, differ from each other and from Americans, and how to deal with them more effectively.

Unknown as Eastern Europe may be, most of the big wars over the centuries have begun there, and many of the minor ones as well. The Thirty Years War (1618-48) that devastated much of Europe began in the Czech lands. The centuries-long struggle between the Muslim Ottoman Turks and Christian Europe was fought in Eastern Europe, as were many battles of the Napoleonic Wars. Two Balkan wars in the early years of the twentieth century were a precursor to World War I, which began in Bosnia's Sarajevo with the assassination of Austrian Archduke Franz Ferdinand. World War II had its prelude in Czechoslovakia and its first battles in Poland. And in our time, Eastern Europe was the battleground for the Cold War between East and West.

More recently, Czechs and Slovaks have dissolved their union, albeit in a peaceful and civilized manner. To their south, however, Yugoslavia has been fragmented in violence, as Serbs, Croats, and Bosnians have slaughtered each other. Elsewhere in Eastern Europe, ethnic animosities simmer just below the surface and threaten the stability of several states. Clearly, it behooves all Americans to learn more about that part of Europe where ethnicity and national character arouse passions as intense today as in the past.

Some readers may question whether there is indeed such a thing as national character. It is not my intention to stereotype all members of a nation (although stereotypes can be useful indicators of national behavior), but rather to call attention to cultural differences between nations that have lived side by side on the European continent from time immemorial but nevertheless still have distinct lifestyles.

As former *Washington Post* correspondent Dusko Doder puts it:

> Countries, like individuals, usually cut an image of some kind. Out of thousands of elements certain general characteristics or special styles of life become associated with one country or another in a way that commands instant recognition.[1]

Who will deny that Russians differ from Poles, Poles from Czechs, Czechs from Slovaks, Hungarians from Romanians,

Bulgarians from Serbs, and Lithuanians from Latvians and Estonians? The characters of these nations have been shaped by geography, religion, and history. Such legacies are not intractable, but time is needed to overcome them. And in Eastern Europe that time will be lengthy because the histories of those nations go back more than a thousand years.

The book is based on my more than thirty years of day-to-day contact with the East Europeans, facilitating people-to-people exchanges in culture, education, and science during assignments with the Department of State, the U.S. Information Agency, the Commission on Security and Cooperation in Europe (U.S. Congress), and the National Endowment for Democracy.

People-to-people exchanges were long considered by government policymakers as marginal activities in East-West relations—a means of interaction that most Americans supported but also a window dressing that enabled heads of government to sign agreements at summit meetings. Real strength, they claimed, was in military force, nuclear missiles, and raw power.

But almost twenty years before Detente—the relaxation of tensions between the United States and the Soviet Union—the West had been practicing detente in Eastern Europe. Communist governments there had earlier accepted the idea that states with different ideologies and politics could nevertheless cooperate in such areas as culture, education, and science, and that people-to-people exchanges could be a useful adjunct to traditional diplomacy. It began in Poland and Yugoslavia in the 1950s, and then in Romania, before it was accepted by most of the other states of the region.

That approach, eventually accepted by the Soviet Union as well, facilitated an expansion of contacts between the peoples of East and West that bridged the Iron Curtain. The objective was mutual understanding—to learn more about other countries and their people. But, in the process, the peoples of Eastern Europe and the Soviet Union began to understand their own countries better and to question what they were being told in their government-controlled media. The more they learned about life in the West, the more they questioned what they were told at home. The human contacts established by those exchanges helped to bring about the political transformations of the 1980s. The costs of the exchanges were small, but the rewards great.

Now that barriers to contacts with all nations of Eastern Europe have fallen, opportunities for cross-cultural communication are far greater than ever before. Still remaining, however, is the challenge of mutual understanding, as the East Europeans move from *Da*—subservience to the East—to "Yes"—cooperation with the West.

In the spelling of names and words from East European languages, the diacritical marks that give different phonetic values to the marked characters have been eliminated (with one exception—the Polish ó, pronounced "oo"). This may cause some discomfort to readers who are familiar with those languages but should not present problems for those who are not. Spellings of place and proper names are those generally used by the media except for Ukraine and Belarus where place names are given in Ukrainian and Belarusian for the most part, rather than Russian, such as *Kyiv* for Kiev and *Miensk* for Minsk.

I hope that readers will enjoy reading this book as much as I enjoyed writing it and that it will help to facilitate their visits to Eastern Europe and make their stays there more productive. I had to learn the hard way, and it took me thirty years.

Yale Richmond
Washington, D.C.

---

[1] Dusko Doder, *The Yugoslavs* (New York: Random House, 1978), 18.

Acknowledgments

Many, many people have contributed material for this book—former Foreign Service colleagues, American volunteers in Eastern Europe, businesspeople, scholars, East Europeans, and Americans of East European descent who are familiar with the languages and cultures of their ancestral homelands. They include, among others, Monika Agopsowicz, Mary Catherine Andrews, Nicholas G. Andrews, Joseph Arciuch, Vaclav Aschenbrenner, Leonard J. Baldyga, Arthur A. Bardos, Harry Barnes Jr., Rudolf G. Barta, Faith Beane, Asta Bedonis, Elez Biberaj, Andrew Bihun, Martha Bohachevsky-Chomiak, Adele Bohmerova, Rodica C. Botoman, Huba Bruckner, Kyra A. Buczko, Stephen Buff, Janusz Bugajski, Brian E. Carlson, Holly Cartner, Terrence F. Catherman, Thomas M. Claflin, Karen Clark, Tibor Csipan, Andrzej Dakowski, Richard T. Davies, John Dalton, David P. Daniel, Orest Deychakiwsky, Nadia Diuk, Maiga Dzervite, Milan Erban, Cheryl Fackler-Hug, John Fay, Zvi Feine, Aurelius Fernandez, Jeff Ferry, Michael Flack, Roy and Ann Freed, Bohdan A. Futey, Robert E. Gordon, A. K. Grina, Paul Hacker, Oleg Havrylyshyn, Christopher Hill, Nora Hlozekova, Stanley W. Hosie, Dennis P. Hupchik, Merit Ilja, Catherine Imholz, Micaela Iovine, Kempton B. Jenkins, Ray Johns, Joseph V. Julian, Vladimir M. Kabes, Philip M. Kaiser, George Kamen, John Karch, James Kenney, Vitaut and Alice Kipel, Mary E. Kirk, Gail

xvii

Kligman, Linas Kojelis, Vilija Jonkaityte, George J. Kovtun, Alan Kulakow, Irena Lasota, Ernest H. Latham, Jerry W. Leach, Leon G. Leiberg, Jeff Levine, Ann G. Lien, Georgene B. Lovecky, John Lukacs, Charles T. Magee, Stephen McLaughlin, Gifford D. Malone, Leonid Murog, Brian C. Murphy, Victor Nakas, James and Amy Osbsorn, Kathy Packer, Predrag Paul Pajic, Marta M. Pereyma, Orysia Pylyshenko, Rodger Potocki, Randall R. Rader, Richard Rahn, Veljko J. Rasevic, Edward Rakosh, Nestor Ratesh, Maire Reichenau, Stefanie Rubin, Nikolai E. Rudensky, Halina Russak, Edward Salazar, Irwin T. Sanders, Ivan Sanders, John D. Scanlan, Janet Sperber Schwartz, Adam Seligman, William Sheehan, John W. Shirley, Vinca Showalter, Jay S. Siegel, Ann M. Sigmund, Frantisek and Larisa Silnicky, Joseph G. Simanis, Elehie N. Skoczylas, Zdenek J. Slouka, Laura Szkrybalo, Martin Sletzinger, Orest Subtelny, David H. Swartz, Julia Stefanova, Vladimir Tismaneanu, Brian Toohey, Ronald D. Utt, Jaroslav J. Verner, Gabor Peter Vermes, Diane Bielauskas Vidutis, George and Helen Viksnins, Mark Warschauer, Thomas Wentworth, William Whitman, Roger Whittaker, Naomi Woronov, Kay Yankosky, Bohdan Yasinsky, Ferenc Zsigo, and Martins Zvaners.

Also helpful were officials of the State Department, the U.S. Information Agency, the Department of Commerce, the U.S. Peace Corps, and the Library of Congress. To those who took the time to review individual chapters and make helpful suggestions, I owe special thanks.

The Woodrow Wilson Center of the Smithsonian Institution provided the opportunity to hear the views of many visitors from Eastern Europe, and the weekly *RFE/RL Research Report* provided much of the data and statistics used.

The editors of the Intercultural Press, David S. Hoopes in particular, provided thoughtful guidance and constructive criticism as well as an eagle eye for my manuscript.

To Paul A. Goble, I am indebted for the story of how the Lenin statues were removed in the Baltic states. Richard T.

Davies provided the anecdote about alcoholic fault lines. Larisa Silnicky inspired the title.

The views expressed are, of course, my own but I believe they are shared by most informed observers of the East European scene.

Yale Richmond

Introduction:
Encountering East Europeans

The problems of Central and Eastern Europe are prover-
bially unintelligible in the West, because various races
live there in an old mosaic pattern, in medieval disre-
gard of the territorial conventions which, since the days
of the Renaissance, have prevailed in the West.

—Elizabeth Wiskemann, *Czechs and Germans*

When I first arrived in Poland in 1958 to take up an assign-
ment as cultural attaché at the American Embassy, I called
on the embassy's political counselor to seek advice on how far
I could go in accomplishing my mission—to expand cultural
exchanges between Poland and the United States. Two years
earlier, Poland had undergone a revolution which ousted a
Stalinist regime and replaced it with a government of national communism. The new government wanted to reestablish Poland's traditional contacts with the West but was
apprehensive lest it go too far and antagonize its Soviet
patron.

"You can do almost anything you wish here," my embassy
colleague advised, "as long as those who run this country
believe that you really like Poland and its people."

1

That advice still stands, in all the other countries of Eastern Europe as well as in Poland. Small nations with long histories and old cultures, they respond readily to foreigners who know something of their history, speak a few words of their language, and show an interest in their people. And they all seek recognition in a part of the world where, as Columbia University historian Istvan Deak explains, "...all peoples tend to feel unrecognized, unrewarded, and unloved."[1]

Europeans All

> No one can be a European in the abstract. It is membership of one of the nations living in Europe and having one's roots in one of the national cultures whose diversity and richness make up the common European heritage, that makes one a European. European culture is not merely the mechanical sum of those cultures nor some sort of common denominator, but a living organism growing in time through the fertile interaction of its national elements.
>
> —Jerzy Turowicz, *Karol Wojtyla*

Some call it Eastern Europe; others, Central Europe; and still others who seek more geographic precision, Central and Eastern Europe. The choice here, for reasons of simplicity as well as convenience, will be Eastern Europe. But whatever it is called, these terms refer to the heartland of the European continent, home to the many nations that live between Western Europe and Russia.

What they do not want to be called is "postcommunist" or "former members of the Warsaw Pact." As Czech President Vaclav Havel remonstrates:

> From the Czech Republic to Kazakhstan we are, and will no doubt remain for some time, "post-communist countries" and "former members of the former Warsaw Pact." I am guilty of having used these expressions myself, but I must admit an increasing aversion to them. After all, we did not go through

the trouble of liquidating the Warsaw Pact only to have it remain—even with a prefix—forever sewn to our coats....(Not long ago I observed, somewhat undiplomatically, that we do not refer to the United States as a "former British colony.")[2]

Historically and culturally a part of Europe, those nations in our time have been isolated from the West by half a century of war and communist rule, an Iron Curtain, and their forced inclusion (Albania and Yugoslavia excepted) in what was known as the "Soviet bloc." But with the breakup of the Soviet Union and the collapse of communism, Europe is no longer divided, and the nations of the East are now returning to a Europe from which they were arbitrarily separated. As noted in the preface, *Da*—subservience to the East—has become "Yes"—cooperation with the West.

Central to the region are the peoples of Poland, the Czech and Slovak republics, Hungary, Romania, and Bulgaria. To the east, other nations newly independent of Russian rule— Estonia, Latvia, Lithuania, Belarus, Ukraine, and Moldova— also reassert historic and cultural claims to be seen as European. To the south live the peoples of the former Yugoslavia which in the past proudly proclaimed its independence and sought neutrality and nonalignment in the Cold War between East and West. That Yugoslavia, however, has disintegrated, a victim of internecine warfare that has highlighted, all too tragically, the cultural differences that can exist between peoples with a common ethnic heritage. Even little Albania, fiercely independent and disdaining membership in any bloc, has ended its self-imposed isolation and has now returned to Europe.

Who are these peoples with exotic languages and unpronounceable names, from whom so many Americans are descended? They are predominantly Slavic, but they share their East European space with several non-Slavic nations including, among others, Hungarians, Romanians, Moldovans, Albanians, Balts, and Gypsies. Together, they number nearly

4

two hundred million, more than three-fourths the population
of the United States but packed into an area less than one-
fourth its size. Although neighbors in contiguous states, they
all have their own languages, cultures, and traditions, as well
as historic rivalries and, in some cases, long-lasting enmities.

No "End of History"

...we will find a long-forgotten history coming back to haunt
us, a history full of thousands of economic, social, ethical,
ethnic, territorial, cultural, and political problems that remained latent and unnoticed under the surface of totalitarian
boredom.

—Vaclav Havel

It was once said of Zbigniew Brzezinski, President Carter's
national security adviser, that when he opened his mouth,
900 years of Polish history came rolling out.[3] Mr. Brzezinski,
who was born in Warsaw, would certainly point out that
Poland has more than a thousand years of history, but the
anecdote does point out the importance of history in Eastern
Europe. Contrary to the predictions of one pundit, the collapse of communism has not led to an end of history.

East Europeans have a sharp sense of history, and foreign
visitors who do not know something of that history will be
found wanting. History, they tell us, is something that Americans read in school texts, while East European have lived it.
Dates and events long past will be cited in conversations with
Americans not accustomed to thinking in historical perspectives. Visitors to the region will find it prudent to learn
something of that history and how it has shaped the characters of the peoples they will be encountering.

Susan Sontag, for example, when she visited Poland in
1980 with a group of American writers, became the "darling"
of the delegation because she had done her homework and
immersed herself in Polish history, culture, and literature

before winging to Warsaw. She could talk with Poles on their own terms.

In these lands, great states have risen and fallen. Nations have known sovereignty and subjugation, at times thriving and at other times suffering. Fought over and partitioned, they have been ruled by Tatar-Mongols, Germans, Swedes, Russians, Austrians, and Turks. And over the centuries these lands were a battleground between Christianity and Islam for control of Europe.

In 1683, the Muslim Ottoman Turks marched to the very gates of Vienna before their advance was turned back by Christian armies led by a Polish king, Jan Sobieski. In this century Eastern Europe has been a battleground in two world wars and the Cold War. And as these pages were being written, Christians and Muslims were once more literally at each other's throats, this time in Bosnia.

American historiography in the past has neglected Eastern Europe, emphasizing instead relations with Western Europe. This is understandable because, as Polish historian Oscar Halecki has pointed out, the nations of Eastern Europe disappeared from the map at the same time the United States was being formed.[4]

The United States, however, from its early years has played a role in the region. The American experience served as inspiration for many of the independence movements in Eastern Europe. From those lands, waves of immigrants came to our shores, contributing much to our economic, cultural, and political life. Under the leadership of Woodrow Wilson the United States was instrumental in establishing several of these nation-states and shares some responsibility for the patchwork borders that were delineated between them. Wilson himself, however, wondered whether he "had taken on too much territory," noting that "...these ancient wrongs, these present unhappinesses, are not to be remedied in a day or with a wave of the hand. What I seem to see—I hope I am wrong—is a tragedy of disappointment."[5]

In the 1990s, the nations of the region again look to the United States for political and economic models. Americans are working as advisers and partners in business, government, academia, and science. Private voluntary organizations are providing much-needed humanitarian and technical assistance, and Americans are returning to the region in search of their roots. They should know something of the history of the nations they will be visiting.

As Michael Shafir, a scholar of Eastern Europe, replied when asked if we are witnessing today a return of history, "Eastern Europe is not going back to itself; it has always been itself."[6]

Friends First...

> It is good to have friends, even in Hell.
>
> —Bulgarian proverb

East Europeans have picked up many Americanisms. They dress informally and wear blue jeans; they eat hamburgers and pizza, and drink Coke and Pepsi; they listen to rock music and jazz; and they watch American TV programs. But beneath the facade of fads and pop culture are many aspects of their lives that may seem strange to Americans. One of them is the networking of family and friends.

Family and friends are a heritage of an older clan society where extended families shared a common existence in agriculture. During the communist years, family and friends became even more important because no one else could be trusted. Today, families and friends are still important, and obligations toward them take precedence over other relationships. East European hosts will inquire about the families of visitors, and Americans should bring family photos to show them.

Rather than going through official channels to get something done, East Europeans will first network their families, friends, and personal contacts who owe them a favor. Do a favor for someone and receive a favor in return. Such friendships, as well as business and professional relationships, are best established over a dinner table and bonded with alcohol. Once a good personal relationship has been established, based on friendship and trust, the job is half done and success is assured.

Transactions between people are made on a personal basis after credibility and trust have been established. That requires time and explains why it takes weeks, months, and sometimes years to get things done, and leads to the "familiar face syndrome."

The familiar face has a built-in advantage in Eastern Europe. American organizations hoping to establish ongoing programs and to achieve results that will stand the test of time should be aware that one-time visits of a few days will be of limited value unless there is follow-up. And, to build trust and confidence, the follow-up visits should be by the same person.

Friendship in Eastern Europe is not to be taken lightly. Americans are accustomed to meeting someone and in the next breath describing that person as a friend. In Eastern Europe, such a newly met person would be called an acquaintance rather than a friend, and there are indeed different words for the two in their languages. Friendships take longer to develop and are made only after some bonding event has occurred. At that point, the two persons are on a first-name basis and will address each other with the equivalent of the Old English "thou" or the French "tu."

Americans are also accustomed to using first names or nicknames in addressing persons they have just met or are doing business with. East Europeans may be uncomfortable with such informality, and it is best to let them take the initiative for first-name familiarity.

...and Contacts Second

After friends come contacts, what Americans call "networking." Eastern Europe is run by networks of personal contacts. Knowing the right people can mean the difference between success and failure, and sometimes even doing the impossible. But more important than merely knowing the right people is cultivating those contacts over a period of time through favors, smiles, drinks and food, and gifts.

Gifts open doors, including those in hotels. One frequent visitor to Eastern Europe reports that he can always get a room at his favorite hotel, no matter how full it may be, because he sends Christmas gifts to the staff each year, and they remember him.

The payoff may not come immediately, but come it will some time in the future when it is most needed. Be aware, though, that one favor requires another, and those East Europeans who do a favor for a visiting American will expect one in return, a form of indebtedness.

There may be times when a visitor cannot grant the favor requested and must say no. Not to worry. A "no" need not end the relationship, and the indebtedness will be carried over for another day.

Follow the Facilitator

First-time visitors to Eastern European countries should hire a facilitator—someone on the ground who speaks the language, knows who is who, is at home with customs of the country, speaks English, and who also knows the United States and what Americans want. A few years ago it might have been difficult in many countries to find such a person but today, with exchanges proliferating, there are many students and young professionals who meet these requirements, and the cost in dollars is low. To find such people, check with visitors who have been there before you.

A good facilitator will help to organize your schedule, advise whom to see and not to see, have a feel for the politics and "connections" that may be involved, and can double as an interpreter if necessary. In scheduling appointments, aim high—ask for the director of an institute or enterprise, or the person in charge. In countrywide activities, try to meet with someone on the staff of the president or prime minister. The higher the better.

Customs of the Countries

In every proverb there is a grain of truth.

—Slavic proverb

American visitors may regard as quaint and old-fashioned many of the practices, traditions, and proverbs which, at one time, were common to all of Europe and may still be so in some West European countries. But these practices stand out in countries that have been isolated from the West for fifty years, where the pace of life is slower, and things are more traditional. And people are very polite; basic courtesies are routine.

Writing about Poles, although the same could be said, more or less, for all East Europeans, Laura Klos-Sokol writes:

A Polish man who doesn't extend the basic gentlemanly courtesies is thought *prymityw* (primitive), *zle wychowany* (badly brought up) or *cham* (a clod or a boor). Foreign men who don't are, well, foreign.[7]

Handshaking is obligatory both on arrival and departure. The visitor shakes hands with more senior and older people first, and it may take some quick judgment to determine who outranks whom. In greeting a woman, however, a man waits for her to offer her hand. Close friends and relatives, both male and female, greet each other with embraces and often kisses on both cheeks, and sometimes on the lips as well. Visitors introduce themselves by giving their first and family names but not the titles "Mr.," "Ms.," or "Mrs."

Elders are deferred to. In many cultures they speak first and start to eat before others. The older person also takes the initiative in changing from the formal to the informal mode of address.

Calling cards are exchanged liberally in business and professional encounters as well as on social occasions. They should include academic degrees and titles, as appropriate, but be careful about abbreviations which may not be understood everywhere (such as "Int'l" for "International"). Titles are also used in addressing people—"Doctor," "Professor," "Engineer," etc. Those who expect to work for some time in one country may wish to print their calling cards double-sided—English on one side and the local language on the other.

Language is often indirect and imprecise, and purposely so. Watch for allusions and hidden meanings, and listen to what is not said as well as what is said. Understatement is usually the rule. East Europeans consider it impolite to say no directly, and in response to a question Americans may be told "it is still under study," or "we'll have to see," or "we'll try." Some sensitivity will be required to determine whether such responses are a polite no or a cautious maybe.

Americans will find themselves the center of attention when they visit factories, schools, government offices, and other institutions. Custom calls for the welcome mat to be rolled out and generous hospitality to be extended. This may include a ceremony at the entrance, a formal meeting cum briefing and refreshments with the top brass, a tour of the facility, a larger meeting with workers or students, and a long lunch that is sometimes more like a dinner. These events will be more formal than Americans are accustomed to. Speeches will be made and gifts presented. As I have learned on many such occasions, it is prudent for the visitor to have ready some prepared remarks as well as some American souvenirs for presentation. If your outercoat does not have a loop for hanging, be sure to have one sewn in before going to Eastern Europe. Checking of coats is customary in theaters and many public buildings, and if yours does not have a loop you will be berated by the grandmothers who do the checking. Bear in mind that whistling after a public performance is a sign of disapproval in European countries, not approval as in the United States.

Home Hospitality

> You must really eat, you know. They will think you dislike their food if you do not. It is our Slav custom to give our guests too much to eat, as a kind of boastfulness, and of course out of goodwill, and the guests show how strong they are by eating it.
> —Rebecca West, *Black Lamb and Grey Falcon*

Hospitality in Eastern Europe is legendary. When invited to a home, guests should be prepared to eat and drink, and, as Rebecca West wrote in 1941 quoting a Serbian friend, the eating is obligatory. Guests should also expect to be seated; the stand-up cocktail party with its finger food is alien.

The midday meal is the big meal of the day, complete with soup and the ever present bread, and the evening meal is more like a cold supper. Vegetarians, once a rarity in a part of the world where meat is the preferred dish, are now becoming more common. One Peace Corps volunteer, however, reports that she rarely received dinner invitations because her hosts in the village where she worked did not know what dishes to prepare for her.

Meals can last for hours, with animated conversation, jokes, music, and singing, and guests are expected to join in. Have a few American songs ready to render. Dining out, a special treat for East Europeans, can also be lengthy and last the entire evening. In restaurants, tables may be shared with other people but permission should be requested before joining other diners. It is considered rude to eat or drink while listening to someone speak. Callers are always offered something to drink, even on short visits—coffee, tea, juice, soft drinks, or something stronger. Teetotalers can politely decline alcohol and request a nonalcoholic beverage, but it is impolite to refuse a drink. If there are no religious or medical prohibitions, I recommend that guests sample the local wines and liqueurs, especially the regional drinks and home brews which differ from country to country and within countries. The hosts will be pleased, and the drinks savored.

When invited to a home, guests always bring gifts. Food and alcoholic beverages are appreciated, and flowers are always appropriate. Odd numbers only though, and be careful about red roses, which are considered a sign of affection. A husband will not appreciate a male guest who brings red roses for the lady of his house. If there are children in the home, small toys or candy will be welcomed.

In many homes it is customary to remove shoes when entering from a dirty street, especially in winter, and guests may be offered slippers. Foreign guests may be told that it is not necessary to remove their shoes, but hosts will welcome it if they do.

Alcoholic Fault Lines

> Without *rakiya* [brandy], there is no conversation.
>
> —Montenegrin proverb

Eastern Europe, it is commonly said, lies athwart several fault lines. Religious fault lines separate Roman Catholics from Orthodox Christians, and Christians from Muslims. Political fault lines mark the limits of empires—Austro-Hungarian,

Russian, and Ottoman Turk. And then there are the alcoholic fault lines. To the north and west of the Tatras mountain system lies the vodka zone, encompassing Poland, the Baltic states, Belarus, and Ukraine. South of the Tatras, in more temperate climates, lies the fruit brandy zone—the *konyak* of Slovakia, *barack* (pronounced "baratsk") of Hungary, *tsuica* (pronounced "tsooi-kah") of Romania, and the *slivovitsa* of the South Slavs. Another fault line separates the beer drinkers of the Czech lands, Poland, and the Baltic states from the wine drinkers of the nations to their south and east—Slovakia, Hungary, Romania, Bulgaria, and the former Yugoslavia.

Alcohol is a component of culture in Eastern Europe that is not easily avoided. A vital lubricant of social encounters and a necessary ingredient of social life, it is ever present. A U.S. member of an international team monitoring elections in Yugoslavia has related how election officials at each polling place visited would produce a bottle of home brew which they insisted on sharing with their foreign guests. This was somewhat shocking for the American election monitors who were not accustomed to mixing booze with ballots.

Toasting is spirited and goes with the spirits. It also becomes more spirited the further east you go. Visitors should have a few toasts ready in advance, for they surely will be needed. Not the laconic "cheers" or "bottoms up" of Americans but rather a short speech to the health of the host and his family, appreciation for their hospitality, the success of whatever joint endeavor may be embarked upon, and the benefits of the cooperation to future generations. Give vent to your emotions and let your imagination soar. The more emotion, the better the toast. Make eye contact with the people being toasted, and clink glasses before drinking.

Since alcohol is difficult to avoid, it should at least be enjoyed. But know your limits. Beware of the sweet-tasting fruit brandies which can cause a headache and more when drunk to excess. And be careful with the home brews that can be very potent and will not bear labels indicating their alcoholic content.

By tradition, toasts are not made with nonalcoholic drinks or water. However, American teetotalers have been known to raise their glasses in a toast, and East Europeans will accept this as another strange custom of their visitors from across the Atlantic.

Visitors determined to avoid alcohol can plead that they are driving, or they can bring along a medication container with a label, "Do not drink alcoholic beverages when taking this medication." It will help to convince hosts that you should not drink. And those who want to limit their intake should remember that an empty glass is promptly refilled. Protect yourself by not draining your glass.

A Tangle of Tongues

As long as the language lives, the nation is not dead.

—Czech proverb

In 1986, a group of twenty-eight Belarusian intellectuals sent a petition to Mikhail Gorbachev detailing the forced decline in use of the Belarusian language and calling for measures to improve the culture, education, and language of their nation. In an introduction to the petition the Belarusians wrote:

Language is the soul of a nation, the supreme manifestation of its true spiritual life. A nation lives and flourishes in history while its language lives. With the decline of the language, culture withers and atrophies, the nation ceases to exist as a historical organism....[8]

The petition was not well received in Moscow, and each of the signatories paid a penalty of harassment, demotion, or job loss. Their petition, however, began a movement for the rebirth of the Belarusian nation, which was in danger of extinction. It also pointed up the importance of language to all nations of the region.

Eastern Europe is an inlay of languages, the bond that binds people together and has kept each nation distinct from others throughout the centuries. Although these are languages that we Americans do not study in school, those who expect to spend some time among these nations should make an attempt to learn at least the rudiments of elementary conversation. Those, however, who do not speak the local language need not feel tongue-tied.

English, the language of choice, is becoming the lingua franca of Eastern Europe, the language Balts use to talk with Bosnians. In most countries, English has become the second language for the younger generation, who wear it on their T-shirts and listen to it in their popular songs. Those under thirty are likely to have studied English in school, as have professionals who need it in their work—scholars, scientists, medical doctors, teachers, businesspeople, government officials, and media personnel. Older people are more likely to know German or French. And all of them will have studied Russian, although in most countries they are reluctant to speak it. Interpreters, when necessary, are readily available.

Interpreters, however, should be used with caution. Their quality can vary greatly, and some ideas and expressions in English simply do not exist in other languages. When using an interpreter, speak slowly, avoid complicated words, repeat important ideas in a slightly different fashion to make sure you are getting through, and look at the person being addressed, not the interpreter. Even when an interpreter speaks English well, you may not be understood and your respondent will be too polite or embarrassed to tell you so, as an American ambassador in Prague once learned.

During a call on the minister of foreign affairs, the ambassador raised a subject which the minister was not prepared to discuss officially at the time, and he so informed the ambassador. "Well," replied the ambassador, "we'll have to discuss that over a beer some time." Confusion ensued on the other side of the table, and the Czechs huddled in conference trying to fathom what the ambassador had meant. A junior official hurriedly left the room, and a few minutes later a waiter entered with glasses of good pilsener beer to slake the ambassador's presumed thirst.

In Slavic languages several words may be used in place of one English word, and those words can all have different meanings. And some grammatical constructions may be confusing to Americans in translation, such as the use of reflexive verbs. More than one American has been puzzled by being asked, "How do you feel yourself?"

The language of public discourse, moreover, has been corrupted by decades of communist rule which altered the meaning of words and introduced alien expressions which became part of the local languages. As Hungarian social scientist Agnes Heller explains:

> We use words and know the words are lying. Then we get so accustomed to these lying words that we become entwined with them. And if someone else speaks out against these words, then you defend the words which you know to be lies. Since you can no longer speak any other language, you forget that you can use your own head for thinking.[9]

Be sure that your words are understood and taken seriously. In some countries, as the United States learned in Bosnia, people do not always mean what they say, and promises should be taken with a grain of salt. If there are penalties involved in failing to fulfill an agreement or contract, make certain that the consequences are fully understood and appreciated. And don't make promises that can't be kept.

Capital Cities

Americans know that New York is not the United States, nor is Washington, D.C. But capital cities in Eastern Europe do represent their nations, much more so than any single American city could. East European capitals are centers of government, finance, culture, the media, and often industry as well. It's as if, for Americans, all their major cities were merged into one—New York, Chicago, Detroit, Los Angeles (and Hollywood), San Francisco, and Washington, D.C., as well as Cambridge and Berkeley.

In Eastern Europe the action is in Warsaw, Prague, Budapest, Kyiv, Sofia, and other capitals. These are the cities of the people who matter, those who make decisions that count and set the standards for the rest of the country. Hungary is the best example, where two million people—20 percent of the country's population—reside in Budapest.

Because of this capital-city concentration, great differences exist between capital cities and the provinces, and between urban and rural areas. City inhabitants are more urbane, cosmopolitan, middle class, up-to-date, and European. Rural inhabitants are more provincial and more likely to represent the traditional cultures of their nations. An American sociologist, who in 1994 returned to the Galician countryside of Ukraine that she had left as a child, remarked how little the villages had changed. The peasants spoke, dressed, behaved, and walked the streets much as they had fifty years ago.

Visitors trying to find their way around those capital cities today may have some difficulty locating street addresses because many street names have been changed since the collapse of communism. Marx, Lenin, and other communist icons are out, replaced by names from the precommunist years. Make sure your city map is up-to-date.

When you ask for instructions on how to get to a particular address, get all the details. East Europeans are casual about giving such instructions, assuming that visitors know more than they actually do about the locations they are seeking.

A Man's World

...there are so many poets among women in my land.
The mute whose speech is suddenly restored
will rend the air with a moan or a shout—
centuries of silence crying to come out.

—Blaga Dimitrova,
"The Women Who Are Poets in My Land"

Poetess Blaga Dimitrova was vice president in the first democratic Bulgarian government after the fall of the communist regime. In her poem she predicts restored speech to

...the cruel silences:
the girl grown mute in wedlock,
so as not to talk back;
and the bride sworn in her home
to be dumb as a doornail all her life,
and not bother her mother-in-law;
the lonely schoolteachers in every little town,
pale-lipped, home-bound.[10]

Eastern Europe is still very much a man's world. Women are flattered to excess, have their hands kissed, are presented with flowers, and are given other deferential treatment, but traditional attitudes toward the female sex still prevail. Women attempting to work professionally must prove themselves before they are accepted as equals. Feminism, moreover, is in its early stages and does not have much popular support. It is a nonissue for most East European women, who do not comprehend the passions it arouses in the United States and some countries of Western Europe.

Women and men in communist states were equal under the law, not because their leaders believed in equality but because gender equality meant a larger labor supply for industrialization. To prove their equality, writes Croat author Slavenka Drakulic, women had to work like men—on construction sites, in mines, in fields, and in factories—but they were far removed from the seats of political power and carried the biggest burden of everyday life. Even when women participated in the revolutions that overturned communism, they were less active and less visible in the aftermath of those revolutions. After the revolutions, writes Drakulic,

>...women still didn't have time to be involved; they still distrusted politics. At the same time, they deluded themselves that the new democracies would give them the opportunity to stay home and rest for a while. There was something else too: somebody had to take responsibility for finding food and cooking meals, a task made no easier—indeed, in some countries made more difficult—by the political changeover.[11]

Women in Eastern Europe do, however, have equal access to higher education and are found in all professions and occupations but usually in secondary and mid- or low-level positions. There are exceptions, to be sure—Prime Minister Suchocka in Poland and Deputy Prime Minister Schmoegnerova in Slovakia—but leadership positions are filled mostly by men.

Conservative political parties throughout the region are calling for a return of women to their traditional roles of childbearing and homemaking. Given that choice, many women would gladly return to those traditional roles, for most of them have filled two jobs, one at the workplace and the other at home, both equally demanding. In Poland, according to a recent survey, 60 percent of women believe the ideal family situation is to have the woman at home cooking, cleaning, and bringing up children.[12] In Czechoslovakia, said a report given by Ludmila Venerova at a United Nations regional seminar on the status of women, "A professional career does not rank supreme in the scale of values of Czechoslovak women." In Romania, Mariana Celac stated at the same seminar, "...women [now] see staying home as 'fashionable, new and progressive.' "[13]

Most women work not for professional fulfillment but for financial need. Moreover, in the transition from a state-controlled economy to a market economy, women's liberation is considered a mixed blessing; as budgets are tightened, gains in women's status in society have been offset by losses in social services provided by the state.

The job choice for women today is being made by the economy. In the downsizing of industrial enterprises, women are the first to be fired. Female unemployment, as a consequence, is much higher than male. By necessity, therefore, many women are again becoming full-time homemakers. In the absence of dependable birth control devices, abortion is the most common form of birth control, and in many countries the number of induced abortions equals—and in some cases exceeds—the number of live births.

Despite these handicaps, many women have achieved prominence, particularly among the intelligentsia—the informed and committed class that has been in the forefront of change. Women are recognized throughout Eastern Europe for their roles in revolutions, dissident movements, and the struggle for human rights where women and men have fought side by side.

As Eva Hoffman points out with regard to Poland, "...in the elusive realm of cultural values there seems to be less of a division between 'male' and 'female' virtues here—and female valor, intelligence, and strength of personality are as highly prized as the male versions."[14]

One final caveat. In Eastern Europe women do not go into bars alone.

Environmental Degradation

An American economist, when asked what advice he would give travelers to Eastern Europe, replied without hesitation, "Don't drink the water." Water drinking is not traditional in that part of the world, and in many countries today it can be downright dangerous.

Untreated sewage is dumped into rivers in some countries, and water supplies are polluted; and where the water source is safe, it can be polluted by faulty pipes. Tap water and unpasteurized milk are best avoided. Equally dangerous, especially for children, is the pollution from industrial chemicals that cannot be filtered from water and food supplies. What to do? Bottled water and soft drinks, both domestic and imported, are available in hotels and stores. Tap water should be boiled.

In the rush to industrialize, communist governments neglected environmental protection and public health considerations. Soil is contaminated, air is foul, and health statistics are shocking. Infant mortality is rising, and longevity is falling. In the former Czechoslovakia, the most developed East European state, longevity is two to three years lower than in Western Europe. Hungary and Poland have the highest heart disease death rates in Europe. In Belarus and Ukraine, the medical fallout from the Chernobyl nuclear disaster will be seen for generations to come.

Fallout from another cloud—tobacco smoke—is also hovering over Eastern Europe, and there is almost no way to avoid it. East Europeans smoke more heavily than Americans, and smokefree areas are few and far between. In Bosnia, writes *New York Times* correspondent Chuck Sudetic, "...anyone who proposed, or God forbid, tried to enforce a smoking ban in restaurants, offices or anywhere else would surely find himself gazing down the wrong end of a gun, to the glee of everyone present."[15]

The Communist Past

The recent revolutions in Central and Eastern Europe have not eliminated the East of which I speak, which is permanently set in the soul of my generation now coming into power.
    —Andrei Codrescu, *The Disappearance of the Outside*

Progress in casting off the communist past varies from country to country, but many of the attitudes shaped by forty-five years of communist rule still prevail. Moreover, in many countries the transition from authoritarian to democratic government and from central planning to market economies has not been smooth, and the outcome is still uncertain. The slogans of building socialism have been replaced by those of building democracy, and the buzzwords of the transition—democracy, pluralism, civil society, freedom of choice, tolerance, human rights—are heard everywhere but are poorly understood.

Freedom of choice presents problems for people accustomed to being told what to do. Largely lacking are open debate, pluralism, and respect for the positions of political opponents. The intrusion of government in the lives of people is pervasive. Government officials are unaccustomed to criticism by the media. A legal system that recognizes private property is not everywhere in place, and when new laws are passed there is often no mechanism for enforcement.

The element of risk in business is poorly understood. Most entrepreneurs want a sure thing and a quick profit. Success in business, moreover, is regarded by the popular cultures in some countries as unethical. With the exception of the Czech Republic, the lack of a democratic tradition handicaps the transition to democracy.

The communist leaders who ruled these states are gone now, replaced in some states by dedicated democrats, and in others by former communists and neocommunists. In all countries, however, the legacy of communism continues in the attitudes of the people.

As Polish writer Ryszard Kapuscinski explains:

> The problem is that communism has not only taken root in the institutions that have remained behind it, but that it has formed the attitudes of the people, continues to influence their behavior and habits, and determines their scale of values and way of thinking.[16]

Put another way, it is not too difficult to change the ideology from communism to democracy but it is much more difficult to change the mentality of a people. As Croat writer Slavenka Drakulic defines it:

> Just how many "iron curtains" still exist? What are they made of? Sometimes it seems to me they are made of a material stronger than iron itself: our memories.[17]

Those memories include a distrust of institutions of civil society—political parties, parliaments, trade unions, the media, and the judicial system—institutions that were coopted by the communist regimes. Courts are seen as places of punishment, not places to seek justice, since most court cases result in convictions. Moreover, there is a belief that every problem has one correct solution, and all that is needed is to find the right experts to discover those solutions—let the experts run the government and the economy. As Eastern Europe moves from a command economy to a market economy, there is also a distrust of private enterprise or *biznes*, as it is called.

The *"Biznes"* Presence

> Bargaining is a repulsive habit; compromise is one of the highest human virtues—the difference between the two being that the first is practiced on the Continent, the latter in Great Britain.
>
> —George Mikes, *How to Be an Alien*

"Who bargains, buys," a Montenegrin maxim admonishes. Bargaining over price is the accepted way of doing business in Eastern Europe. The asking price is merely the opening bid in a negotiation in which the two parties attempt to narrow the difference between the "bid" and the "asked," as in an Eastern bazaar or a Western stock market. The seller will not be offended if the asking price is rejected. In fact, the seller will be very much surprised if the initial price is accepted without the customary bargaining. And Americans should be aware that for them the asking price is usually inflated and should be firmly but politely rejected.

In Eastern Europe people are accustomed to doing business, not by fax, or E-mail, or Internet, or even phone, but by face-to-face meetings, and that is not likely to change quickly. Telephone technology is archaic and is only now being upgraded (with the help of U.S. firms). Moreover, everyone seems to have a television but not everyone a phone. In 1993, only 10 to 12 percent of Hungarians had a phone line. As one joke had it, half the people were waiting for a phone, and the other half for a dial tone. Telephones, moreover, are suspect—they may still be bugged. Improved technology, however, is not the only answer.

The business culture differs in Eastern Europe, as it does in many other countries around the world. The pace is slower, and deportment more polite. Business practices are more formal, and decision making more hierarchical and lengthy. Titles and honorifics are important. Letters are answered late, if at all. Since most business is conducted on a personal basis, a potential partner will want to sit across a table from a Western visitor, preferably in a restaurant, before making a business decision.

Legislation and regulations are changing rapidly, and it is difficult to get up-to-date information on how to proceed, especially in small towns. In a Hungarian post office, as a Peace Corps volunteer relates, different clerks would give different answers to the same question. The dilemma was solved, she explained, by questioning as many clerks as possible and accepting the majority opinion.

The sanctity of the contract is poorly understood. A contract or agreement will be negotiated to the last detail, with every i dotted and every t crossed before it is signed and sealed. Yet shortly after signing, the signatory may ask to reexamine its contents, raise questions about interpretation, or sidestep implementation. The entire contract may come into question because of new legislation passed after it was signed, or if the signatories change their minds.

A Western company reports that it submitted the best bid on a contract, met all the requirements, and was pleased by a ministry announcement that it would be awarded the contract. But then the ministry received a better offer from another firm and sought to back out of its commitment. In another case, a U.S. government agency negotiated and signed a rental lease and occupied the premises, only to be harassed by the landlord when a better offer was received. The electricity was turned off and other forms of annoyance were used in an effort to get the tenant to voluntarily break the lease and vacate the premises.

An American business executive reports that East Europeans have difficulty drafting meaningful plans for business endeavors and considering various options in cooperating with a foreign firm. Moreover, their plans will emphasize the upside and deemphasize the downside risks. They will not always be clear about what they themselves seek in a joint endeavor, and they can change their minds quickly. To make certain that they really mean and understand what they say, one should ask them to repeat the details of their claims.

Proposals for business projects will be made with little capital to finance them, and some of the proposals may not be well thought-out. Potential partners will seek to give the impression that they understand everything, but the understanding will often be superficial. They should be queried again and again to make certain that they do indeed understand. To ensure that they know what they are talking about, one American business executive recommends that every deal be preceded by a feasibility study.

On-time delivery may be a problem, as one American business executive learned. He had signed a contract to distribute tourist buses in the United States and had several prospective customers lined up. The first bus, a prototype, was to have been delivered by a certain date but that date came and went without any sign of a bus. When he complained to his South Slav partner, he was told that the manufacturers had liked the prototype so much that they decided to exhibit it at several European trade fairs rather than ship it to the United States. To prevent such occurrences, purchasers should not allow manufacturers to draw down the full amount of their letters of credit in advance of delivery. Pay as you go.

Another American reports signing a contract to act as U.S. distributor for a Balkan product. When her American lawyer asked whether she had confirmation that her prospective partner had the right to license the product for distribution in the United States, she inquired and learned that the firm indeed had no such right.

A few more caveats. Young entrepreneurs entering into negotiations with a Western firm may have an office, a fancy calling card, and big plans, but little or nothing to back them up. Prospective investors should personally check out whatever has been promised—capital, land, property, experience, etc. Business language, moreover, may not have the same meaning as in other countries where there is a longer tradition of private enterprise. Presenters of cost estimates, for example, should be asked how they arrived at their figures. The response "no problem" is a warning sign to be careful.

Many new entrepreneurs are engineers or scientists by training in fields given priority by communist regimes in their rush to industrialize. Those fields attracted the gifted and talented, people who are experts in their specialties but inexperienced in the ways of a free market. Graduates of business schools they are not.

Competitive bids should be obtained from several firms, advises another American. Before finalizing a deal, see how they perform on a trial basis over a period of several months. Take your time and play it cool.

Deals can be done on a handshake but should be followed

up in writing. If and when an agreement or contract is not implemented, negotiators should be prepared to return to Eastern Europe again and again. This cannot be done from a distance. When things go wrong, what to do? There are of course legal recourses which may work in theory but not in practice. Newcomers to the East European "biznes" scene are advised to withhold some sums from payment until complete satisfaction has been obtained. Find an East European partner is another valuable piece of advice. A local partner, in addition to understanding the language and business culture, will also know all the potential pitfalls and how to avoid them.

Many East Europeans fear the uncertainties of competition and the free market. Government officials, managers, and workers, after years of communism, are not accustomed to notions of productivity, accountability, cost controls, lean management, and honest reports to stockholders and investors. Profit and loss are concepts only beginning to be understood. Laws and regulations on business are not always in place and, when they are, they can change from day to day.

Managers and supervisors have difficulty in accepting responsibility and making decisions. They can talk at length about problems but have difficulty focusing on solutions. For many years it was safer to sit and talk than to make decisions or express their own views. Decisions that in the United States would be made at an intermediate level are usually passed up the line to top management for resolution.

Georgina Wyman, a Canadian managing director of Bata's shoe factory and stores in the Czech Republic, reports that her employees expect her "to spell out the minutest details of their responsibilities to make sure they won't get into trouble." Changing such ingrained habits, she adds, takes time, sensitivity, and patience. "When people come in with a question, I ask them, 'What is your opinion?' Once they have told me, I say, 'If that's your opinion, why don't you go ahead and do it.?' "[18] Work forces are inflated, and Western analysts believe that many East European industries could be productive with far fewer employees than their present number. Finally, in some countries free enterprise is still suspect and is challenged by an older belief that it is immoral for some people to get ahead at the expense of others.

Germans have been trading in Eastern Europe since the industrial revolution and their products are well known. Germany, moreover, is nearby, and a German can catch a plane in Frankfurt or Munich and fly to any of the East European capitals in an hour or two and resolve any problems that may have arisen. Americans, however, also have advantages. American business is highly regarded, and American technology is believed to be on the cutting edge.

Eastern Europe has highly skilled workers and well-trained engineers, a vast market with great potential, and a younger generation that is committed to change. The younger generation understands that new ways of doing business must be learned; it also recognizes that it won't be easy and will take time.

A European business executive with long experience in Eastern Europe advises using the "partnership" approach, not in a contractual sense but rather in accepting East Europeans as partners and treating them as equals, as you would someone at home.

Some potential partners, however, should be treated with caution. Bribery and corruption are widespread, and in some countries they are standard procedure. And then there is the mafia.

The Mafia

Thieves increase with the making of new laws.
—Romanian proverb

The term "mafia" is heard everywhere in Eastern Europe, not the Italian Mafia but a homegrown variety. The term is confusing, however, because it can encompass a wide range of activity from outright racketeering to legitimate business.

In most countries the mafia are the newly rich members of the former *nomenklatura* (the communist elite) and their children, who have managed to reemerge high on the heap after the recent political upheavals. (Mid-level people in government are likely to be the same as before.) In the private sector, however, former high communist officials may now be corporate chief executive officers, having privatized their firms early on by issuing stock which they sold to themselves, thus giving rise to the term "nomenklatura capitalism." The term "mafia" may also be applied to legitimate businesspeople who are resented for their entrepreneurship and success.

On the extreme fringe of the mafia are those who would be gangsters and racketeers in any country, providing protection to those willing to pay for it and retribution to those who are not. They dress well, drive costly Western cars (Mercedes and BMW preferred), have expensive lifestyles, and never go anywhere without their cellular phones.

Mafia machinations include extortion, kickbacks, and protection as well as gang warfare for control of restaurants, nightclubs, prostitution rings, drug traffic, and other businesses, legitimate as well as illegitimate. Foreigners doing business in Eastern Europe should be sensitive to the people they deal with and understand exactly what is required of them and the retribution they might expect for failing to carry out their half of a deal.

Organized gangs have weapons which are easily available from the military. Well-armed men walk the streets at night, and caution is advised. Street crimes and burglaries are on the rise, and residents have installed double and triple doorlocks. Local police are understaffed, inadequately paid, poorly trained, and unable to control the criminals and racketeers.

Such crimes, however, appear more numerous than they really are because they are a relatively new phenomenon in

Eastern Europe and did not exist on the same scale a few years ago. Moreover, under the communists crime was rarely reported, whereas today it is given broad coverage by a free press. While crime in Eastern Europe is increasing, it is still much lower than in U.S. and West European cities. And looking at it somewhat cynically, increased crime is another sign that Eastern Europe is becoming more Western.

Blame Others

> The easiest thing is always to blame strangers.
> —Eric Hobsbawm,
> in a lecture opening the 1993-94 academic year
> at the Central European University, Budapest

East Europeans have a tendency to blame others for their misfortunes. There is, of course, some historic reason to do so. All of these nations were under foreign rule for much of their history and were not masters within their own borders. And after World War II, a victorious Soviet Union imposed communist regimes and ruled through local parties.

The practice of blaming others, however, continues today. Slovaks blame Czechs for having failed to provide full equality within the Czechoslovak Republic. Romanians and Hungarians blame each other for their troubles in Transylvania. Ukrainians and Poles blame Russians for centuries of oppression. Lithuanians blame Poles for treating them as second-class citizens during the interwar period. Croats and Serbs blame each other for their long history of animosity, and Muslims blame Christian Serbs for their fratricidal war. All blame the Soviets for having imposed communism, and whatever blame is left over is heaped upon Gypsies and Jews.

The tendency to blame others is difficult to discard, and it is often the minorities and neighboring nations on whom the onus is placed for today's troubles. This has caused open warfare in the former Yugoslavia and Moldova. In other countries of the region, however, ethnic intolerance simmers just below the surface and could erupt if living conditions deteriorate and extremist politicians take advantage of public discontent.

Crossing Cultures—Two Views

In conducting interviews for this book I encountered two views on how to provide technical assistance to East Europeans. Basically, the difference is whether to "talk with" or "talk to."

The "talk with" view is taken by an American business executive experienced in providing technical assistance to fledgling firms in Eastern Europe. His advice is to listen a lot before giving advice. Talk first with each member of the business to be advised, he suggests, "from the chief executive officer to the janitor," and solicit their views on what changes should be made in the firm. Most employees will have never before been asked for their views and will be reluctant at first to make suggestions to a supervisor or outside consultant. They are quick to learn, however, and appreciate being asked. Concentrate on one change at a time to make certain it is fully understood. Keep your expectations modest and follow up your recommendations to make sure they are implemented correctly. Treat the East Europeans as equals and you will be respected and your advice followed.

The "talk to" view is given by an equally experienced and successful technical assistance provider. These people, he says, have been told what to do for more than forty-five years, and they have little experience in making their own decisions. You can't ask them what should be done because they simply do not know. Instead, he counsels, do some preliminary research on the country, the enterprise, the people, and the market, and be prepared to present a plan for them to follow.

Who is right? The author suggests that both of these diametrically different views may be valid, but in different coun-

tries and with different people. Eastern Europe is not a uni-
form region. There are differences—cultural, political, and
economic—between nations that are closer to Western Europe and those that are further east, those that are more
developed and those that are less developed, and between
those that are Catholic, Protestant, or Orthodox; and there
are also differences in their experiences under communism.
Some states were able to break away from or moderate the
Stalinist system imposed by the Soviet Union; others were
more Stalinist than the Soviets.

Common to all, however, is a decline in the work ethic, a
result of years of working against the communist system within
a narrowly defined area of responsibility. "This is my area of
competency" is commonly heard among workers and office
personnel, and they are reluctant to do anything outside that
area. Each employee is accustomed to doing one type of
operation and then passing the product on to the next employee. The idea of seeing a job through from start to finish
is alien.

Also alien is decision making at lower levels. In the past,
decisions were made at higher levels of management and
carried out at the lower levels. Employees at mid- and lower
levels are unaccustomed to making decisions on their own.
Moreover, under the communists, decisions were made by
committees rather than individuals, and responsibility was
avoided. That system is proving difficult to change.

With the collapse of communism, East Europeans experienced an initial euphoria. The wealthy West would come to
their rescue, and the transition to a free market and democratic governance would be relatively painless.

Today, they are disappointed and discouraged. Euphoria
has given way to cynicism, and inflated expectations of foreign assistance to hardheaded realism. It is now realized that
there are no quick cures for economic ills nor magical recipes
for reconstruction. Through experience, East Europeans now

know that there are good and bad foreign consultants, and they no longer accept foreign advice without question. Western visitors should show respect for such attitudes, be patient and understanding, and recognize that their successes and failures will be judged by severe standards. And show some respect for history. American historical memory is measured in years; in Eastern Europe it goes back for centuries. Grievances there are older than our own nation.

---

[1] Istvan Deak, "Survivors," *New York Review of Books* (5 March 1992): 51.

[2] Vaclav Havel, "A Call for Sacrifice," *Foreign Affairs* 73, no. 2, (March/April 1994): 2-3.

[3] *New York Times*, 12 August 1993.

[4] Oscar Halecki, *Borderlands of Western Civilization: A History of East Central Europe* (New York: Ronald Press, 1952), 3-4.

[5] Woodrow Wilson, cited in Mark Sullivan, *Our Times: The United States 1900-1925* (New York: Charles Scribner's Sons, 1926), 535.

[6] Michael Shafir, in a lecture at the Wilson Center, Washington, D.C., 2 February 1994.

[7] Laura Klos-Sokol, *Speaking Volumes about Poles* (Warsaw, Poland: IPS Wydawnictwo, 1994), 88.

[8] "Letter of the Twenty-eight," in Jan Zaprudnik, *Belarus: At a Crossroads in History* (Boulder, CO: Westview Press, 1993), 125.

[9] Agnes Heller, quoted by Joe Julian in "Reflections on the Political Reconstruction of Hungary, *Kettering Review* (Winter 1993), 64.

[10] Blaga Dimitrova "The Women Who Are Poets in My Land," trans. Niko Boris and Heather McHugh, in *Ms* 3, no. 1 (July/August 1992): 17.

34

[11] Slavenka Drakulic, *How We Survived Communism and Even Laughed* (New York: Harper Perennial, 1993), xv.

[12] *Economist* (12 December 1992): 60.

[13] United Nations Regional Seminar on the Impact of Economic and Political Reform on the Status of Women in Eastern Europe and the USSR, Vienna, 8-12 April 1991.

[14] Eva Hoffman, *Exit into History: A Journey Through the New Eastern Europe* (New York: Viking Penguin, 1993), 81.

[15] Chuck Sudetic, *New York Times*, 5 September 1993.

[16] Ryszard Kapuscinski, in foreword to Edward Behr, *Kiss the Hand You Cannot Bite: The Rise and Fall of the Ceausescus* (New York: Villard Books, 1991), xii.

[17] *New York Times*, 11 December 1993.

[18] Sonja Sinclair, "The Best Revenge," *Canadian Business* 67, no. 2 (March 1994): 26.

1

Slavs and Other Peoples

> The East begins on the *Landstrasse*.
>
> —Metternich

Eastern Europe, as noted earlier, is divided by historical and cultural fault lines. One of the more important lines marks the limits of the conquests of the Muslim Ottoman Turks, limits that were not very far from the *Landstrasse*, a southeast suburb of Prince Metternich's Vienna. Another important line separates Western and Eastern Christianity. These two fault lines have shaped the nations of Eastern Europe and, to a great extent, they account for the cultural differences between them today.

The terms "East" and "West" are of course relative. In a religious-cultural sense, the West is the world of Western Christianity which experienced, in turn, a Renaissance, Reformation, Enlightenment, and modernization brought by the industrial and scientific revolutions. The East was the world of Orthodox Christianity and the Ottoman Turks, which experienced none of the above. *Oesterreich*, the German name for Austria, originally meant Eastern Realm, the eastern outpost of the Holy Roman Empire. Similarly, *Ukraine* in Slavic languages indicates a "borderland," which it indeed was to

Poles and other Christians who lived to its west. Those cultural borders were recognized by the Polish historian Oscar Halecki in the title of his classic history of East Central Europe, *Borderlands of Western Civilization.*

Geography and Ethnicity

...geography, at least European geography, doesn't leave history very many options.

—Joseph Brodsky

In geographic terms, Europe is the western extremity of the vast Eurasian landmass that extends from the Atlantic to the Pacific Ocean. Along the plains and grassy steppes of this landmass—the natural routes for people on foot or horseback, in railway cars, and more recently in tanks and trucks— nations have migrated and armies have marched throughout history.

In prehistoric times these plains were the main routes for migrations from east to west in what historians call the *Voelkerwanderung* (migration of nations). But migration and wandering, by connotation more or less peaceful in nature, are misleading terms, for these mass movements of people were anything but peaceful.

Along these routes in prehistoric times came Scythians, Sarmatians, Goths, Alans, Huns, and Avars in their westward migrations. Along these same routes in the ninth century came the Magyars, Ural-Altaic people who were the ancestors of today's Hungarians. In the thirteenth century came Mongol-Tatars who ruled Russia and parts of Eastern Europe for more than two hundred years, penetrating as far as Poland, Hungary, and the Adriatic Sea. The Ottoman Turks came in the fourteenth century at the start of their relentless advance into Europe.

But there were also migrations from west to east. The Teutonic Knights and other military-religious orders used the North European Plain in the thirteenth century when they began the German *Drang nach Osten* (drive to the East) at the start of their conquest and colonization of parts of Poland and the Baltic states. Austrians also moved from west to east, advancing to the borders of today's Russia in their campaign to drive the Ottoman Turks from Europe. Napoleon's armies passed this way on their ill-fated march to Moscow in 1812. In the twentieth century, German and Russian armies fought their way across Eastern Europe in two world wars. After all these travails, the mere survival of the East European nations is testimony to the durability of national cultures in the face of continued colonization, persecution, and mass violence.

Scholars give various reasons for the migration of nations—famine, pestilence, pressures from neighboring peoples, as well as a vital urge to conquer, proselytize, and enrich themselves. Whatever the reasons, the indigenous peoples they encountered in Europe were conquered, subjugated, and at times annihilated. In most cases, however, the invaders from the East were assimilated over time and, with the exception of the Magyars, took on the languages and cultures of the lands they had overrun.

The Slavs

> Above all, there is no clearly defined or universal Slav attitude. The aspirations and trends of the different Slav nations are varied and often contradictory.
> —Hans Kohn, *Pan-Slavism: Its History and Ideology*

Since at least the sixth century, the Slavs have lived in Eastern Europe where they have been the predominant ethnic and linguistic group. They are divided into three branches. The West Slavs are the Poles, Czechs, Slovaks, and some smaller nations in eastern Germany. The South Slavs are the Slovenes, Croats, Serbs, Bosnians, Montenegrins, Macedonians, and Bulgarians. The East Slavs are the Russians, Ukrainians, and Belarusians.

These nations all speak closely related Slavic languages, some of them mutually intelligible, others not; some written in Latin script, others in Cyrillic. But while they all share common cultural and linguistic roots, it would be a mistake to speak of a common Slav race. Each differs from the others, in culture as well as language, a difference they proudly maintain. Indeed, each nation has been sustained by its language and religion.

The entry of the Magyars into Central Europe at the close of the ninth century determined the history and ethnicity of the region for the next thousand years. A nomadic people, the Magyars had migrated earlier from the Ural Mountain region of today's Russia to the steppes north of the Black Sea, where they remained for three hundred years before moving on to Europe. They spoke a language related to that of the Finns from whom they had separated during their earlier migration.

The Magyar advance into Europe was stopped in 955 at Augsburg in today's southern Germany. But rather than return to their homeland in the Dnieper River region, the Magyars settled permanently in the Central Danubian Plain, a fertile land between the Carpathian Mountains of Slovakia and the Dinaric Mountains of the former Yugoslavia.

The Magyarization of the Central Danubian Plain permanently divided the West Slavs from the South Slavs and brought about the development of the West and South Slavic language groups. These languages have many words with common roots but differ in grammar and pronunciation.

...And Other Nations

The Balkans...is, or was, a gay peninsula filled with sprightly people who ate peppered foods, drank strong liquors, wore flamboyant clothes, loved and murdered easily and had a splendid talent for starting wars.
—C. L. Sulzberger, A Long Row of Candles

To the east of the Hungarians live the Romanians, a non-Slavic people who trace their origins to the intermingling of indigenous Dacians and Roman settlers in the eastern limits of the Roman Empire. One remnant of that Roman colonization is the Romanian language which, despite its admixture of Slavic and Turkish words, is regarded as a Romance language because of its Latin roots.

Other non-Slavs include the Albanians and the three Baltic peoples—Lithuanians, Latvians, and Estonians. The Albanians, who speak an Indo-European language, are descendants of an Illyrian people who lived in the region before the arrival of the Slavs. Lithuanians and Latvians speak old Indo-European languages belonging to the Balto-Prussian group. Estonians speak a Finno-Ugric language that is close to Finnish. And to further complicate this linguistic and ethnic mosaic, in most states of the region there are also national minorities—Gypsies, Germans, Turks, Greeks, Armenians, and Jews, as well as members of neighboring nations of the region.

No nation of Eastern Europe can claim to be racially pure. Each is a mixture of indigenous peoples and the invaders who periodically migrated across the region.

Gypsies are the second largest ethnic minority in Eastern Europe (after the Russians in Ukraine), which is home to more than half of the world's estimated eight to ten million Romany or Roma, as they are also known. They are found in all the states but their exact numbers are in dispute. Romania has the most—some 3.5 million—followed by Hungary, Slovakia, Bulgaria, Bosnia, and Ukraine.

Gypsies left their ancestral home in northwest India around the tenth century and arrived in Eastern Europe some three to five hundred years later. Used as slave labor in the Ottoman lands of the Balkans, they were emancipated only in the nineteenth century.

Wherever they lived Gypsies have encountered hostility because of their nomadic ways, resistance to assimilation, and different appearance, dress, lifestyle, and language. During World War II, some 500,000 were exterminated in Nazi death camps. Communist efforts to integrate them into local societies—in some cases by force—met with failure, as have similar efforts by postcommunist governments. As a result, Gypsy unpopularity persists. They continue to be victims of violence and discrimination and are the last hired and first fired. In contrast to the romantic Western view of Gypsies, they are the poorest, most disadvantaged, and most disliked ethnic group in Eastern Europe.

Germans also resisted integration. For centuries they have lived in these nations, and in considerable numbers in Estonia, Latvia, Poland, the Czech lands, Hungary, and Romania. After World War II most of the Germans were repatriated to West Germany but some still remain.

Germans were early colonizers and rulers in the Baltics and parts of Poland. In the Czech lands, they were the majority in the Sudetenland, an area adjacent to Germany, and in many cities of Bohemia and Moravia. German-speaking people also lived in large numbers in Hungary, where they were, however, assimilated over time. Lutheran "Saxons" have lived in Transylvania since the twelfth century, prospering as farmers in the countryside and as merchants and manufacturers in cities that were German-speaking. The Catholic "Danube Swabians" have lived since the eighteenth century in the Banat region of Romania and Serbia, where they were invited to settle by the Habsburgs after the area had been liberated from the Turks. And in modern times German princes were invited to rule over many of these East European nations.

Wherever they lived, Germans constituted the middle class. As educated urban residents, successful businesspeople, skilled artisans, and prosperous farmers, Germans dominated cultural life in many of the areas where they resided and tended to look down on their indigenous neighbors.

Crossroads of Empires

> Southeastern Europe is a caldron of history—of unresolved border disputes and nationality questions created by the collapse of the multinational Hapsburg [sic] and Ottoman empires.
>
> —Robert D. Kaplan

Eastern Europe has been a political crossroads, a geopolitical fault zone where great powers over centuries have confronted each other—Russia, Poland, Germany, Austria, Sweden, and Turkey—causing tectonic tremors and changing political frontiers as they skirmished and fought for territory and influence. Over the centuries these great powers have warred against each other and the nations of Eastern Europe, vanquishing and partitioning, and leaving a lasting legacy of instability.

As a result, East Europeans have a deep sense of history, much more so than Americans, whom they regard as ahistorical. This is understandable when one considers that East Europeans have been living in the same places for more than a thousand years whereas most Americans have been in their land for a much shorter period of time.

The first known Slavic political entity was formed in the ninth century, the Great Moravian Empire which united Czechs, Moravians, Slovaks, Croats, and some south Polish tribes. The most powerful state in Eastern Europe at the time, it eventually succumbed to pressure from Germans and Magyars. The Hungarian state that followed, encompassing the Central Danubian Plain, lasted more than a thousand years before being dismembered at the end of World War I.

To the east, the great Polish-Lithuanian Commonwealth, which evolved at the end of the fifteenth century, stretched from the Baltic to the Black Sea and from the Oder to the Dnieper River. One of the largest and oldest states of Europe, it lasted until the end of the eighteenth century when it was partitioned between Russia, Prussia, and Austria and disappeared from the map of Europe for 123 years.

As the twentieth century began, much of Eastern Europe remained partitioned between Russia, Germany, and Austria-Hungary. When these empires, in a quirk of history, all collapsed at the same time in 1917-18 (Germany and Austria-Hungary to defeat in the Great War, and Russia to revolution), the subject nations of Eastern Europe reemerged as sovereign states. Benefiting from the self-determination policy of Woodrow Wilson, they enjoyed twenty years of independence until World War II brought a return to imperial rule, first by Nazi Germany and then by a communist Soviet Union. In the late 1980s, history was repeated once more as communism collapsed, the Soviet Union split asunder, and independence was restored once more to Eastern Europe.

The empires, however, left a cultural heritage that continues. Austrian influence can be seen today in the architecture and cultures of the region—from Kraków, Lviv, and Chernivitsi in the east to Prague, Ljubljana, Zagreb, and Sarajevo in the west. The Ottoman Turks left behind pockets of Muslims in Yugoslavia, Bulgaria, Romania, and Albania. Russian influence can be seen in Ukraine, Belarus, and the Baltic states, while Germans left a legacy in Bohemia, Poland, Latvia, Estonia, and Romania.

Wars, conquests, and partitions are continuing themes that have left their marks on the peoples of Eastern Europe. Another mark has been left by religious rivalry.

...And Religions

In the course of the post-Napoleonic settlement at the beginning of the nineteenth century, Eastern and Southeastern Europe was divided among three great empires.... Each of them was based on a faith: one on Sunni Islam, another on Counter-Reformation Catholicism, and the third on Orthodoxy. Not one of them was legitimated by ethnic homogeneity. All of them included complex patchworks of populations of diverse languages and religions, often distributed by social role rather than territory.

—Ernest Gellner,
"Ethnicity and Faith in Eastern Europe"

Five of the world's major religions have contributed to the diversity of Eastern Europe—Roman Catholicism, Eastern Orthodoxy, Protestantism, Judaism, and Islam. Politics and religion together have left their mark, confirming the Latin saying, *cuius regio eius religio* (who rules determines the religion). Moreover, through the region runs the historic divide between Western and Eastern Christendom, a north-south religious as well as cultural demarcation, confirmed in our time by the violence between Serbs and Croats.

Poland, Lithuania, and Slovakia are Catholic; the Czech lands and Hungary are Catholic and Protestant; Romania, Bulgaria, and Serbia are mostly Orthodox Christian; Croatia and Slovenia are mostly Catholic; Bosnia, the remaining republics of the former Yugoslavia, and Albania are a mix of Orthodoxy, Catholicism, and Islam; Estonia and Latvia are historically Lutheran but today are half Russian Orthodox; Belarus is Orthodox; Western Ukraine is Greek Catholic (Uniate) and Ukrainian Autocephalous Orthodox but the rest of the republic is a mix of Ukrainian Orthodox and Russian Orthodox. And, as a reminder of centuries of rule by Ottoman Turks, there are pockets of Muslims in Romania, Bulgaria, the former Yugoslavia, and Albania.

Jews have lived in Eastern Europe for centuries. Before World War II the region was home to the largest concentration of Jews in the world—estimates run as high as 50 percent of world Jewry—numbering in some countries as much as 10 percent of the population and concentrated mainly in cities and small towns. From early years Jews were prominent in trade, arts and crafts, and later in commerce, finance, law, medicine, and journalism, exerting an influence far beyond their numbers.

Most of the Jews are gone now, victims of the Holocaust and the emigration of its few survivors. But small numbers remain in all countries; Ukraine has an estimated 500,000 and Hungary an estimated 100,000. Remnants of the Jewish past may also be found today in many of the indigenous cultures and languages of the region. Another remnant of the past that has returned with democracy is anti-Semitism. Now nonviolent, it persists in some countries, despite the small numbers of Jews.

Ethnic Cleansing

> Myth and invention are essential to the politics of identity by which groups of people today, defining themselves by ethnicity, religion, or the past or present borders of states, try to find some certainty in an uncertain and shaking world by saying, "We are different from and better than the Others."
> —Eric Hobsbawm,
> in a lecture opening the 1993-94 academic year at
> the Central European University, Budapest

Minorities are not minor problems in Eastern Europe. Whether religious or ethnic, minorities are major concerns for many of these nations and, for some nations, "ethnic cleansing" has been the solution. This, in contrast to the West where several peoples have been fused into one— France, Britain, Italy, Canada, and the United States.

Ethnic cleansing is today's term to describe the violence used to rid territories of ethnic and religious minorities—Serbs in Croatia, Croats in Serbia, and Muslims in Bosnia, among others. As shocking as these actions are in the 1990s, they are not new to Eastern Europe. The history of the region is replete with massacres, pogroms, and the forced resettlement of peoples because of wars and shifting borders and alliances.

Nazi Germany resorted to the most brutal form of ethnic cleansing, the Holocaust, in its campaign to rid Europe of Jews and Gypsies. The Soviet Union committed ethnic cleansing when it executed 15,000 captured Polish officers and 11,000 other Polish citizens at Katyn forest in 1940. During the war the Soviets deported entire nations—Crimean Tatars and Volga Germans, among others—suspected of sympathies for Germany. After the war, another form of ethnic cleansing—forced resettlement—was used to rid Czechoslovakia, Poland, Hungary, Romania, and Yugoslavia of Germans who had lived in those lands for centuries. In Czechoslovakia alone, more than three million Sudeten Germans were resettled to West Germany. Also in 1945, another ethnic cleansing occurred when Poland's borders were shifted 150 miles to the west, with a resultant forced exodus of 5.5 million Germans from East Prussia, Pomerania, Silesia, and other parts of Poland. To replace the Germans, Poles were resettled from Poland's eastern territories that had been transferred to the Soviet Union. Today, for the first time in its long history, Poland is an ethnically homogeneous state—98 percent of the population is ethnically Polish—and has thereby been spared the ethnic strife that has plagued other East European states.

In the other states, however, ethnic and religious minorities continue to cause social and political tension. Some three million Hungarians live in neighboring states—more than two million in Romania, 600,000 in Slovakia, 350,000 in Serbia, and 160,000 in Ukraine. Bulgaria has almost one million Turks, as they are called, although many of them are ethnic Bulgars who converted to Islam under Turkish rule.

In Estonia and Latvia, close to half the population is Slavic and Russian-speaking. Lithuania has 250,000 Poles. In Ukraine, 22 percent of the population is Russian, and another 12 percent are Ukrainians whose first language is Russian. And the Romanian citizen you meet may also be a Hungarian, Gypsy, German, or Jew.

In all states, ethnic and religious minorities are potential sources of unrest and violence. In some states, the minorities have not given up hope that their lands will some day be rejoined with their "home" countries.

2

Poles

Poland has not yet perished
So long as we live.
—Refrain from the Polish national anthem

Poland has come close to perishing several times in its long, turbulent, and tragic history, but never did. Poles repeat this refrain from their national anthem whenever the nation is in danger. However great that danger, they know that Poland will survive as long as they live—and fight.

History is very important to Poles, and visitors will be surprised how often dates and events from the past of Poland and other countries will be cited in conversations. In particular, Poles will recall their traumatic experiences during and since World War II. No country in Europe suffered so much during the war as Poland, and Americans can expect to see and hear some of that history in their business and social encounters with Poles. Almost everyone will have a story to tell, even those born long after the war had ended.

"For your freedom and ours" is an old Polish revolutionary refrain. Poles have fought not only for an independent Poland but for the freedom and independence of many other nations as well. It is not by coincidence that Solidarity, the first nonviolent mass movement to challenge a communist government, arose in Poland. Nor that Solidarity's success started a chain reaction that ended with the collapse of communism throughout Eastern Europe and the Soviet Union as well as the breakup of Russia's Eurasian empire—no mean achievement for a country of thirty-nine million that did not even exist from 1795 to 1918.

In 1241, Poland saved much of Europe by absorbing the shock of a major Mongol-Tatar invasion that threatened to overrun the entire continent. In 1683, Polish arms broke the Turkish siege of Vienna. Poles fought for the American colonies in their war of independence. In the nineteenth century, they fought for freedom in Belgium, Spain, the Balkans, and Italy. In 1812, Poles formed the vanguard of Napoleon's march to Moscow and protected the rear on his retreat. In 1848, they fought with Hungarians for their independence, and in the American Civil War they served on both sides, but mostly with the Union Army.

In World War I, a Polish army fought with the Allies on the Western Front—although Poland as a state did not even exist—and suffered enormous casualties. In World War II, Polish armies fought in the Middle East, Africa, Russia, and Western Europe. Poles flew with the Royal Air Force (RAF) in the Battle of Britain where one Polish squadron had the highest number of "kills" of any RAF squadron, shooting down nine German planes for every plane it lost. Poles landed in Normandy with the Allies and stormed Monte Cassino in Italy. More than six million Polish citizens perished during the war, one of every five inhabitants, half of them Jews.

More recently, the Polish will to resist, by force if necessary, deterred the Soviet Union from invading Poland three times—in 1956, 1980, and 1981—when communist rule in Poland was threatened. The thousand-year nation has been sustained by the courage of its people, a hope that has defied the odds, and their romantic nationalism.

Romantic Nationalism

> Poland is a very touching, proud little country. They have something in common with the Spaniards, a certain noble pride. A bit stupid, some practical people might say. They will go a thousand strong against an army of a million, fighting with forks and spoons and I don't know what.... They are the only ones who opposed Hitler from the first to the last.
>
> —Artur Rubinstein

Poles have a reputation for being romantic nationalists. This is not to be confused with patriotism as Americans understand the term. Polish romantic nationalism transcends patriotism and is a far more emotional and mystical phenomenon permeating Polish culture and behavior.

To understand the emotions aroused by Polish nationalism, listen to Chopin, the national composer, whose music combines the romanticism and nationalism that explains its popularity in Poland and elsewhere. Polish history is replete with rebellions and revolutions against foreign rulers, most of them failed. Poland was the first major state to be excised from the map of Europe, and during the 123 years of its partition there were four major insurrections and many more minor rebellions against the occupying powers of Russia, Prussia, and Austria.

In our time, there is the heroic image from a Polish film—whether real or apocryphal is not clear—of Polish cavalry charging German tanks in the early days of World War II. During six years of occupation and suffering, and despite the loss of 20 percent of its population, underground opposition to the German occupation never ceased, and there were no Polish Quislings. The Warsaw Ghetto rose up in 1943—the first major Jewish resistance to Hitler's "Final Solution"—and was completely destroyed. In 1944, the city of Warsaw, led by Poland's Home Army and other underground military forces, rebelled against its German occupiers. In sixty-three days of fierce fighting, Warsaw paid with 18,000 dead and

25,000 wounded among its Polish combatants, and close to 200,000 dead among its civilian population. Warsaw, nevertheless, was mercilessly leveled to the ground by the Germans, while advancing Soviet forces paused on the other side of the Vistula River.

Another uprising was staged in 1956 by striking Polish workers, causing the fall of Poland's Soviet-imposed Stalinist government and its replacement by a government of national communism and reform. In 1970, Polish workers struck again, bringing down the government they had brought to power fourteen years earlier. And in 1980, they struck once more when they formed Solidarity, the first free trade union in the Soviet bloc.

Poland defied the odds again in 1989 when it became the first nation to depose a communist government. And when all other former East European satellites were tearing down their statues of Stalin, Poland had none to topple. It was the only Soviet bloc nation that had never erected a monument to Stalin.

Poles take immense pride in these achievements. They also glory in the election of a Polish pope; Nobel prizes in literature for Wladyslaw Reymont, Henryk Sienkiewicz, and Czeslaw Milosz; and a Nobel peace prize for Lech Walesa.

The Szlachta

...the Polish gentry are eager for glory, keen on the spoils of war, contemptuous of danger and death, inconstant in their promises, hard on their subjects and people of lower orders, careless in speech, used to living beyond their means, faithful to their monarch, devoted to farming and cattle breeding, courteous to foreigners and guests, lavish in hospitality, in which they exceed other nations.
    —Jan Dlugosz, Polish chronicler, 15th century

Many mannerisms of today's Poles may appear outmoded to visitors from abroad. Women can expect to have their hands kissed, receive compliments on their dress and appearance, and be given deferential treatment. A love of horsemanship and the cavalry continues; Solidarity underground activists would proudly and symbolically wear—and some still do— riding boots, called *ofycerskie*. The archaic third person form is used in addressing persons in the formal (impersonal) mode. Rather than ask "Do you want...," Poles will say "Does the lord (or lady) wish...." Even the simplest worker or peasant will use forms of speech and behavior derived from the *szlachta* (pronounced "shlakh-tah"), the landed nobility and gentry who ruled Poland until the end of the eighteenth century.

During the communist years, Polish officials at formal state dinners would at times wear tuxedos when such attire was disdained by Russians and other communists as a sign of bourgeois decadence. Such ideals are a heritage of the szlachta.

Noble titles were rare in Poland and membership in the szlachta class was not limited to a small circle of aristocratic families ranked according to their titles. The szlachta numbered 10 to 12 percent of the population of historic Poland but up to 25 percent of its ethnic Poles, and all members enjoyed equal rights. Strong believers in personal liberty, republicanism, and individual rights, they set standards of behavior for all classes of society, then and now. Not all Poles whom Americans meet will be of szlachta descent but all will display many of the characteristics described here. Like the szlachta, today's Poles show an independent spirit and are ready to express their personal opinions on any subject raised.

The szlachta decline began in the seventeenth century with the start of "the deluge," denoting the downfall of Poland, at that time the largest state in Europe, stretching from the Baltic to the Black Sea and from the Oder to the Dnieper River. After Poland was partitioned at the end of the eighteenth century, the szlachta retreated to their country estates where impoverishment awaited many of them. Their ideals, however, became the model for a new class of Polish leaders, the intelligentsia, a group which transcends class barriers but retains many of the szlachta ways. As former *New York Times* Warsaw correspondent Michael T. Kaufman explains it:

> The role of the szlachta is one of the things that has made Poland very different from its neighbors. The gentry made up a higher percentage of feudal society in Poland than anywhere else and their influence was paramount for centuries. There has never been a period of bourgeois dominance in Poland as there was, for instance, in Czechoslovakia. Under partition and foreign domination, the gentry often led rebellions and uprisings. As urbanization and industrialization were advanced, to a large extent by Jews and Germans, the often impoverished rural-based aristocracy set standards of grace and behavior in ways that echo the life of the American South after the Civil War.... William Styron once told me that when he came to Poland to do research for *Sophie's Choice*, he was struck by how much the Polish countryside reminded him of his native Virginia.[1]

Sense of Honor

> For "honor," an important value guiding Polish life, people have sacrificed their personal freedom, economic interests, and even their lives.
>
> —Janine Wedel, *The Private Poland*

Czlowiek honoru (person of honor) is a Polish expression that does not exist in other Slavic languages. Another heritage of the szlachta, the Polish sense of honor—to do what is right— requires a Pole to do things that most Americans would consider foolhardy or at least unwise. Yet, for Poles the honorable course of action is often the only one to take.

During the early weeks of martial law in 1981, relates American anthropologist Janine Wedel, a Solidarity activist purposely arrived at the doorstep of a Solidarity leader who, it was reasonable to assume, had just been arrested. The activist went, knowing that police were most likely waiting for anyone who might come to the apartment. He went anyway, as a matter of honor, he explained to Wedel, adding "I was rather conscious I might pay the price."[2] In another instance related by Wedel, a respected Polish journalist who, on principle, had resigned his position after the imposition of martial law, placed an ad in the leading Warsaw newspaper. "Looking for honest work," he wrote, followed by his name and phone number. Overnight, he became a national hero, and Poles delighted in his clever poke at the government printed in an official newspaper. The journalist received some thirty job offers, including several from state agencies (190-91).

Poles are often compared with the Spaniards and Irish, two fellow Catholic nations. Poles and Spaniards, writes American historian M. K. Dziewanowski, have "...an exalted sense of honor and suffer from an exaggerated sensitivity. Both are fatalistic and tend to have a cavalier attitude toward death." Polish and Spanish men have "...preserved a highly ritualistic, ceremonial, old-fashioned gallantry toward women."[3]

With the Irish, Dziewanowski continues, Poles share

> ...a zealous, traditional, ritualistic Roman Catholicism, with its strong devotion to the Holy Virgin...an exhibitionistic, masochistic enjoyment of sufferings inflicted on them by foreign rule...proclivities toward capricious moods, highly critical, often negative spirits, bellicosity, and a love for singing and strong drink, apparently as an outlet for their frustrations (252-53).

As a consequence of foreign rule and economic exploitation, concludes Dziewanowski, Poles and Irish became nations of emigrants, with the largest segments of their diaspora located in the United States (252).

Another definition of the Polish sense of honor—with its pluses and minuses—is given by Krystyna Carter, a Polish-born translator and interpreter, who describes it as:

...grace, high-mindedness, often generosity, defence of the powerless, chivalry towards women, self esteem and family loyalties. It may also reflect bad features like arrogance, indifference, xenophobia, intolerance and snobbery.[4]

Russia or Germany—the Geographic Dilemma

The Poles are a middle-sized but old nation, settled between two great nations whose influence on the fate of the world has been, is and will continue to be extremely important.

—Andrzej Szczypiorski, *The Polish Ordeal*

The tragedies of Polish history, Poles say, result from geography—Poland's position between two great powers, Russia and Germany. Faced with adversaries on two indefensible borders, Poland has often had to choose between the two. And when it was unable to make that difficult choice—as its national traditions dictated—it had to contend with adversaries on both borders, and Polish independence was lost.

An American who visited Poland in 1991 was surprised by the interest Poles demonstrated in the nations to their east—Lithuania, Belarus, and Ukraine. With full independence having been achieved, the visitor had expected Poles to be more interested in countries to their west. Again, history provides the explanation.

Poland's historic expansion was to the east. Bordered on the west by a rising Germany, and on the east and southeast by lands decimated by Mongol-Tatar invasions, Poland's natural expansion was in the latter direction. Its dynastic union with Lithuania in 1386 led to a Polish-Lithuanian Commonwealth which encompassed today's Lithuania, much of Latvia, Belarus, and Ukraine, and parts of Russia.

In an historic sense, Poles see their nation as a defender of the Christian West against the barbarism of the East; and in a religious sense, as the "Christ of nations," making the supreme sacrifice for the salvation of others.

Refreshingly Unpredictable

...a certain Polish lightness of mind, a complex of impulses, frivolous and unserious, that are characteristic of this community on the Vistula.

—Tadeusz Konwicki, *Moonrise, Moonset*

Among their fellow Slavs, Poles have a reputation for being light-minded and frivolous, as Tadeusz Konwicki, Poland's leading postwar novelist, puts it. Poles are high-spirited, full of vitality and zest. Reserved and restrained they are not. British writer J. B. Priestly, visiting Poland in 1972, described Poles as:

> ...more alive than most people, less inclined to turn themselves into zombies and robots.... They are very brave, tenacious, quite clever, and at the same time slightly daft and refreshingly unpredictable.[5]

Russians, in particular, regard Poles as unserious people, perhaps because Russians, by comparison, are themselves so serious. The Bolshoi Opera's production of *Boris Godunov* portrays Poles whose only interests seem to be dancing, drinking, and "demoiselling."

Poles do not hesitate to speak out and tell foreign visitors what's on their minds, even when they run the risk of getting themselves into trouble. During the Vietnam War, when the communist regime staged "spontaneous" demonstrations—as they were described in the Polish press—in front of the American Embassy in Warsaw, Poles would alert the embassy in advance.

On one such occasion, after a Polish television crew took up a position outside the embassy to film the expected event, I ventured forth from my office and asked the startled crew what time the "spontaneous demonstration" was scheduled to start. They laughed and gave me the exact time.

During the communist era, Poland amply demonstrated its divergence from the policies of other communist countries. Polish national communists were purged in 1948 and imprisoned but not executed as in Czechoslovakia, Hungary, and Bulgaria. After the "Polish October" of 1956, reforms were initiated by a government of national communism. The Catholic Church was given more freedom than in any other communist country. Cultural and scientific contacts with the West were reestablished. Artists, scholars, and writers were able to maintain a degree of independence and intellectual freedom unequaled in the communist world. And in a major ideological shift, the forced collectivization of agriculture was reversed and, after 1956, some 85 percent of Polish farmland was in private hands.

These reforms were unique in the communist world, Yugoslavia excepted. It took another twenty or so years before similar reforms would come to other East European states and thirty-five years before they would come to Russia.

Poles are proud of their "Polish way." They take risks and are not intimidated by rules and regulations. They also have a flexibility that makes them relatively easy to negotiate with. A Polish *nie* is almost never a firm no but more likely to become a "maybe," or "perhaps." Differences with Poles can usually be worked out, and when they have the will, they find a way.

Religion

> The history of Poland is to a large degree the history of Christianity in that area of Europe. Even today, Catholicism and Polish identity are to a certain degree the same thing.
> —Andrzej Szczypiorski, *The Polish Ordeal*

Catholic Poland's dilemma, resulting from its geographic location between Germany and Russia, was aggravated by religious differences—Prussia was Lutheran and Russia was Orthodox. This has caused Polish nationalism to be identified with Catholicism, the religion of almost all ethnic Poles. Historically, the Polish church has provided moral and spiritual values for the nation. During the partition years, the church held the nation together and gave Poles their sense of being Polish. During the communist years, wrote former U.S. Ambassador to Warsaw Jacob D. Beam, the church was "...Communism's strongest competitor," and Cardinal Wyszynski, Poland's primate, was "...his country's single most influential figure."[6] Although harassed by the authorities, the church was allowed a degree of independence. It was able, for example, to maintain a Catholic university, in Lublin, the only Catholic and private university in a communist country, and to publish a Catholic weekly, *Tygodnik Powszechny*, in Kraków.

Religion today has lost some of its importance in society, and many Poles have differences with their church over such issues as contraception and abortion (which is widespread). While most Poles profess to be believers, economic conditions and changing lifestyles of late have caused them to take positions and actions which are not always in accord with the church's teachings. Taking the longer view, however, in times of stress and hardship, Poles have always turned to their church as the symbol of all that is Polish in their culture and history.

Historic Poland included many people of other religions—Ukrainian and Russian Orthodox, Greek Catholics (Uniate), Jews, Lutherans, Calvinists, Polish Brethren, Armenian Orthodox, and Muslims. With such a multiplicity of religions, laws were passed by the parliament in 1573 and endorsed in the constitution, protecting citizens from persecution and punishment because of differences of faith. This occurred, as historian Adam Zamoyski points out, at a time when people for religious reasons were being executed in England and burned at the stake in Holland.[7]

Refuge was provided for persons persecuted in other lands.

When Jews became victims of the Crusades in Western Europe, they found sanctuary in Poland where they were welcomed for their ability to aid in the country's development. A charter issued in 1264 promised them complete freedom and opportunities for economic livelihood. When Jews in Europe were blamed for the Black Death, they were again welcomed in Poland. Polish history is entwined with that of the Jews.

In the fourteenth century, under the enlightened rule of King Casimir the Great, Jews were invited to aid in the development of Poland's eastern territories, newly liberated from Tatar rule. Casimir's liberal policies toward serfs and Jews earned him the title, "King of the Jews and the Serfs." He also had a Jewish concubine, Esther, who bore him a son on whom he bestowed a coat of arms. With protection under the law, more than half of world Jewry found a home in the multinational Polish-Lithuanian Commonwealth.

Jews who believe that their family roots are in Russia, Ukraine, or Lithuania should understand that most of the Pale of Settlement, to which Jews were restricted in the Russian Empire, was a part of historic Poland before the partitions. Thus, the roots of most American Jews are in Poland, not Russia.

Despite the loyalty of Poles to their church, the Inquisition never reached Poland. In the sixteenth century, writes Zamoyski, the last two Jagiellon kings

> ...allowed their subjects to do anything they wanted—except butcher each other in the name of religion.... They institutionalized a spiritual and intellectual freedom which still lives.... It was principally owing to the efforts of the last Jagiellons [a Polish dynasty] that the murderous Reformation and Counter-Reformation never grew into anything more dangerous in Poland than a squabble over seating arrangements at a family wedding (73-74).

In 1791, a new constitution, the first written constitution in

Europe, guaranteed freedom of religion, gave townspeople the same rights as the szlachta, recognized Jews as citizens, and provided protection to peasants. That constitution, however, proved too democratic for Poland's neighbors and led to Poland's final partition a few years later and its disappearance from the map of Europe.

Toleration, to be sure, deteriorated in later years. Jews, along with Germans, were members of the small middle class, serving a useful role in the economy as traders, stewards of estates, innkeepers, artisans, and tax collectors. Several factors, however, placed severe burdens on Polish society and caused changes in the protected status of Jews—a deteriorating economy caused by the loss of Poland's eastern territories, the impoverishment of the szlachta, and the emancipation of serfs and their migration to the cities. The new Polish middle class of former szlachta and peasants found itself in competition with the urban Jews. Rising nationalism, which identified with Polish ethnicity, gave rise to intolerance and anti-Semitism.

Although almost all of Poland's Jews, who constituted 10 percent of the 1939 population, are now gone (only some 5,000-10,000 remain), a residue of anti-Semitism remains. There is no simple explanation for such intolerance in our time but it reflects, in part, the increased freedom of expression which permits such views to be openly espoused. At the same time, however, young Poles are showing new interest in the culture and history of the Jews who lived in their midst for a thousand years. And, in the 1991 parliamentary elections, two parties that used anti-Semitism in their campaigns failed to win a single seat.

Intellectual Freedom

> Even during the worst periods…totalitarianism was never able to completely suppress the residues of independent culture….
>
> —Stanislaw Baranczak, *Breathing under Water and Other East European Essays*

Polish elites have a tradition of intellectual and cultural individualism, and among Poles a variety of views can always be expected. After the first free elections in 1991, twenty-nine political parties (including a Beer Drinkers Party) were represented in the new *sejm* (parliament), no one of which held more than 13 percent of the seats. Some were called "sofa parties" because all the members could fit on one sofa. Poles can be deadly serious when discussing domestic politics, international affairs, history, the arts and sciences, and whatever else may be of interest to them and their nation. Visitors will be expected to participate in these discussions, and their opinions will be sought and heard with interest and attention. Be prepared, however, for a multiplicity of views and sharp but polite debate. Subjects of interest to Poles include their neighbors—Russia, Germany, Ukraine, Belarus, and Lithuania—Polish membership in European organizations such as NATO and the European Union, and U.S. domestic politics and how they may affect Poland.

One theme likely to arise in discussions with Americans—and on which all Poles are united—is the importance of Poland in East-West relations and their fear that the United States will again focus its attention (and resources) on Russia to the detriment of Poland. This fear reflects not only the Polish grand view of their role in the world but also their expectations of a special relationship with the United States based on history and the many Americans of Polish descent.

Scholars and creative artists have provided much of the intellectual leadership in Poland, and they enjoy a degree of respect seldom experienced by their American colleagues. Kraków's Jagiellonian University was established in 1364, before the universities of Vienna and Heidelberg, and its most famous student was Mikolaj Kopernik (Nicolaus Copernicus), the medieval astronomer. When the Germans took Kraków in 1939 in the early days of World War II, the first people rounded up for imprisonment in concentration camps were not the Jews of Kraków but the professors of the university.

The intellectual tradition lives on in Poland today but intellectuals are no longer a minor segment of the population. Poles today are a highly educated people, thanks to the expansion of higher education and the democratization of educational opportunities over the past forty-five years. They are very knowledgeable, not only about the history and culture of their own country, but of other countries as well, and the United States in particular.

Culturally Creative

The intensity, versatility, exuberance of Poland's cultural life, the puzzling combination of tradition and avant-garde, of pathos and irony, of sentimentality and whimsical wit, does not cease to astonish Western intellectuals.

—M. K. Dziewanowski,
Poland in the Twentieth Century

In the 1950s, the British Broadcasting Corporation (BBC) played a hoax on its audience at the expense of Poles. Broadcasting a cacophony of noise and sounds, BBC described it as a new piece of music by an avant-garde Polish composer. Many in the radio audience fell for the spoof, and some musicologists even found the music interesting. What is interesting for us here is that the BBC chose to identify the composer as a Pole.

Poles do have a reputation for being in the avant-garde of artistic creativity. Their annual music festival, Warsaw Autumn, is devoted to contemporary classical music, and in the 1950s and 1960s it served as the main means of introducing modern music to the entire Soviet bloc. Receptive to new trends, Poles have been innovators in the plastic arts, literature, music, theater, and film, and in the vanguard of scholarship and science. The names of prominent Poles in these fields include—to mention only a few—Chopin, Mickiewicz, Sienkiewicz, Korzeniowski (Joseph Conrad), Modrzejewska

(Modjeska), Wieniawski, Paderewski, Szymanowski, Rubinstein, Lutoslawski, Grotowski, Wajda, Polanski, and Milosz.

After 1956, when Stalinist conformity was still the rule in other communist countries, creative freedom was enjoyed by Polish writers, scholars, artists, and musicians. Cultural and scientific exchanges with the West were resumed, and many Poles were free to travel abroad. Polish publishers printed books by Western authors who could not be published elsewhere in the bloc—Saul Bellow, for example. Polish universities enjoyed considerable autonomy from the government, and their scholars, academic freedom. Polish film and theater directors, composers, and artists gained worldwide recognition.

Polish cultural creativity was due in the past, in no small part, to the multiethnic character of the society and the creative mix that resulted from interchanges between ethnic Poles and the many minorities. It can also be seen as a Polish response to successive campaigns of Prussianization, Russification, and Sovietization by Poland's occupiers.

Language

W Szczebrzeszynie chrzaszcz brzmi w trzcinie.
(In Szczebrzeszyn, a beetle is heard in the reeds.)
—Polish tongue twister

Visitors will be playfully asked by Poles to repeat the tongue twisters that foreigners find so difficult to articulate. Failure to pass these tests today, however, is not so drastic as in the year 1312 when Polish Duke Lokietek retook Kraków in his campaign to reunite the country after the Tatar invasions. In a sure test of nationality, Kraków residents were rounded up by Lokietek and asked to repeat Polish tongue twisters. Those who could not pass the test were promptly beheaded (34).

Polish is a subtle language that can seem purposely ambiguous at times. Thoughts are often expressed in an indirect and roundabout way in the expectation that the real meaning will be somehow understood. Visitors should listen carefully for hidden meanings.

A Slavic language, Polish is one of the West Slavic subgroups and is written in the Latin alphabet. The grammar is complex and the pronunciation difficult, with many soft sounds—*s, sh, cz,* and *szcz*—which pose problems for the foreigner, and for English speakers in particular.

In compensation for the difficult pronunciation and grammar, Polish has many words from Western languages—Italian, for example. In the sixteenth century, Poland had an Italian queen, Bona Sforza, who brought with her to Poland a retinue of Italian architects, artists, and humanists who introduced the Italian Renaissance to Poland. One result is the many Italian words and terms that were adapted to the Polish language. The Polish word for oil, *oliwa* (oh-lee-vah), is from the Italian for "olive"; *kolacja* (ko-lat-si-yah, supper) is from the Italian *colazione*, but in Italy it is lunch or breakfast.

As with other Slavic languages, it takes more words to say something in Polish than in English, and many English words and expressions simply do not exist in Polish. The language, moreover, is more formal than English, and elegant salutations are used in addressing people of equal or higher social status.

In speaking, the stress is always on the next-to-last syllable, which gives Polish the melodious and rhythmic sound of Italian. When I made this observation once to my first Polish teacher, Ludwik Krzyzanowski, he beamed and replied with obvious pleasure, "That is the influence of the Italian Renaissance on our language!" Also influencing the Polish language have been French, German, and English. Polish aristocrats spoke French, reflecting the long and close relationship of Poland with France—separated as they were by Germany—and many French words have come into the Polish language. Medical and technical words are mostly from the German. More recently, English terminology has been adopted for business and science.

Most educated Poles have some knowledge of one or more West European languages, which they need to communicate with the world beyond their borders. The study of Western languages is encouraged and English is today the most popular foreign language in Polish schools. Visitors will find, however, that many Poles still have difficulty communicating in English.

For those Americans who plan to study Polish, the challenge is formidable but well worth the effort. Knowing another European language will be helpful in learning Polish. When I first began to use Polish many years ago, I found that I could take the corresponding word from French, German, or English, add a Polish ending, and usually come up with a word that was comprehensible to Poles and was often the correct word in Polish.

Sense of Humor

...there are two ways to surmount the triteness and tragedy of existence—heroism and humor. The Poles have frequently been called upon to display both.
—Stewart Steven, *The Poles*

Humor is another Polish staple, particularly political humor. During the most difficult of times, Poles can find something to make fun of and laugh at. Many of the anticommunist and anti-Soviet jokes that circulated throughout the Soviet bloc had their origins in Poland. One favorite was: "Why is a Pole like a radish? Because he is red on the outside and white on the inside." Red and white are also the national colors of Poland.

Political cabaret that lampoons politics is an art form. Guests are seated at tables in crowded, smoke-filled rooms and entertained by actors who irreverently poke fun at prominent political leaders and the country's travails.

Poles appreciate humor but not when they are the butt of the jokes. The "Polish jokes" heard in the 1970s were particularly offensive, as I personally learned during official talks with the Polish government in 1975 on U.S.-Polish cultural relations. At those talks, the Polish Ministry of Foreign Affairs requested that the U.S. State Department take steps to stem the Polish joke syndrome in the United States. In response, I attempted, without much success, to explain that the State Department had no authority to control humor in the United States or elsewhere. Informally, I also explained that ethnic jokes came and went in American humor, and the Polish joke would soon play itself out. This indeed came to pass when Cardinal Karol Wojtyla, archbishop of Kraków, was elected pope, and Polish jokes became passé.

At Home

Learn in Italy; clothe yourself in Germany; flirt in France; banquet in Poland.

—Polish proverb

Americans will feel at home in Poland. There are some countries in which they are disliked, others in which they are tolerated, and others in which they are welcome. In Poland, Americans are genuinely welcome.

In contrast to some other European countries, it is customary for Poles to invite visitors to their homes to eat, drink, and engage in long conversations, another heritage of the szlachta. The main meal of the day, as in many other European countries, is in the early afternoon, at 2:00 or 3:00 P.M., and the evening meal is likely to be a cold supper. For guests, both will be delicious. Poles know how to feast, even in difficult times.

The gift you bring to a Polish home need not be expensive; almost anything will be appreciated, but especially items that may be difficult or costly for Poles to obtain. Flowers (except for red roses) are traditional, and can be purchased year round. Western goods, especially American, enjoy a special status. If a guest arrives a little beyond the appointed hour, it will not matter. Poles are not punctual, and time for them is not money (although that may be changing as the economy is privatized).

Handshaking is customary and obligatory with the hosts and other guests, as elsewhere in Europe, on both arrival and departure, and women should expect to have their hands kissed. Men whom Poles feel close to should be prepared to be kissed by other men on the cheek three times, alternating from cheek to cheek. Another sign of affection for those whom Poles particularly like is a rendition of the song *Sto Lat* ("One Hundred Years"), and its wish that the person so honored should live that long.

Americans should expect to be queried about many things. Poles are very curious about the United States and will ask visitors about their lifestyle, how much they earn, and their opinions on politics, the latest books, and films; and foreign visitors will eventually be asked: "What do you think of Poland?"

Social life evolves around so-called "circles"—networks of family, close friends, professional associates, old schoolmates, war veterans, Solidarity associates, and others with experiences in common. These are the friends to whom Poles turn in times of need for assistance and favors. Foreigners can break into these networks, but it will take time before they are accepted as genuine members. Doing small favors for Poles will help.

Such networks are used to solve all kinds of problems, personal as well as professional. Do a favor for someone and expect a favor in return, not immediately but sometime in the future. The favor is not given as a quid pro quo but it is understood that it will be returned. Visitors will find it much easier to get things done by working through networks of friends and acquaintances than by going through official channels.

With persons they do not know well, Poles are reserved. On the street they appear grim; strangers are not greeted, and eye contact with strangers is considered rude. Eye contact with strangers, when made by women, may also be interpreted as a come-on. However, if a foreigner should ask directions of a Pole, the assistance rendered will be helpful and warm.

The formal mode of address will be used initially and may continue to be used for some time until the friendship stage is reached. First names should not be used until that stage *has* been reached, usually after a measure of trust, confidence, or intimacy has been established or after a long and festive evening.

Poles have two codes of behavior, one public and the other private. In public, they can be pushy, demanding, distant, abrupt, and rude. In private, they are warm, generous, hospitable, and loquacious. Conversations are lengthy, and goodbyes never seem to end. As the Poles say, "The English leave without saying goodbye. The Poles say goodbye but do not leave."

Negotiating with Poles

If there is any secret to Polish diplomatic success it is the Polish warmth and responsiveness which turns visitors to Poland into friends of Poland.

In 1008, when the Holy Roman Emperor Otto III visited Poland, he was delighted with Poland's ruler, Boleslaw the Brave, and addressed him as his brother and friend.[8] Eight years later, another emperor, Henry II, sent a German noble, Bruno of Querfurt, as his emissary to Boleslaw. Bruno was similarly charmed and wrote that Boleslaw "became as dear to him as his soul and more than his life" (30).

In our time, diplomats who have served in Poland have found the Poles to be equally attractive and have come away with a special feeling for the country and its people. One

Polish ambassador to Washington, Romuald Spasowski, jokingly referred to State Department officers who had served in Warsaw as "my Polish Mafia."[9] As in other Slavic lands, the human dimension is important in all aspects of interpersonal relations, including business. Poles will strike a deal when they feel right about it, and not before. Very big deals are being struck these days between Poland and the West, but Polish officials making these deals will want to have trust and confidence in their prospective partners before they sign and put their careers on the line.

Caring for people is seen by Poles as a strength, not a weakness, and persons most likely to do well with Poles are those who respect emotions and who care. Caring is believing in the deal you are proposing and in convincing Poles that it is in their interest as well.

Those who hope to do business in Poland should be prepared to spend some time developing a good personal relationship, and only then should business be discussed. Gifts are given, not as bribes but as a means of establishing a relationship that may later lead to something more concrete. Poles are less inclined than Americans to focus on the details of a deal, and if details are important they should be spelled out in an agreement.

Negotiating tactics differ little from those of other European nations, but protocol is important in business and professional relations. Discussions should be initiated as high up as possible in an organization's hierarchy, preferably with the person in charge, even if only a courtesy call. To do otherwise might be interpreted as a snub.

Alcohol

Good God, how they drink. They drink without interruption, ceaselessly, for hours on end. Have Poles developed a special gene adapted to the vodka environment?
—Eva Hoffman, *Exit into History*

When Pope Innocent III, in the thirteenth century, wrote to Prince Leszek of Kraków requesting Polish participation in a crusade to the Holy Land, Leszek replied that "neither he nor any self-respecting Polish knight could be induced to go to the Holy Land where, they had been informed, there was no wine, mead, or even beer to be had."[10] Mead, made from honey, can still be found in Poland today, but the drink of preference is *wódka* (pronounced "vood-ka," the diminutive and endearing term for water).

Wódka is a passion Poles share with their Slavic neighbors. Poles claim, however, that their wódka is better than the Russian—and after extensive field-testing, the author agrees, particularly when it is made from rye, a grain grown in northern climates. A vital component of Polish social life, wódka establishes a sense of intimacy and community, and it is difficult for visitors to avoid. Wódka is drunk straight, ice cold, in small glasses, in one "bottoms up" gulp, with food and with other drinkers. One does not drink alone. Rather, someone at the table will raise a glass, make a toast or say *na zdrowie* (to health), make eye contact with each of the other guests, and all will drink together. Tap water, as in most European countries, is not taken with meals and, with today's pollution, is best avoided.

Beer is becoming more popular now that its quality has improved, but wódka is still the Polish drink of choice for meals, celebrations, business deals, and conviviality in general. It is also the adhesive that bonds people together. As one prominent Pole has put it, "When we Slavs drink, we open our hearts."[11]

Enjoy it, in moderation, but be aware that a wódka bottle, once opened, will be drunk to the last drop and never put back on the shelf.

Moderation in drinking is not customary for Poles. Since the fall of communism, alcohol consumption has risen 40 percent, and in 1989, the average Pole drank the equivalent of nearly two gallons of pure spirits. By 1992, average annual consumption had risen to almost three gallons.[12]

Cigarette smoking has also increased. According to the World Health Organization, Poles are the world's heaviest smokers, with adults fifteen years or older smoking 3,620 cigarettes each year.[13]

Whither Poland?

Poland faces West with its hopes, and East with its fears.

—William Safire

Poland is once more confronted by its age-old geographic dilemma. As New York Times columnist William Safire says, it looks west, with its hopes for security and economic stability, and east to nuclear-armed Russia and its questionable political future.

Self-preservation as a nation has been Poland's guidepost through history, expressed in opposition to foreign rule and hostile neighbors, and more recently in resistance to communism.

But as Wiktor Kulerski, a former Solidarity leader, writes:

Suddenly, here we are with no enemy in sight. The Russian and German empires that had invaded us are no more. Nazism and communism no longer threaten us with extinction. There is no longer pressure from the Orthodox Church, Protestantism, or atheism. We no longer live in fear of invading armies or foreign occupiers and the discriminatory laws they impose. An international security system protects us and our smaller neighbors. Ethnic minorities are protected by international law. But we remain as we had been, still shaped by our two centuries of struggle. We have no enemies left and cannot fashion enemies out of those who are weaker than us. What are we to do?[14]

This presents a challenge for a nation whose raison d'être has been based on opposition. The Solidarity movement, which once bound Poles together in opposition to communism, is no more. The Catholic Church, although still strong, no longer commands the allegiance of all Poles. The ethnic homogeneity of the population and the absence of minorities have diminished the appeal of nationalist parties. Where will Poles now turn in their efforts to build a new national identity?

The American Connection

> Oh, the shades of Washington and Kosciuszko,
> Statesmen, who from different foreign nations
> Came to nurture you in their youth, America,
> To acknowledge as their own someone else's freedom...
> —Cyprian Norwid, *John Brown*, 1859

Visitors to the museum at Harpers Ferry, West Virginia, will find there the above excerpt from a poem by Cyprian Norwid, the Polish poet of freedom who lived in the United States from 1852-54. As a Polish patriot preoccupied with his own nation's struggle for freedom, Norwid was moved by John Brown's aborted uprising to free the slaves. He also honored Polish patriot Tadeusz Kosciuszko for his service with George Washington in the war for independence.

Some ten million U.S. citizens can trace their origins to Poland. Poles identify with Americans, and many of the Poles whom Americans meet will boast a cousin in Chicago, the city which for many years had the largest Polish population after Warsaw. Canada also has many citizens of Polish descent, a million or more.

Of all the East European nations, Poland's history is most intertwined with that of the United States. As Americans will be reminded by their Polish acquaintances, the struggle for freedom and independence are common themes that run through both the American and Polish past. In the eighteenth and nineteenth centuries, the United States was a symbol in Polish romantic literature for the freedom and democracy to which Poles aspired.

Tadeusz Kosciuszko, a professional military officer, served in the Continental Army in 1776 and was instrumental in its victories at the battles of Saratoga and West Point. He later led the failed Polish insurrection against Russia which ended with the third and final partition of Poland in 1795 and its erasure from the map of Europe. A statue of Kosciuszko, a general in both the American and Polish armies, stands near that of Lafayette in the park across from the White House in Washington, D.C.

Another Polish officer, Casimir Pulaski, a brigadier general in the Continental Army and commander of its cavalry, saved Washington's army at the Battle of Brandywine and gave his life, at the age of thirty-one, leading a charge at Savannah. Known as the "Father of the American Cavalry," Pulaski's statue stands in Washington on Pennsylvania Avenue, two blocks from the White House.

Poles first came to the New World in 1608 with the soldier adventurer Captain John Smith as skilled artisans at Virginia's Jamestown Colony, twelve years before the Pilgrims arrived in Massachusetts. The first in a long line of Polish immigrants included a glass blower, a pitch and tar maker, a soap maker, and a timberman.

The first purely Polish settlements in the United States were farming communities in Texas, settled in 1854 with names such as Kosciuszko, Polonia, and Czestochowa. Other agricultural settlements followed in Nebraska, Virginia, Wisconsin, and the Connecticut Valley of New England. From 1870, however, emigration was largely to the industrial cities of Chicago, Buffalo, Baltimore, Cleveland, and Milwaukee, where burgeoning industries presented opportunities for employment. Among U.S. cities and counties that bear Polish names there are fourteen Pulaskis, eight Warsaws, but only two Kosciuszkos (perhaps because it is so difficult for Americans to pronounce).

Ignacy Jan Paderewski, Poland's premier pianist in the early 1900s, performed widely in the United States in the years before and during World War I, gaining sympathy for his country's struggle for independence. His most important audience, however, was President Woodrow Wilson, whose support was instrumental for a united and independent Poland. When Poland's independence was restored in 1918, the premier pianist became the *Premier Ministre* of the newly reconstituted state. Paderewski died in New York in 1941 and was interred in Arlington National Cemetery. In 1992, his remains were returned to a free Poland.

Prominent Americans of Polish origin include former secretary of state and senator, Edmund S. Muskie; Zbigniew Brzezinski, national security adviser to President Carter; Czeslaw Milosz and Isaac Bashevis Singer, Nobel laureates in literature; Hilary Koprowski, virologist; John Cardinal Krol, archbishop of Philadelphia; Wanda Landowska and Artur Rubinstein, pianists; Richard Pipes and Adam Ulam, Harvard professors; Stan Musial, St. Louis Cardinals slugger and Hall of Famer; Bronko Nagurski, all-time football great; and Carl Yastrzemski, Boston Red Sox star; and many members of Congress.

---

[1] Michael T. Kaufman, *Poland: A Nation in Conspiracy* (New York: Random House, 1989), 124.

[2] Janine Wedel, *The Private Poland* (New York: Facts on File, 1986), 184-85.

[3] M. K. Dziewanowski, *Poland in the Twentieth Century* (New York: Columbia Univ. Press, 1977), 252.

[4] Krystyna Carter, *Simple Etiquette in Poland* (Folkstone, Kent, England: Simple Books, 1992), 16.

[5] J. B. Priestly, in M. K. Dziewanowski, *Poland in the Twentieth Century*, 253.

[6] Jacob D. Beam, *Multiple Exposure: An American Ambassador's Unique Perspective on East-West Relations* (New York: W. W. Norton, 1978), 93.

[7] Adam Zamoyski, *The Polish Way: A Thousand-Year History of the Poles and Their Culture* (New York: Franklin Watts, 1988), 91.

[8] S. Ketrzynski, "The Introduction of Christianity and the Early Kings of Poland," in *The Cambridge History of Poland: From the Origins to Sobieski (to 1696)*, edited by W. F. Reddaway et al. (Cambridge, England: University Press, 1950), 23-24.

[9] Romuald Spasowski, in a meeting at the State Department in the 1970s which the author attended.

[10] Zamoyski, *The Polish Way*, 34.

[11] Jacek Kuron, in a talk at the National Endowment for Democracy, Washington, D.C., 11 November 1994.

[12] *New York Times*, 28 March 1993.

[13] *New York Times*, 6 June 1994.

[14] Wiktor Kulerski, "The Post-Totalitarian Syndrome," *Uncaptive Minds* 5, no. 2 (1992): 112.

3

Czechs and Slovaks

...in discussing the past or present, one more properly
speaks of a Czech heritage and a Slovak heritage that
are occasionally identical, frequently similar, but more
often than not different in important respects.

—Bruce Garver,
"The Czechoslovak Tradition: An Overview"

At first glance Czechs and Slovaks are indistinguishable. The
two peoples are look-alikes, their languages are mutually intelligible, and in this century they have lived together in one
state for sixty-nine years. And because intermarriage has
been high, many Czechs and Slovaks have lived under the
same roof as well. A closer look, however, will disclose under-
lying differences that brought their cohabitation to an end in
1993 and resulted in two separate states, a Czech Republic
with 10.3 million people and a Slovak Republic with 5.3
million.

Czechs are pragmatic rather than idealistic. As products of
an urban European culture, they are an "early to bed and
early to rise" people. They care about work, order, and fi-
nances and are without strong likes and dislikes. Good with
their heads and hands, their personality is closer to the Ger-

mans—staid, stolid, and steady—and, when you get to know them well, loyal and honest. All of these traits contribute to their reputation as the most orderly people in Eastern Europe (as well as the most orderly drivers in a part of Europe not known for defensive driving).

The cultural scene is active. Music, theater, and dance are popular and on a level as high as anywhere in Europe. Czechs are also a bookish people. Bookstores are found everywhere in the cities, and new titles are snatched up as soon as they appear.

A thrifty people, Czechs spend only what they earn, and it is not in their tradition to borrow. In 1994, their government had a tight money policy, a budget surplus, healthy foreign currency reserves, a strong export market to the West, and low unemployment. It also had the fastest pace of privatization of state-owned industries in Eastern Europe—some 80 percent of its enterprises were expected to be in private hands by early 1995. An island of political, economic, and social stability, the Czech Republic had one of the few governments in Eastern Europe that was not made up of former communists. Prime Minister Vaclav Klaus has described it as a "non-leftist island" in Central Europe.

Czechs speak softly, without emotion, and take their time. Nothing is done precipitously, and time is not money. They can sit for hours, talking over drinks in coffeehouses or pubs, without getting drunk as can happen in some other Slavic lands. Pubs (*pivnices*) and wine restaurants (*vinarnas*) are central to social life in Czech and Slovak cities and are a good place to meet people over a beer, a glass of wine, a snack, or a full meal.

In conversations, Czechs tend to be contemplative—talking about issues at great length but without reaching conclusions. On public transportation, there is no pushing and shoving as in some other Eastern countries. Relations with others are correct, and friendships are formed slowly. Once formed, however, friendships are taken seriously and are long lasting.

Although society is male-dominated, the Czech Republic has been described as the least macho country in Eastern Europe. Sexual harassment is rare, and men do not accost unescorted women in cafes and public places nor whistle at them on streets. The moderate Czechs have no forbidden attitudes toward sex. Homosexuality is accepted, and there is less blatant pornography than in other East European countries.

Feminism is stronger than in nations farther east but Czech women are turned off by radical feminism, regarding it as an ideology that forces them to be either for or against something. Czechs today have had enough of ideologies.

They are a polite people, and visitors should watch their manners and speak softly. A Prague joke asks why Americans speak so loudly. Answer: "So they can be heard over their clothes."

Nominally Catholic or Protestant, Czechs are more likely to be nonreligious or even agnostic. A 1993 public opinion survey showed that 20 percent believe in God, 30 percent are not sure, and 50 percent are nonbelievers. Moreover, according to Catholic bishop Frantisek Lobkowicz of Prague, of the 40 percent who declare themselves to be Catholics, only 2 or 3 percent are practicing.[1] The suicide rate is high in the Czech lands, as it was under the Austrians.

A passion for gardening is shared by both Czechs and Slovaks. Some see gardening as an attachment to the land; others, as an escape from the ills of society—social, economic, and environmental. Whatever the reasons, it is a national pastime.

An American teacher of English, to start his Monday conversation class, recalls how he would ask his class of middle-aged Czech men what they had done over the weekend. "Worked in my garden," was the inevitable answer and the subject for that lesson's conversation.

Old World formality continues. People dress for theater and concerts. Handshaking is standard, both on greeting and taking leave, even for children. Frowned on are such acts of American informality as putting feet up on desks, standing with hands in pockets, and lounging in public places. In contrast to many of their neighboring nations, Czechs are punctual. People invited for dinner at eight o'clock will show up exactly at eight, or even fifteen minutes early; and, in contrast to Slavs who live further east, it is not customary for Czechs to invite to their homes people they do not know well. Invitations to homes come only after a closer relationship has developed.

Czechs and Poles

> Elsewhere men have died for the honor and welfare of their fatherland; the same reason impels us to live for it.
>
> —Karel Havlicek

Havlicek was a celebrated leader of the Czech national revival of the nineteenth century, a movement that eventually ended three hundred years of Austrian rule of the Czech lands. His views epitomize the differences between Czechs and Poles.

Poles, as we have seen, were always prepared to rise up and fight for their independence and freedom. Czechs have consistently chosen a more cautious course and, they might argue, with similar results.

While Poles in the nineteenth century were openly rebelling against their occupying powers, the Czech national revival was proceeding without violence, based, as historian Hans Kohn has put it, on "a realism which abhorred rash adventures and grandiose hopes...and remained free on the whole from those messianic dreams and claims which characterized some of the noblest and most prominent Poles."[2]

Czechs are also a moderate people, seeking gradual and peaceful change. They are, writes Flora Lewis,

...more stolid, cautious and practical than other Slavs, without the streak of wild passion, gaiety and cruelty.... There is a sense of measure about almost everything, which can be considered stodgy or admirably rational according to the point of view, but it doesn't provoke strong feeling.[3]

Moderation paid dividends in the period between the two world wars. When all other states of Eastern Europe had succumbed to authoritarian rule, the Czechoslovak Republic remained the only fully functioning democracy in the region, with a standard of living much higher than its East European neighbors. "[T]he moderate disposition of the Czech people," writes political scientist Paul Zinner, "safeguarded them from the misfortunes of adventurism and extremism."[4]

In 1938, they chose not to resist and sacrifice their country's youth when their republic was dismembered by Germany, albeit after Britain and France, preferring "peace in our time," had accepted Hitler's demands. Nor did the Czechs resist with open force when the Soviet Union invaded in 1968 and ended the reform movement known as Prague Spring.

Czechs and Slovaks can be criticized, as former BBC correspondent Misha Glenny does, for "...the weakness of the resistance during the war and the absolute passivity of most of the population."[5] During the communist years, opposition to the regime was muted, and *samizdat* (undergound publishing) was less widespread than in Poland. Czech passivity has been criticized by President Vaclav Havel: "[T]he members of our resistance movements against both the Nazis and the Communists enjoyed little public support—in fact, people avoided contact with them."[6]

Czechs and Slovaks, however, can boast of their Velvet Revolution which ended communist rule in 1989 and regained without bloodshed the independence and freedom they had long sought. And Czechs and Slovaks, in 1993, dissolved their sixty-nine-year union in a legal and civilized manner, without violence, in contrast to the savage ethnic warfare raging at the time in Yugoslavia and various republics of the former Soviet Union. The intent here is not to imply that Polish militancy is preferred over Czech caution. Each nation's behavior is understandable in terms of its history and cultural values. Each achieved its objectives in its own way, and at the price it was prepared to pay.

Czechs and Germans

> The Czech cultural and national tradition, the Czech way of thinking and reacting to reality is close to the tradition, customs, habits and emotions of the Germans, although the Czechs are Slavs, and their language seems somewhat similar to the Polish language.
>
> —Andrzej Szczypiorski, *The Polish Ordeal*

Visitors to the Czech lands of Bohemia and Moravia will agree with contemporary Polish writer Andrzej Szczypiorski. Except for the Slavic language spoken by Czechs, visitors might believe that they are somewhere in the Germanic world.

Like the Germans, Czechs are dependable and skilled workers, punctual and businesslike people, possessing traits not always encountered in the Slavic world. Czech cooking is similar to the German, and Czech beer, the nation's drink of preference, beats the best of Bavaria. (Moravians tend to favor wine.) It is not surprising, therefore, that to other Slavs, Czechs appear German-like. But the Bohemians are not bohemians. In fact, they lead very conventional lives. They are, as one American who worked in Czechoslovakia has put it, quietly civilized.

Tadeusz Konwicki, Poland's leading postwar novelist, sees the Czechs as "Germans amid delightful Slavs," but adds:

Meanwhile, the Czechs have a literature any nation would be proud of; meanwhile, the Czechs have music which the whole world plays from morning till night; and meanwhile, the Czechs are no slouches at painting either.... I wanted to know how that small Central European nation, so oppressed by German culture, could generate so much artistic power, such poetic freshness, such intellectual and aesthetic universality.[7]

Geographically, Czechs are the most western of the Slavic nations. Their capital, Prague, described by Thomas Mann as "one of the most magical cities on earth," is actually farther west than Vienna. When Czechs are described as Germans who speak a Slavic language, the implication is that Czechs are more Western than other Slavs, and in ways other than geographic.

Surrounded as they are on three sides by German-speaking people, the history of the Czechs has been closely intertwined with that of the Germanic world. Bohemia lies on the road from Vienna to Dresden and from Munich to Wroclaw, wrote British historian Elizabeth Wiskemann, and "...long ago became the battleground *par excellence* between the Germans and the Slavs."[8]

For almost a thousand years, Bohemia was a part of the Holy Roman Empire, and in 1346 a king of Bohemia was crowned Holy Roman Emperor as Charles IV. Two years later, Charles founded the Empire's first university, in Prague, and presided over his country's golden age as Prague became one of the great cultural centers of the West and one of Europe's most beautiful cities. The university still bears Charles's name, and parts of Prague today still look much as they did six hundred years ago, having been spared the ravages of war and the neon lights of the modern world.

The Czech Hussite movement of the fifteenth century began as a campaign for religious reform but soon became a civil war between Czechs and Germans. The Hussite reforms presaged the Reformation in Germany almost a century later. Indeed, it can be said that the Reformation began in Bohemia.

Also beginning in Bohemia, in 1618, was the Thirty Years War, the great German religious struggle that shook Europe. Two years later, Czech sovereignty ended when the Protestant Bohemian nobility were defeated by the Catholic Austrians at the Battle of White Mountain outside Prague. The effect of that cataclysmic event on Czech history and character, even today, should not be underestimated. When the war ended in 1648, the population of the Czech lands had declined almost by half, due to military casualties, famine, disease, and emigration. "The defeat and its long-lasting tragic aftermath," writes Flora Lewis, "affected the Czech character, leaving a lack of self-confidence, a sense of historic victimization and of a need to seek accommodation."[9]

After the war the Czech lands were absorbed into the Austrian Habsburg Empire where they remained for the next three hundred years. Most of the Czech Protestant nobles were executed or exiled, and their castles and lands given to nobles from Germany, Austria, and other lands of the Habsburg Empire. Waves of German immigration followed, and German became the language of the townspeople, the privileged, and the educated. Czech was spoken mainly by peasants, workers, and servants. With the loss of their native nobility, Czechs were deprived of leadership and a sense of nationalism for the next two hundred years. Only in the nineteenth century, under, by then, benign Austrian rule, was there a revival of Czech schools, language, and the intelligentsia, and the beginnings of a new national spirit.

In 1938, the German issue once more became a casus belli when the so-called Sudeten Germans in Czechoslovakia, numbering more than three million, were the immediate cause of the Munich *Diktat* and Nazi Germany's dismemberment of the Czechoslovak Republic. The age-old problem of Czechs and Germans was resolved only at the end of World War II when most of the Sudeten Germans were expelled to Germany.

On May 5, 1945, in the closing days of World War II, American troops under the command of General George Patton liberated western Bohemia and the city of Plzen from German rule. The Americans were within forty miles of Prague and could easily have liberated it but, in accordance with an Allied agreement, they paused to allow Soviet troops to take the city on May 9 after four days of a local uprising by Prague citizens. The Soviet troops were to remain in Czechoslovakia for the next forty-six years.

The Slovak Difference

Where there is a Hungarian, there is anger; where there is a Slovak, there is a song.

—Polish proverb

Slovaks are more like their Polish neighbors—spontaneous, warm, generous, outgoing, relaxed, without affectation, and less inhibited. In a word, they are more Slavic than the Czechs. Their pace of life is slower, and they seem to enjoy it more. Music is deeply rooted in the Slovak soul, and they have a song for every occasion. Friends and family (extended as well as nuclear) are important, and Slovaks seem to have them everywhere.

Foreigners may find it difficult to break into these circles of close friends and family, since Slovaks do not generally invite foreigners to join in. One Fulbright lecturer who spent a year in Slovakia reports that he was never invited to the homes of his professional colleagues but was invited to the homes of his wife's English-language students, her local greengrocer, and even complete strangers. Another Fulbright lecturer advises Americans to take the initiative with their Slovak colleagues. Invite them to lunch, he suggests, or for a coffee or drink. Your invitation will most likely be returned and you will be on your way to establishing close relationships.

Slovaks party a lot, on birthdays, name days,[10] holidays, and comings and goings—almost any excuse will do for a party, which can last all afternoon or evening. Parties are taken seriously. There is much food and wine, as well as stronger drinks, and preparations for them, as one American put it, are as thorough and detailed as for D-day. In their homes, Slovaks are obsessively hospitable. They will insist that guests have a drink, and it will be more than one. Glasses and plates will be continually refilled. To survive this hospitality visitors are advised never to completely empty their glasses and plates. Bear in mind that the abundant cold cuts, pickled vegetables, and other cold delicacies that will be served are only the first course, and will be followed by a hot dish, dessert, and more drinks. Guests should also be careful about what they admire in a Slovak home, for it is likely to be presented to them as a gift.

Wine, beer, and hard liquor are the drinks of choice— vodka, cognac, rum, and the Slovak *Borovicka* (a juniper-flavored gin). Slovak food is tasty, but theirs is a country diet, long on fat—sausage, pork, head cheese, lentil and tripe soups—but short on vegetables other than cabbage, peppers, potatoes, and root crops. Bread and soup are staples of the dinner table. Americans watching their cholesterol level will have to be careful, especially because the food is so delicious.

Caution should be shown about making remarks that might imply criticism. Among themselves, Slovaks are critical of their own society and how it functions, but they are very sensitive to remarks by others that seem to question their abilities. They react strongly to those who try to lecture them, and criticism by foreigners may be regarded as attempts to discredit Slovakia abroad. Insult is seen where none is intended.

Slovaks understandably see themselves as victims, rather than makers, of history. A nation of grumblers and complainers, they feel put upon by others and are envious of the more successful. A common response to a request is *neda sa* (it can't be done).

"A lack of repentance" is how one Slovak describes it. As Emil Komarik, vice chairman of the Christian Democratic Party of Slovakia explains:

> The Slovak people were never able to exercise political choice. The nation's destiny was usually determined by external influences, and Slovaks never experienced politics as a consequence of their own choices and decisions. We thus believe that we have always been in the right. This attitude has led to a weak sense of political responsibility—to a lack of repentance—and is a genuine threat to any democratic government.[11]

Slovaks, however, do know how to work the system, a legacy of their rule by Hungarians, Czechs, and communists—how to put to good use their charm, good manners, hospitality, and personal contacts. To get things going they may offer a "small token of appreciation," a gift or a bottle but never cash. Such gifts are usually seen as attempts to establish a sense of bonding. Caution is advised, however, because some may be seen as bribes. The difference is how it is done.

For most of its history Slovakia was a society of peasants and workers; serfs were emancipated only in the 1860s. Today, after an education explosion, society is mostly middle class and well educated but with a small-town, country atmosphere. City dwellers maintain a strong attachment to native villages and regions, and in Slovakia (as well as the Czech lands) many city people have a weekend *chata* (a cottage, usually self-built) on a small piece of land not far from town. At the first sign of spring they begin to garden, and on weekends the cities empty to the countryside.

Because of its higher birthrate, Slovak society is younger than Czech. It is also more male-dominated. Slovak women are busy with work and home. They have little time for other activities, and feminism is a non-cause. Invitations to official receptions do not include wives unless specifically mentioned by name.

Catholicism is the religion of 60 percent of the Slovaks. More religious than the Czechs, Slovaks identify with their Catholicism; and being Catholic is equated with nationalism, although most leaders of the Slovak movement for national identity have come from the Protestant intelligentsia. In contrast to the Czech lands, suicide in Slovakia is low.

Slovaks tend to spend and borrow, and these characteristics are reflected in government policies. In 1994, Slovakia had a weak currency, a large budget deficit, precariously low reserves, a declining economy, and high unemployment. Moreover, privatization was proceeding slowly, and most of the economy was still state-owned. Contributing to this economic malaise were gigantic and unprofitable state-owned steel and textile mills, inherited from the communist years, and a vast and outdated weapons industry.

Oppressed as they have been throughout their history, it is all the more remarkable that Slovaks have been able to maintain with tenacity their national identity. Their warmth, however, is tempered by uncertainty about the future. Younger people, as elsewhere in Eastern Europe, are more optimistic. Older people, too old to change and with families to support, are unsure about what the future will bring and how they will fare in an independent Slovakia.

No-Fault Divorce

> ...if there is one thing that underlies the split between Czechs and Slovaks, it is their long and troubled history, extending as far back as the Austrian and Hungarian empires.
> —Theodore Draper

Two closely related Slavic nations have chosen to end their sixty-nine years of cohabitation. Their divorce, however, has been celebrated in only one state. At a time when Europeans are seeking strength through economic and political union, nationalism has proven more powerful for Slovaks and, somewhat reluctantly, for Czechs as well.

Slovaks deny the divorce analogy, since the two nations of the Czechoslovak Republic were never really equal and Slovaks regarded the federation as Czech-dominated. The rift, Slovaks say, is more like a younger brother escaping from the domination of a stronger and more successful older brother. One thousand years ago, Bohemians, Moravians, and Slovaks, as well as some south Polish tribes, were united in the Great Moravian Empire with its capital in the Slovak city of Nitra. The largest political entity in Central Europe at the time, it succumbed in 906 to pressure by Magyars from the east and Germans from the west. Faced with that choice, Czech leaders swore allegiance to the Frankish (German) emperor while the Slovak lands became part of the multiethnic Hungarian state founded and ruled by the Magyars, recently arrived from the steppes of Asia.

Czechs and Slovaks lived in two separate worlds for almost a thousand years. The Czech lands, under German and Austrian influence, became urban, modern, industrialized, and prosperous, with a populace that was well educated and thoroughly Western. The Slovak lands, colonized by Hungarians, remained predominantly rural, agricultural, and much poorer than the Czech lands, belonging more to Eastern than to Central Europe.

In the Czech lands the religious reforms left a legacy of tolerance; Catholics were in the majority but Protestants wielded political and economic power. Slovakia remained staunchly Catholic, although many of its writers and leading personalities were Lutheran.

The Czechs benefited from the moderate and enlightened rule of Austria which permitted a Czech national revival in the nineteenth century. The Slovaks suffered under a heavy Hungarian hand that ruthlessly repressed their culture and language during the late nineteenth and early twentieth century. The language of instruction in schools was Hungarian, and use of the Slovak language was confined to the home. The growth of an educated class was limited largely to those Slovaks willing to identify with Hungarian language and culture. Intellectual life and commerce were dominated by large Hungarian, German, and Jewish communities. Despite such handicaps the Slovak language was codified, political organizations emerged, and Slovak nationalism gained strength.

The collapse of the Austro-Hungarian Empire at the end of World War I brought the Czech and Slovak lands together once more in the Czechoslovak Republic, but the differences resulting from the long separation proved difficult to bridge. Two agreements signed in Cleveland and Pittsburgh by Czechs and Slovaks during the war provided for a federal state with separate administrations, parliaments, and courts, and the use of the Slovak language in Slovakia. But the hyphenated "Czecho-Slovak" state foreseen by the agreements was not to be, and a unitary state was created. "The Czechs," writes historian Bruce Garver, "by virtue of their greater numbers, wealth, and political experience, and often with the best of intentions, insisted upon being the senior partner."[12]

After their union in 1918, the Czechs dispatched a swarm of officials to help build Slovak local government, schools, and the economy. The officials, however, remained long after reconstruction had been completed and were strongly resented by the Slovaks. Leadership remained with the Czechs.

The Slovaks chafed under Czech dominance, and their desire for increased autonomy was exploited by ambitious political leaders. In 1939, after Czechoslovakia was dismembered by Germany, the Czech lands were occupied by German troops and became a German protectorate. Although nominally independent, Slovakia was little more than a puppet state of Nazi Germany.

The policy of the Allies, as well as of the Czechs, was the reestablishment of the Czechoslovak Republic, which was accomplished in 1945 with Slovakia promised a measure of autonomy, a promise that was not realized. In the elections of 1946, the Communist Party lost decisively in Slovakia but received a plurality in the Czech lands.

After the communist takeover in 1948, Slovak resentment against Czech dominance continued, under the communists as under the democrats. This led to the creation in 1990 of a Czech and Slovak Federal Republic and, following a bitter debate, to the establishment of two independent republics on January 1, 1993.

Doing Business

> The Czechs and Slovaks are not passionate people. They seldom get worked up about anything.
>
> —Vaclav Havel, *Stories and Totalitarianism*

When the Czech composer Antonin Dvorak lived in New York a century ago, he wrote that he was puzzled and bewildered by the "capacity for enthusiasm," the "American push," and the "eagerness to take up everything."[13] Czechs and Slovaks, by contrast, are neither enthusiastic, pushy, nor eager. Rather, they are a polite and modest people who take things slowly. With them, the "soft sell" will be more successful than the "hard sell."

Czechs and Slovaks conduct their business seriously. They have a good sense of humor but they joke after, not during, business, and they do not appreciate the American habit of cracking jokes and making humorous comments during business meetings. Because they are nonconfrontational, it can be difficult to determine where they really stand on an issue. Often, they will appear to agree because it is the easier thing to do. Rather than respond with a flat no, they are more likely to say *uvidime* (we shall see).

Academic titles are also taken seriously, as in Germany, and are used in addressing people in business and social settings. A graduate in economics, engineering, or technical sciences, for example, gets the title *inzenyr*, and is addressed as *pan inzenyr* (Mr. Engineer) or *pani inzenyrka* (Ms. Engineer). For those who have more than one title, all will be used.

"The Czechs love titles," writes Karen von Kunes, who teaches Czech at Harvard, "so don't be surprised to be handed a business card that reads Prof. PhDr. Ing. MUDr. med. h.c. Jan Novak CSc. DrSc."[14] But don't call him Jan for short— first names should not be used unless specifically requested to do so.

Long-term prospects are more important than short-term gains. Czechs and Slovaks will agree to do many things for a visitor, but don't expect anything to happen by the date agreed to. It will be necessary to follow up (over and over and over).

In both countries there is inordinate state intervention in business and the lives of people, a legacy of the Austro-Hungarian bureaucracy that was exacerbated under the communists. Officials and managers are reluctant to give up control.

Private enterprise, moreover, is developing differently in the two states. In the Czech lands, industrialization began in the late nineteenth century under Austrian and German influence, and in the 1990s it is following these models, spurred on by a government committed to rapid privatization and the free market. Slovak industrialization, based on military production, began in 1950 with the Soviet Union as the model; and this has made the transition to a free market more difficult. Slovakia has preferred to privatize at a slower pace.

Newfound capitalism in both countries is described by one American businessman as "a jungle." Contracts are legally binding but laws are not yet fully in force to protect investors, and there are still gaps between legislation of the old Czechoslovak Republic and the new Czech and Slovak republics.

Czechs and Slovaks generally can be expected to operate aboveboard. They may test the waters to see what they can get away with but if some incorrect action is pointed out they will quickly make the necessary changes. The term *chytry* (clever) is used in a positive sense; the opposite is *svinarna* (dirty tricks, from the German *Schweinerei*). Americans are assumed to be loaded with dollars, and caution is advised.

Women in business are the exception rather than the rule, and getting to the top level of management for women is very difficult. However, those who do succeed are reportedly very impressive. To compete successfully, American women will have to be forceful.

Forty-five years of communist rule have made it difficult for Czechs and Slovaks to accept responsibility. Sensitive and proud, they want to be treated as equals and do not appreciate a condescending attitude. They want to do things the right way, but in the transition from a command to a market economy it is sometimes difficult for them to know what the "right way" is.

In many state-owned supermarkets, for example, customer access was controlled by shopping carts, and no one was allowed into a store without one. Since the number of carts was limited, customers often had to wait outside the store until someone exited with a cart. This served as a form of crowd control and prevented shoplifting. But when a chain of stores was privatized by Kmart in 1993, the same system at first continued—no entry without a cart—and the fact that this limited the number of customers and profits to the store did not seem to matter.

Despite the Czech reputation for orderliness, things don't always go as planned; and it is easier to understand Kafka, knowing he wrote in Prague where there is often no straight line from A to B but rather a series of frustrating detours.

One such detour was encountered in a Prague office I visited. The phones were out and it appeared that someone had cut the line. When the host inquired at the telephone company as to when service would be restored, he was told that before making the repairs they would have to find out who had cut the line!

Another Kafkaesque experience was encountered by an American who needed a work permit for a job he had found in Prague. He first made an appointment with an official at the *Pracovni Urad* (Work Office) to find out what forms he had to fill out. That could not be done by phone and required a personal appearance. Returning to the office with the completed forms, he learned that there was still another form to complete. On his third visit he was told that one of his documents had to be an original—a copy would not do. And so it went. With each visit he would see a different official and get a different response or learn that regulations had changed and a new requirement had to be met. By the sixth visit all his papers were finally in order, but he was told that twenty-one days were needed to review his case before a decision could be made. By the end of the review period six weeks had elapsed since his first visit to the Work Office but still no permit had been issued. Not to worry though; the applicant had been working during those six weeks and was confident that the permit would be issued. In the meantime, he was learning to cope with the Czech bureaucracy.

Despite the bureaucratic hassle, foreign visitors will have no difficulty conversing with Czechs and Slovaks. English is making rapid progress in both countries. Ask a question in English, and the reply, from Czechs and Slovaks under age thirty, is likely to be in English. For those over thirty, German is the more common second language.

The Czech and Slovak languages, as noted earlier, are mutually intelligible for the better educated although there are differences in spelling, vocabulary, and grammar. Slovak has been called the Esperanto of Slavic languages because it is the most understandable Slavic language to speakers of other Slavic languages—because of its affinity with both West Slavic and South Slavic languages. Czech and Slovak are pronounced as they are written although the consonants are much different from those in English, and diacritics placed over some letters give them a different sound. The stress is on the first syllable; if placed elsewhere, spoken words may not be intelligible. Somewhat disconcerting for foreigners is the running together of consonants without vowels, especially in Czech, as in the city names Plzen (Pilsen) and Brno.

Truth and Tradition

> Seek truth, listen to the truth, learn the truth, love the truth, speak the truth, keep the truth, defend the truth with your very life.
>
> —Jan Hus

Morality and the search for truth are traditions traced to Jan Hus, the fifteenth-century reformist preacher, father of the Czech Reformation, and a major shaper of the Czech national spirit. His words are recalled in the motto of the Czechoslovak Republic, "Truth will prevail."

A follower of the English religious reformer John Wycliffe, Hus challenged papal authority by protesting against the moral decay of the church at the time and the misuse of its wealth and privilege. Although Hus was excommunicated and burned at the stake, the reform movement that bears his name continued, encouraging Czech national consciousness and use of the Czech language in churches, schools, and public life. The bloody religious wars that followed Hus's execution caused future generations of Czechs to question the use of force to achieve their ends. Instead, Czechs have developed a trust that truth and moral authority will eventually prevail.

The spirit of Hus was epitomized by the philosopher Tomas Garrigue Masaryk, a founder of the Czechoslovak Republic and its first president in 1918. Masaryk's father was of Slovak descent, and his mother of mixed Czech and German ancestry, but he opted politically to be a Czech. Like Hus, Masaryk believed in a higher morality as the decisive element in religion. He called for a moral rebirth and urged that politics be based on work, humanity, justice, and the search for truth.

In our time, the tradition of morality and realism in politics and government continues with Vaclav Havel, the playwright who helped found the Charter 77 human rights movement, led his country's Velvet Revolution of 1989, and became its president after the collapse of communism. "[W]e still don't know how to put morality ahead of politics, science, and economics," said Havel in an address to the U.S. Congress in 1990. "We are still incapable of understanding that the only genuine backbone of all our actions—if they are to be moral—is responsibility."[15]

Svejk, Good or Bad Soldier?

"Svejkism"...is characterized by elements of both collaboration and resistance, blended together in such a way as to suggest an unusual, if not unique, feature of the Czech national character.

—David W. Paul,
The Cultural Limits of Revolutionary Politics

Svejk is the "bumbling, imperturbable, contemptible-but-lovable hero..." of *The Good Soldier Svejk*, the World War I novel by the Czech writer Jaroslav Hasek. A Czech folk hero, Svejk (or Schweik, as he is known in German and English) is a favorite, although controversial, character in Czech literature, a grotesque exaggeration of reality, as David W. Paul describes it, "...but like all good fictional characters, he embodies certain profound truths of human nature."[16]

In the novel, Svejk is the symbol of Czech opposition to Austrian rule during the war. His military misadventures follow one after another in hilarious sequence, illustrating the senselessness of established military, political, and religious order. As Czech writers Zdenka and Jan Munzer explain, Svejk is

...the little man lost in the labyrinth of world politics and universal confusion who guides himself by common-sense and whose weapon against oppression is a slightly foolish guile which is perhaps more effective than wisdom in a world not ruled by reason."[17]

American readers will recognize the similarities to Joseph Heller's *Catch-22*, the World War II novel. Ever the "artful dodger," Svejk battles the bureaucracy by appearing to be in step with it, but he actually marches to his own tune. As David W. Paul explains,

Svejk...is a secret rebel who fundamentally rejects the world around him. The world is oppressive and absurd, and he is aware of that. Instead of fighting it, however, Svejk chooses to ridicule it together with all its established values...and Svejk's special talent is uncovering the many absurdities that surround him.[18]

Svejk twists the bureaucratic world around his finger. He neither gets down on his knees nor stands up, but stoops and survives.

Svejkism stood the Czech people well during the communist years when they were ruled by the most conservative and cautious communist government in Eastern Europe. It enabled them to collaborate and resist at the same time, to find humor in misfortune, and to survive as a nation as they had done under the Austrians and Germans, and as they are likely to do in the postcommunist era, whatever it may bring.

The debate over Svejk continues today among Czechs, many of whom still question the 1938 decision not to resist German demands for dismemberment of Czechoslovakia.

When I asked three Czech scholars in Prague whether Svejkism still exists, they fidgeted in their chairs and replied somewhat reluctantly, "Yes, there is something of Svejk in all of us."

Janosik, the Slovak Robin Hood

Janosik was a brigand who loved freedom, music, and gaiety. ...His love of life, the pathos of his situation, his vibrant, young personality and daring had a strong emotional appeal to the Slovak people.

—Peter P. Yurchak, *The Slovaks*

Folk heroes tend to symbolize the character and spirit of their people, and this is true of Juro Janosik (1688-1713), the Slovak Robin Hood, leader of a band of brigands who robbed from rich Hungarian landowners and distributed their spoils to destitute Slovak serfs.

In the latter part of the seventeenth century, the Slovak peasantry suffered in virtual bondage, a condition that led to increased brigandage by bands based in Tatra Mountain hideaways. Generations of Slovaks have been brought up on Janosik's exploits, in stories, songs, poems, paintings, and films where he is portrayed as a fighter for social justice. His name is embodied in the Slovak word *janosikovsky* (heroic).

Born into a poor peasant family, Janosik served in the Hungarian army. With his mother gravely ill, his father was flogged for missing fieldwork in order to help her. Both parents died, the mother before Janosik returned home, and the father shortly after. With great resolve, Janosik embarked on a mission to avenge his father's death and ameliorate the frightful economic, political, and social injustices perpetrated by the feudal overlords on the Slovak people. The band that he led caused consternation among the Hungarians who were robbed and fueled the imagination of the suffering Slovaks who received their booty. Eventually betrayed, Janosik was captured, tried, and convicted as a lesson to others. Rejecting a pardon offered in return for revealing the whereabouts of his band and their cache, he is said to have shouted (in words reminiscent of our own Patrick Henry), "Give my people liberty or let me die" before killing himself.

More than any other person, Janosik symbolizes Slovak history and the character of its people—their perseverance through centuries of foreign oppression; their struggle for social justice, autonomy, and finally independence; their resilience and patience; and their positive outlook on life as evidenced in their music, dance, enjoyment of food and drink, and cheerfulness during years of oppression.

The American Connection

...I accepted the principles of American democracy. I can say that these principles have been and ever will be the policy of my government and my life. They appeal to our people, our people have adopted them as their own and through them we shall for ever be united with the American people, united with them in the spirit of liberty and democracy.
—Tomas G. Masaryk, Fourth of July Address, Prague 1919

Schoolchildren know that "Good King Wenceslas went out on the feast of Stephen," as the old English Christmas carol would have us believe. They may not know, however, that Vaclav, as Wenceslas is known in Czech, was a Slav and prince of Bohemia and Moravia in the early tenth century. The great square in the center of downtown Prague bears the name of this patron saint of the Czechs.

The modern patron saint, however, is Tomas Garrigue Masaryk, founding father of the Czechoslovak Republic. Philosopher, university professor, and first president of Czechoslovakia, Masaryk devoted his life to one task, according to Hans Kohn, "...to align his people in the spiritual battle between East and West, morally, culturally, and politically, with the West.... In the center of his philosophy stood the Western concept of the dignity of the individual and of the objectivity of truth."[19] Masaryk's model was American democracy.

Masaryk knew America well. He had visited the United States several times and took as his own the family name,

Garrigue, of the American woman he married. The new Czechoslovak state would resemble America, Masaryk wrote, because:

>...we, too, have no dynasty of our own and dislike a foreign dynasty; we have no aristocracy, no army and no militarist tradition...and we do not have an intimate relationship with the Church—a minus point unless we realize that a democracy and a republic must be based on morality.[20]

Together with President Woodrow Wilson, Masaryk was instrumental in founding the Czechoslovak state. Indeed, the intellectual compatibility of the two university professors and practical politicians surely played a role in their synergism.

When the United States entered World War I, Wilson initially opposed the breakup of Austria-Hungary in the hope of negotiating with it a separate peace and ending its alliance with Germany. Point Ten of Wilson's Fourteen Points on U.S. war objectives called for autonomous development for the peoples of Austria-Hungary but not their independence. But when secret peace negotiations with Austria failed, U.S. policy began to shift and soon thereafter came to support freedom for all Slavs in the German and Habsburg empires.

Masaryk helped draft the Czecho-Slovak Agreement, signed in Pittsburgh on May 31, 1918, which united Czechs and Slovaks in support of a unified democratic state. Declared president of the new republic on November 14, 1918, at the age of sixty-eight, he served for the next seventeen years, always reelected by a landslide vote. A railroad station in downtown Prague is named after Masaryk, and adjacent to the station is a street named for Woodrow Wilson.

Wilson is also respected by the Slovaks. When the Austro-Hungarian Empire disintegrated in 1918, Slovaks sought a new name for their leading city, refusing to call it by its German name, Pressburg, or its Hungarian name, Pozsony. They decided, instead, on the name Wilson, which the city bore for several months before reverting to its historic Slavic name, Bratislava.

The Moravian Brethren were among the earliest immigrants to the United States who can trace their origin to the Czech lands. Forced by the Counter-Reformation to leave their homeland in 1620, the Moravians first found refuge in other European countries, and it was from Germany that a group of them, by then Germanized, arrived in Pennsylvania in the early eighteenth century.

Czech emigration to the United States rose rapidly in the second half of the nineteenth century following the failed revolution of 1848 and the economic dislocations caused by the industrial revolution. Many of the immigrants were skilled artisans and tradesmen who settled in Chicago, St. Louis, New York, Cleveland, and Milwaukee. The farmers among them migrated westward, settling in rural areas of Iowa, Nebraska, and Texas. Literate and skilled in their professions, Czech immigrants were easily assimilated and soon became a part of the growing American middle class, owning their own homes and farms, and forming social, educational, and fraternal organizations. Czech pioneer life in Nebraska was vividly portrayed by Willa Cather in *My Antonia*, a classic of American literature.

The Czechs were also active in public life. Adolph J. Sabath, who arrived in Chicago in 1881 as a youth of fifteen, was the first U.S. congressman from the Czech lands. Elected to the House of Representatives in 1907, Sabath represented Chicago for forty-six years, establishing a reputation as an advocate of social legislation. He was followed by other notables of Czech origin, including Anton J. Cermak, mayor of Chicago from 1931 to 1933, until he took a bullet intended for President Franklin D. Roosevelt; Senator Roman Hruska of Nebraska, and Representative Charles Vanik of Ohio. Other prominent Americans of Czech origin include musicians Rudolf Friml and Rafael Kubelik, and, most recently, Madeleine Korbel Albright, who in 1993 was appointed U.S.

Representative to the United Nations.

The Czechs did well in the United States and documented their successes. A bookish people, they launched more than 340 periodicals and left behind a wealth of material for Americans seeking to explore their Czech roots.

The arts provide another Czech connection to the United States, and to the world. We all delight in the music of Dvorak, Smetana, and Janacek, and in the films of Milos Forman and other cinematographers of the Prague school. And those of us who wear soft contact lenses are grateful to the Czechs who invented them.

Americans today find life in the former Czechoslovakia to be congenial. Some 20,000 now make Prague their home, attracted by the ambiance of life in "Golden Prague."

Slovak emigration to the United States was equally large, if not larger. Some two to three million Americans are of Slovak descent, and one of every three Slovak citizens today has relatives in the United States. Cleveland at one time was the largest Slovak city in the world.

During the fifty years prior to World War I, some 600,000 Slovaks, nearly one-quarter of Slovakia's population at the time, emigrated to the United States. Another 100,000 Slovaks emigrated during the interwar period, and more left after World War I. Early emigrés, largely agricultural, were fleeing abysmal poverty and the inability to acquire farmland in their home country. They settled mainly in the northeast, especially in Pennsylvania, New Jersey, and New York, where they found employment in coal mines and steel mills and became strong union supporters, earning the description "builders of America." Later immigrants, including many artisans and professional people, settled in the western states, especially California, and in Florida.

The early immigrants established Slovak communities centered around their churches and parochial schools. In the 1880s, more than two hundred Slovak-language newspapers and periodicals were published in the United States, an activity which had been forbidden them in their homeland. In the absence of social security and a welfare system, they organized fraternal self-help societies which provided disability insurance and death benefits to workers and their families. They also formed national organizations, many of which still exist today.

Among the prominent early Slovak arrivals were Major John Polorecky and Count Maurice Benyovsky, who fought in the American Revolutionary War, and Colonel Gajza Mihalotzy, organizer of the "Lincoln Riflemen of Slavonic Origin" who fought in the Civil War. The Reverend Joseph Murgas of Pennsylvania was issued two patents for wireless communications before Marconi and transmitted the first wireless signals in 1905. Stephen Banic presented his parachute patent to the Army Air Corps, which made him an honorary member.

More recent Americans of Slovak descent include D. Carleton Gajdusek, 1976 Nobel laureate in physiology and medicine; Jaroslav Pelikan, theologian and Yale University professor; Michael Novak, political scientist and syndicated columnist; Eugene Cernan, lunar astronaut; Robert Urich, Tom Selleck, Sissy Spacek, and Richard Chamberlain, actors; Joe Lapchick, basketball player and coach; Chuck Bednarik, Philadelphia Eagles' Football Hall of Famer; Stanley Mikita, Chicago Blackhawks Hockey Hall of Famer; Bernie Kosar, NFL quarterback; Lou Holtz, Notre Dame football coach; and Elaine Zayak, figure skater.

---

[1] *Prognosis* (Prague), 17-30 September 1993.

[2] Hans Kohn, *Pan-Slavism: Its History and Ideology* (Notre Dame, IN: Notre Dame Univ. Press, 1953), 28.

[3] Flora Lewis, *Europe: Road to Unity*, rev. ed. (New York: Simon and Schuster, Touchstone, 1992), 422-23.

[4] Paul Zinner, *Communist Strategy and Tactics in Czechoslovakia, 1914-48* (New York: Frederick A. Praeger, 1963), 10.

[5] Misha Glenny, *The Rebirth of History: Eastern Europe in the Age of Democracy* (London and New York: Penguin Books, 1993), 28-29.

[6] Vaclav Havel, in a statement broadcast on 29 March 1993, reported in *RFE/RL Research Report* 2, no. 24 (11 June 1993).

[7] Tadeusz Konwicki, *Moonrise, Moonset*, trans. Richard Lourie (New York: Farrar, Strauss, Giroux, 1987), 85-86.

[8] Elizabeth Wiskemann, *Czechs and Germans: A Study of the Struggle in the Historic Provinces of Bohemia and Moravia* (London and New York: Oxford Univ. Press, 1938), 1.

[9] Lewis, *Europe*, 427.

[10] In Eastern Europe, name days (the days of saints for whom people are named) are celebrated rather than birthdays.

[11] Emil Komarik, "Vestiges of Communism and the Dissolution of Czechoslovakia," *Uncaptive Minds* 6, no. 1 (Winter-Spring 1993): 56.

[12] Bruce Garver, "The Czechoslovak Tradition: An Overview," in Hans Brisch and Ivan Volgyes, eds., *Czechoslovakia: The Heritage of Ages Past* (Boulder, CO: East European Quarterly, 1979), 26.

[13] *New York Times*, 21 November 1993.

[14] Karen von Kunes, *Prague Post*, 15-21 September 1993.

[15] Vaclav Havel, address to a Joint Session of the United States Congress, 21 February 1990. *Congressional Record* 136, no. 13, H392-95.

[16] David W. Paul, *The Cultural Limits of Revolutionary Politics: Change and Continuity in Socialist Czechoslovakia* (Boulder, CO: East European Quarterly, 1979), 256-57.

[17] Zdenka Munzer and Jan Munzer, *We Were and We Shall Be: The Czechoslovak Spirit through the Centuries* (New York: Frederick Ungar, 1941), 98.

[18] Paul, *Cultural Limits*, 257.

[19] Hans Kohn, *The Twentieth Century* (New York: Macmillan, 1949), 212-13.

[20] George J. Kovtun, *Masaryk and America: Testimony of a Relationship* (Washington, DC: Library of Congress, 1988), 53.

4

Hungarians

I found on further acquaintance...the passion, the dynamic force which have made Hungary, in its strange isolation, its strategic position in the center of Europe, such a continually erupting crater, such a constantly humming powerhouse, which is also such a constant exporter of power.

—Edmund Wilson, *Europe without Baedeker*

For a Hungarian to understand the United States, a Hungarian once told me in Washington, he should stand on his head. All his preconceptions about the country will be turned upside down.

This is not to imply that Americans should stand on their heads in order to understand Hungary, but rather to consider that in Hungary things really are different and will at least seem upside down.

My first encounter with a Hungarian was in Germany after World War II. He was a displaced person, a lawyer by profession, and my chief employee in a U.S. military government office in a small Bavarian town. Although he did not smoke, my Hungarian always carried a cigarette lighter; when anyone within sight pulled out a cigarette, he was immediately there with a light.

"*Herr Doktor*," I once asked, "since you do not smoke, why do you always carry a cigarette lighter?"

Drawing himself up and looking at me with some disdain, he replied simply but proudly, "I am a Hungarian."

Chivalrous behavior and grace in dealing with people are typically Hungarian. Men still give their seats to women on public transportation, get off buses first in order to help their women step down, and walk to the left of women (to protect them with their swords, of course). Women precede men on entering theaters, cinemas, and private homes, but men go first in restaurants, bars, and cafes.

Courtliness and gallantry are legacies of the Hungarian past, which parallels the lifestyle of the Polish szlachta. The Hungarian and Polish aristocracy and gentry were noted for their lavish hospitality, extravagance, overstatement, sense of honor, and romantic nationalism. This kinship between Hungarians and Poles has a basis in history.

The old Hungarian and Polish societies were similar—a small aristocracy at the top, a somewhat larger landed gentry (5 percent of the population in Hungary), a very small urban middle class, and illiterate peasants or serfs who made up the bulk of the population. With such similarities, Hungary and Poland have been political and military allies more often than not, sharing common adversaries—Russia and the Ottoman Turks. "The Pole and the Hungarian," an old saying goes, "are two brothers in drinking and wielding the sabre." Indeed, Poles have had a better rapport with the non-Slavic Magyars than with any of their Slav neighbors.

Poles and Hungarians also share a common attitude toward West and East. Their historic role—which they believe is not properly appreciated—has been to protect the West from Mongols, Russians, Turks, and other "barbarians" of the East.

The Hungarian Difference

> Outside Hungary there is no life; but if there is, it is not the same.
>
> —old Hungarian saying

Hungarians do not have an identity crisis. They know who they are. The first great Hungarian, they say, was Attila. To be sure, Attila was a Hun, not a Hungarian, but the Asian despot who ravaged much of Europe before settling in what is now Hungary in the fifth century is seen as a hero, and his name is borne by many Hungarians today.

The nomadic horsemen who founded the Hungarian state one thousand years ago originated in the Ural Mountain region of Asia and migrated to Central Europe in the ninth century from the steppes of what is now southern Russia. The Magyars (pronounced "Mudyars"), as they called themselves, were known in the West as *Onogurs* ("ten tribes," in Turkic), "Hungarian" in English, *Hongrois* in French, and *Ungar* in German. But in contrast to most other Asian tribes that migrated to the West, the Magyars left an imprint on Europe—and the rest of the world—that is still with us today.

Toward the end of the ninth century the Magyars began to move through Carpathian Mountain passes and settle in the Roman province of Pannonia in the Central Danubian Basin. With that incursion they split the West Slavs from the South Slavs and prevented henceforth the formation of a greater Slav state. From their Danubian base the Magyars were the scourge of Central and Western Europe, raiding as far as Rome, Bremen, Verdun, and the Pyrenees in the West, and Constantinople in the East, until their defeat by Germans and Czechs in 955 at Lechfeld near Augsburg in today's southern Germany.

The Magyars retreated to their settlements in the Central Danubian Basin where they founded the largest state in Central Europe and extended their rule over an area that included today's Hungary, Slovakia, Croatia, Transylvania, parts of Serbia and western Ukraine, and a small part of today's Austria. Scholars differ in explaining why the Magyars chose to remain in Europe. Most likely their return route to Asia was blocked by other advancing tribes. Some Hungarians, however, claim that it was because the women they found in the Danubian Basin were so beautiful. That too is a very Hungarian response which, based on my field research, is completely credible.

Despite their Asian origins, the Magyars have identified with Europe for a thousand years. Today's Hungarian, living in the heart of the continent, is actually an ethnic mix of Huns and Avars, Magyars, Slavs, Tatars, Turks, Romanians, Germans, Jews, Gypsies, and other ethnic groups that marauded or migrated over centuries to the Central Danubian Basin, "...superimposed and deposited," as Claudio Magris describes them, "one upon another in layer after layer."[1] Moreover, the Hungarians lived on a broad plain, bound together by their Magyar language, a culture and lifestyle that are uniquely Hungarian, a passionate pride in their Hungarianness, and an attachment to their homeland.

Fact and Fiction

Weeping, the Hungarian makes merry.

—Hungarian proverb

Literature abounds with legends about Hungarians, some based on fact and others on fiction—their gallantry, romanticism, traditions of honor, exaggeration, flamboyance, fondness for gypsy music, and a tendency to become maudlin under the influence of wine. This was how the Hungarian looked to other Europeans, and as he may appear today.

"The Hungarian is fond of trappings," says a Hungarian

proverb. This was confirmed by Arthur J. Patterson, an early English expert on Hungary, who wrote in 1869, "In his actions, the Magyar, to whatever class he may belong, is apt to attach too much importance to the effect they will produce on the eyes or imaginations of beholders."[2] "Among the weak points of the Magyar's character," continued Patterson, "must be reckoned that of being peculiarly open to flattery; nor is he averse to display, or insensible to the charms of beauty."[3]

More than one hundred years later much of Patterson's description is still valid. Hungarians still do things with exaggeration, as well as style and dash.

In the mid-1970s, for example, I was traveling by rail from Belgrade to Budapest. My train was rather grimy and without food or beverage service for the long trip. But when we crossed the Yugoslav-Hungarian border, a Hungarian waiter boarded the train. Clad in a freshly starched white linen jacket, and with flair and flourish, he offered good strong Hungarian coffee and cookies to the grateful passengers. Welcome to Hungary!

On another occasion that year, as I was traveling by rail from Bratislava to Budapest, a Hungarian porter boarded my train at the border and announced that he was taking orders for taxis to meet passengers at the Budapest station. This kind of service was unknown elsewhere in Eastern Europe at that time.

Such service is now carried over to air transport. At Budapest's new international terminal, arriving passengers are waved through immigration and customs without hassle. Limousine service to any hotel in Budapest? No problem.

Hungarians take great pride in such achievements and in the recovery of their accustomed lifestyle, which they managed to put together after years of Stalinism and a 1956 revolution savagely suppressed by the Soviet Union. That recovery came much faster than in other East European states, and when the other states were still drab and dreary, Hungary was a pleasure to visit.

For Hungarians, there is more to life than work. Important are poetry, music, and art, as well as the public baths, flowers, dogs, sweets, weekends spent with family, walks in the woods, dachas in the country, and books. In a nation of bibliophiles there are bookstands everywhere on the Budapest streets.

Conversation is an art. Hungarians take great pleasure in sitting and conversing for hours at a time and without getting bored. All this can be summed up in the word *Eletmuvesz* (life artist), a term used to describe someone who makes an art out of life.

Business is conducted indirectly. Money is not passed openly between acquaintances but is first placed in an envelope. Rather than responding directly to a question at hand, Hungarians will talk around it, and visitors will have to be alert to what is said and not said. To say no to a social equal or a superior is not considered polite, so various excuses may be given in responding to a request.

An American scholar, for example, relates how he once asked to borrow a book he saw in the apartment of a Hungarian colleague. "Very sorry," replied the Hungarian, "I am writing a review of the book for a scholarly journal, but please call me in a week." A week later, the American called and was told by the Hungarian that he was going to Vienna for the weekend and would be taking the book with him to read on the train, but please call again. Calling once more, the American learned that the Hungarian's grandmother was deathly ill, and he planned to read her a few choice chapters from the book before she expired. And so it went, each excuse more silly than the previous until the American finally understood that the Hungarian did not want to lend the book but was too polite to say so.

Social settings are influenced by established codes of behavior. As one American said, it's like playing several games of chess at one time. Hungarians, for example, will want to know who you are—your ethnic background and religion, who your grandfather was. In the United States these things may not be very important, but in Hungary they determine how people relate to each other. Social status remains important.

Children are raised to respect age, authority, and power. Students rise when a professor enters the classroom. An American guest professor relates how he would enter an elevator filled with students at his university. The students would be going to the second floor and the professor to the third, but they would allow the professor to go to his floor before they went to theirs.

Such politeness, however, is not universal. At the office or at home Hungarians are most cordial, but on the street they can be quite uncivil to each other. Americans who have worked with Hungarians say they do not return phone calls or reply to letters.

Emotion rather than rational analysis often determines behavior, and self-confidence can exceed self-knowledge. As Hungarian-born American historian John Lukacs says:

> More than one succeeding generation [of Hungarians] were driven astray by their rhetoric of national self-confidence. Alas, that sometimes salutary sense of national self-confidence existed together with a wanting extent of self-knowledge; and with a wholly wanting understanding of the limits of national power, indeed, of Hungary's situation in Europe.[4]

And yet, despite the traditions of romanticism and exaggeration, Hungary in our time has demonstrated pragmatism and efficiency in its economic reforms. During the communist era, Hungary was a mecca for visitors from the East—Russians, Poles, and others—who saw Hungary as a model of Western efficiency and a great big shopping mall where they could purchase items not available at home.

As a Polish friend told me in the 1970s, "How do they do it? They have the same communist system as we, and yet their shops are full and ours are empty." Today, Hungary's greater stability, rule of law, good banking system, skilled workers, and central location are strong incentives for Western investment.

Another truth about Hungarians should be seen as fact rather than fiction. They are smart, sophisticated, and very European, and they do not appreciate being talked down to.

High Achievers

The happy mixture of the many races and nationalities has produced people whose talents are enormous and whose expressive abilities span the cultural and scientific world.

—Ivan Volgyes, *Hungary: A Nation of Contradictions*

Hungarians like to tell the story about one of their physicists who had attended an international scientific congress abroad. When asked, on his return home, how he had been able to communicate with scientists from so many other countries, the physicist replied simply, "We all spoke Hungarian, of course."

There is as much truth as jest in this anecdote. Three Hungarians were leaders in the development of nuclear energy in the United States: Leo Szilard, Eugene Wigner, and Edward Teller. Physicist Theodore von Karman was instrumental in the development of supersonic flight and the science of aerodynamics. Mathematician John von Neumann is known as the father of the computer. John G. Kemeny, a president of Dartmouth College, was the coinventor of BASIC, the most widely used computer language. Biochemist Albert Szent-Gyorgyi discovered vitamin C. Bela Schick devised the Schick test for diphtheria, and Ignaz Semmelweis made childbirth safer through his discoveries in antisepsis. Ladislas Biro invented the ballpoint pen, and Erno Rubik, Rubik's cube.

Hungarians have a well-deserved reputation for being high achievers. Faced with adversaries, real and potential, on all sides—Turks, Romanians, Russians, Slovaks, Croats, Serbs, and Austrians—Hungarians early on developed a militant and competitive spirit, a will to win at all costs in order to survive as a nation. As a Hungarian told me, Hungarians are suicidal perfectionists—they must come out ahead even if they self-destruct in the process. They are, it has been said, the only people who can enter a revolving door behind you and exit ahead of you.

Also remarkable for a nation of only ten million are the stellar achievements of Hungarians in the arts. In music, they have given us composers Franz Liszt, Zoltan Kodaly, Bela Bartok, Ernst von Dohnanyi, Franz Lehar, and Emerich Kalman. Symphony conductors from Hungary include Fritz Reiner, George Szell, Eugene Ormandy, Antal Dorati, and Sir George Solti. Among Hollywood's pioneers were Hungarians Adolph Zukor, the founder of Paramount Pictures, and William Fox, a founder of Twentieth-Century Fox. Other prominent Hungarians in the entertainment industry include film director George Cukor, producers Joseph Pasternak and Alexander Korda, actors Bela Lugosi and Paul Lukas, the three Gabor sisters, as well as master magician Harry Houdini. And that most English of actors, Leslie Howard (who played Ashley Wilkes in *Gone with the Wind*) was of Hungarian descent. Indeed, Hungarians seem to have a talent for absorbing themselves into other cultures and then becoming the prototypes of those cultures, although their unmistakable accent on the first syllable of words often gives them away.

Other celebrated Hungarians include publisher Joseph Pulitzer, architect Laszlo Moholy-Nagy, sociologists Karl Mannheim and Oszkar Jaszi, writer Arthur Koestler, and the founder of the Zionist movement, Theodore Herzl. Many of these scientific and artistic luminaries were of Jewish origin but they were all Hungarian in culture, language, and their drive to high achievement.

Hungarian talent and will to win are also reflected in athletic prowess, as Joe Namath fans will confirm. In the

1992 Summer Olympics, Hungary won thirty medals—eleven gold, twelve silver, and seven bronze—more medals than South Korea, France, Australia, Spain, Japan, Britain, Italy, Poland, Canada, Romania, and Bulgaria in that order. Equally remarkable, Hungary finished third at Helsinki in 1952, behind Germany and the United States, and fourth at London in 1948, Melbourne in 1956, Tokyo in 1964, and Mexico City in 1968.

The striving for achievement is also indicated in the Hungarian language. As Lukacs points out, an American will ask how much do you *make* in a year? A German, how much do you *earn*? The French and Latins use the word *win*. A Hungarian, however, asks how much do you *gather*, a word that in Hungarian originally implied *achieve* (106-7).

Yes, Hungarians are high achievers, as well as being very intelligent, better educated than most Americans, and a match for anyone.

The Dark Destiny of Hungarian History

Arise, Magyars, your country calls you!
The time has come, now or never!
Shall we be slaves or free?
This is the question—choose!
By the God of the Magyars
We swear, we swear
That we will no longer be slaves!
—Sandor Petofi, *Talpra Magyar!*
("Arise Hungarians!"), 1848

Despite their achievements, Hungarians have a reputation for being moody, melancholy, and malcontent. A nation of gripers, they have an ability to turn positives into negatives and appear to delight in doing so. The Hungarian, it is said, will complain if his ice cream is cold.

Pessimism runs deep. When asked how things are going today, a Hungarian is said to have replied, "Worse than yesterday, but better than tomorrow." They are also self-accusing and self-pitying, and overly concerned with death. Personal problems are repressed rather than discussed with friends. Despair and depression are the result and often lead to suicide. According to the Johns Hopkins School of Hygiene and Public Health, Hungary has the highest suicide rate in Europe, 40 per 100,000 of population, followed by Finland with 27. (To put these figures in perspective, the United States and Poland each have 13 per 100,000.)

The public attitude toward politics is apathetic, with little belief that elections can change things for the better. A Peace Corps volunteer reports how surprised her Hungarian friends were by her interest in the 1992 presidential election and her elation over the Clinton victory. They could not imagine how anyone would be so interested in an election.

Much of this mood can be attributed to history and the fact that Hungary in its wars has always chosen the losing side. Holidays celebrate military defeats and failed revolutions. "The great literature of Hungary," writes Claudio Magris, "is not the literature which glories in the splendour of a heroic Hungary, but the one which reveals the misery and darkness of the Hungarian destiny."[5]

Hungarians have a deep sense of history and will speak of events that took place centuries ago as if they had occurred last week. Visitors who have at least a cursory knowledge of Hungarian history will be appreciated.

The symbol of Hungarian nationalism is the crown of St. Stephen, patron saint of Hungary. When King Istvan (Stephen) received his crown from the pope in the year 1000, the Hungarian nation began the process of becoming Christian and henceforth a part of the Western world.[6] Greater Hungary, a multinational state in which the Magyars ruled supreme, was to last almost a thousand years despite devastating invasions by foreign forces.

The Mongols ravaged Hungary in 1241. Next came the Ottoman Turks in the sixteenth century. Hungary's position in Central Europe placed it squarely between the advancing Muslim Turks and an Austria that saw itself as the defender of Christian Europe. In 1526, at the Battle of Mohacs on the Hungarian-Serb border, Hungary suffered a major defeat and the Turks occupied central Hungary for the next 150 years. What remained, when the Turks were eventually defeated by Austria at the end of the seventeenth century, was a wasteland which Austria resettled with Germans, Slovaks, Serbs, and Romanians. In their "liberated" state, which was little more than a colony of Austria, Hungarians numbered only 35 percent of the population.

Another invasion came in 1849, this time from both East and West when Russia and Austria jointly occupied Hungary and brutally suppressed a revolution of the previous year which had sought independence. It has been said that Hungary lost that war but won the peace. Prior to 1848, Hungary had been a backward agricultural state with little industry, few cities, and a largely peasant population. In 1848 the combined population of Buda and Pest—two separate cities at the time and not yet connected by a Danube bridge—was only 150,000. Industry was largely German-owned, commerce was mostly the province of Jews, while the "business" of Hungarians was agriculture.

Modernization began in 1848 with the freeing of the serfs, the development of agriculture on a commercial basis, and a start in industrial expansion. Economic development accelerated after 1867, the year of the Austro-Hungarian Compromise which established a dual monarchy and gave Hungary home rule within its historic territories. Thus the assertion that Hungary "won the peace."

Hungary prospered as partner in the Austro-Hungarian Empire. Highways and railroads were built, industry and commerce expanded, agriculture became more scientific, and cities grew. By the turn of the century, Budapest was a major European metropolis, capital of a multinational kingdom in which Hungarians ruled although they numbered little more than half the population. Beneath the surface, social problems festered, but the future of Hungary looked promising as war clouds ominously gathered over Europe.

Hungary's next defeat came at the end of World War I when it was again on the losing side. Fragmented by the Treaty of Trianon (a nasty word in the Hungarian lexicon), Hungary lost two-thirds of its historic territory and one-third of its ethnic Magyar population to Romania, Czechoslovakia, and Yugoslavia, a debacle from which it has never recovered. Determined never to accept the Trianon losses, *nem, nem, soha* (no, no, never) became the Hungarian national slogan in the interwar years. Today there are an estimated two million Hungarians in Romania, 600,000 in Slovakia, 400,000 in Serbia, 200,000 in Ukraine, 40,000 in Croatia, 16,000 in Austria, and 10,000 in Slovenia. The truncated Hungary is now the size of Indiana.

After World War II, when Hungary was again on the losing side, Soviet troops occupied the country and it fell within the Soviet orbit. In 1956, Budapesters rose in armed rebellion against their Soviet occupiers, only to be crushed once more.

Looking back at their history, Hungarians believe that their ordained role has been to suffer and be abandoned by those in the West whose freedom they have defended. As the final line from the Hungarian national anthem laments, "This nation has already atoned for its past and its future."

The Language

[Hungarian] is not the language of trade, of persuasion, of weighing things, but rather that of pronouncement, of judgment. It is a language which articulates, strongly emphasizing every word. Foreigners, when they first hear it, feel that it is a language of command.

—Gyula Illyes

To Gyula Illyes, one of Hungary's leading twentieth-century writers, Hungarian only *seemed* to be a language of command. Those who fashioned it, he explained,

> have communicated only thoughts that have been completed, already chewed, and then they have said no more. Each of their words has its value. Behind each thought is a real experience, if not a real sorrow. The very word for thought [*gondolat*] is derived in this language from the word for care [*gond*].[7]

Also puzzled by the sound of spoken Hungarian was an American who worked in Budapest in the early 1990s. A Hungarian meeting, she relates, first appeared to her as a group of people sitting around a table shouting at each other, interrupting, not seeming to listen when others were speaking, but then suddenly reaching a decision which seemed to satisfy everyone. Americans in such meetings, she counseled, should be patient, for that is the Hungarian way, and it works.

Quiet and orderly meetings are rare. There is much small talk and humor before getting down to the serious business. Hungarians like to tell jokes, and visitors should have a few of their own ready to tell. Before the serious business, there will be a long introduction that does not really say much but sets the stage for the give-and-take that will follow. And do they give and take! Everything is debated at length, often without regard for time or for the agenda of the day, if one exists.

The Hungarian language is the root of Hungarian behavior, the glue that has bound the people together and given them their distinctiveness. Until the 1830s, Latin was the language of government and law but over the next decade it faded from use and was gradually replaced by Hungarian. It continues to thrive today, and Hungarians cling to it with pride and persistence.

Hungarian is a Finno-Ugrian language, a group of tongues also spoken by the faraway Finns, Estonians, and Lapps. In

1500 B.C., they split into two groups, Finns and Ugrians, with the Magyars among the latter. Finnish and Hungarian today sound similar but are mutually unintelligible and equally difficult to learn. Edmund Wilson, however, found Hungarian much less difficult than Russian. Wilson, who studied Hungarian, has described it as "...an almost perfectly logical instrument, codified as a literary language as late as the eighteen-thirties by a practical committee of scholars, whereas Russian was developed in a hit-or-miss fashion—a language composed of idioms, with a queer and irregular grammar."[8]

Like many Asian tongues, Hungarian is an agglutinative language. The vocabulary, in which verbs predominate, is based on root words with suffixes added to express various nuances. This suggests manifold aspects of action, multiple shades of situations, and a literary enthusiasm that gives Hungarian a conciseness and ability to express much with very few words.

In spoken Hungarian, the emphasis is on the first syllable, which, Lukacs conjectures, explains the "straw-fire nature" of Hungarians, "...the brilliance of short-run effort at the expense of prudence and foresight."[9] The lilt of sentences, in contrast to English, runs from a high of the first syllable down toward the end of the sentence, which makes Hungarian speech and music sound rather wild and strange to the foreigner. Equally daunting is the spelling, with double letters (*cs, sz, zs, gy, ly, ny, and ty*) that express various sounds. The pronunciation is easy, however, once a few rules have been learned.

Hungarian has four words for *you*, each with a plural form, and the choice depends on the social or class relationship between the people who are conversing, whether they are speaking to social equals or to someone of higher or lower class or status. And like Polish, the third person is used in addressing persons of higher status. The style is very literary in both speech and writing.

As in Asian languages, family names precede given names. Bela Bartok, for example, as the Hungarian composer is known in the West, is Bartok Bela in his homeland. Another reminder of Hungary's Asian roots is the many words of Turkic origin, a legacy of the 300 years that the Magyars lived among Turkic peoples in the steppes north of the Black Sea, as well as the 150 years of Turkish occupation of Hungary. When introducing themselves, Hungarians will give their family name first.

Because Hungarian is not related to any major European language group, Hungarians, by necessity, are great linguists. They learn other languages easily and have been called a nation of translators. They are also a nation of raconteurs, and the telling of anecdotes interspersed in speech is an art form. In a cerebral society where intellectuals are highly respected, Hungarians can discuss objectively almost any issue solely on its merits, while separating themselves from the issue under discussion.

Their rhetoric, however, often carries Hungarians away. As Lukacs puts it, "...in public rather than in private speech, the sober and rational element in the Hungarian mind—and the terseness of the language—tend to be overwhelmed by the intoxication of rhetoric." There is little inclination to profit from a dialogue, adds Lukacs,

> ...to find satisfaction in compromise. There is often yawning distance, not so much between thought and speech as between speech and action, between the attraction of ideals and the contemplation of realities, between verbal energy and physical lassitude. The result is a fatal Hungarian tendency to self-centeredness (110).

A similar view was voiced by Antal Szerb, the great Hungarian literary historian. The Hungarian mind, he wrote, "tends to monologue rather than dialogue."[10]

Exaggeration is another tendency of Hungarian rhetoric, epitomized by that hero of Hungarian folklore, Hary Janos, a

Magyar Baron von Munchhausen, a teller of absurdly exaggerated stories. "Hungarians," wrote Patterson in 1869, "....are disposed to exaggerate the efficiency of misrepresentation, and even self-deception, as a means of tiding over present difficulties and acquiring future advantages."[11] Marian Burros of the *New York Times* writes more charitably in 1992. "Hyperbole is to Hungarians," she says, "what understatement is to New Englanders."[12]

As a consequence, there is often a discrepancy between what Hungarians say and what they are able to do. As an American diplomat with long experience in Hungary told me, "At a first meeting Hungarians will promise much. At a second meeting, they are likely to back off from earlier promises. And at a third meeting, their response may well be, 'Yes, it may be possible,' with the emphasis on the *may*."

Negotiating with Hungarians

Bargain like an enemy; pay like a friend.

—Hungarian proverb

Those who negotiate with Hungarians should allow plenty of time. Hungarians are very legalistic in their approach to negotiations. They will want to review the terms of a draft agreement "a hundred times," as one experienced U.S. government official put it, seeking clarification of what each term means and asking "what if" questions.

Such tactics may be due in part to the legalisms of the Austro-Hungarian bureaucracy that still pervade much of Central Europe. Also playing a role may be the Hungarian language with its exactitude and conciseness, and some Hungarians simply enjoy negotiating. Whatever the reasons, negotiations can be long and involved. They do, however, start on time. Hungarians are a prompt people and will even show up for appointments a little early. Americans too should be prompt in Hungary.

The negotiating process becomes most complex in the privatization of state-owned enterprises. The future welfare of work forces will be involved, as well as the survival of firms which Hungarian officials may regard as among the family jewels of the Magyar nation. A particular firm may have once been a part of an historic estate or been regarded as a national landmark—no minor considerations in a small country with a strong sense of history. Such sentimental considerations, however, tend to inflate the true value of an enterprise and make negotiations more difficult.

What to do? Be patient and understanding. Steer the discussions back to practical issues, which Hungarians will understand and appreciate. Once they have been reassured on all points under contention, they will be ready to sign, their word will be good, and the agreement will be carried out as written. But be prepared to sit and wait. And while waiting, have another cup of good Hungarian coffee.

Coffee, Tobacco, and Other Addictions

> Good coffee should be black like the devil, hot like hell, and sweet like a kiss.
>
> —Hungarian proverb

Coffee is the national addiction, and Hungarians have been drinking it longer than most other Europeans, since the sixteenth century when it was introduced by the Turks. Coffee in Hungary, and elsewhere in Eastern Europe, is made in the Turkish fashion—finely ground coffee is brewed *with* sugar; and some of the grounds, after settling to the bottom of the cup, are drunk with the coffee. Hungarians have good reasons for complaining about the bitter Turkish rule, but no grounds for complaint against the strong brew brought by their Turkish conquerors.

Coffeehouses were the centers of social life in old Hungary, rather like English pubs—places to meet friends, eat, drink, and socialize—and at little cost. Many are gone now, victims of a faster way of life; but in those coffeehouses that remain, it is still possible to sit for hours and talk over a cup of coffee, read newspapers or magazines, and do business. Hungarian authors wrote much of their work in coffeehouses, and they were as attached to their coffeehouses as they were to Hungary.

A story is told of Ferenc Molnar, the renowned playwright. In the late 1930s, he had his favorite coffeehouse, and in that coffeehouse his favorite chair in which he would sit for hours, converse with friends, and write. Nazi Germany had just annexed neighboring Austria and a friend asked Molnar (who was a Jew), "Ferenc, aren't you afraid? Why don't you save your neck and emigrate to America?" "It is easy to emigrate to America," replied Molnar, "but it is difficult to get up from this chair." Molnar eventually did emigrate to the United States where, as another Hungarian high achiever, he was as successful in New York as he had been in Budapest.

Hungarian coffee is drunk throughout the day, in small cups, black, sweetened, very strong, and served with a glass of cold water. Visitors in offices and homes should expect to be offered coffee but are warned not to drink too many cups. On a business trip to Budapest once, I had scheduled six meetings in one day, and at each I was served coffee, sweets, and *barack*, the local apricot brandy. At the end of the day my heart was racing, and I badly needed a respite.

Tobacco is another national addiction, and Hungarians are among the world's heaviest cigarette smokers—3,260 per person annually, according to the World Health Organization.[13] Cigarette smoking is declining in the United States and Western Europe but is increasing in Eastern Europe, where there seems to be little concern for its health hazards. For Hungarians, Marlboro is the preferred brand.

Good food with good Hungarian wine and animated conversation are traditional. Hungarian cuisine is in the grand tradition of East European cooking—long on pork and fat, high in calories and cholesterol, enriched with cream sauces, flavored with paprika (sweet pepper) and spices, and, unfortunately, very tasty. In an agriculturally rich country, food is abundant and varied, but for persons on a diet, watching their waistlines, or accustomed to bland food, caution is advised. "Lard, paprika, and sour cream," writes Burros, "is the holy trinity of Hungarian cooking."[14]

Who Is a Magyar?

> Hungarianness is both a fact and a value.
> —Laszlo Ravasz, *What Is a Magyar?*

The term "Magyar" today is applied to anyone who can claim descent from the Magyars, as well as those who are Magyar in language and culture but not necessarily of Magyar descent. This can include Hungarians whose origins are Slovak, Croatian, Turkish, German, or Jewish. Because Hungarians were a minority in their own country, persons of the subject nations who learned to speak Hungarian and assimilated were accepted as Hungarians. As for religion, some two-thirds of Hungarians are Catholics. The other one-third are mostly Protestants (predominantly Calvinists with smaller numbers of Lutherans of German and Slovak origin), and Jews.

Jews have lived in Hungary since the founding of the Hungarian state one thousand years ago, but nowhere else in Eastern Europe did they become so assimilated to the local culture and achieve such prominence in society. Moreover, Hungarian Jews never had to live in ghettos, as elsewhere in Europe.

Jews were emancipated in Hungary in 1867 when an act of parliament gave them full equality with Christians in the exercise of civil and political rights. Moreover, in 1895 the Jewish religion was granted full legal equality with other denominations. This is particularly noteworthy because, during the latter part of the nineteenth century, Hungary had received large numbers of Jews from Galicia and other west Ukrainian provinces under Austrian rule.

Although numbering no more than 5 percent of the population, Jews soon became an important element in the small but growing urban middle class and influential far beyond their numbers, excelling in industry and commerce, fields disdained by the Hungarian nobility and gentry as beneath them. As the economy expanded, Jews also were prominent in banking, law, journalism, medicine, science, and the arts and became fully assimilated Hungarians. Many took Hungarian names, and a few hundred Jewish families were even ennobled and recognized as gentry, adding to their Hungarian names the final *y* which denotes nobility.

Anti-Semitism grew in the interwar period. The small middle class, largely Jewish, was augmented with impoverished gentry, newly arrived Hungarians from the lost territories, and upwardly mobile peasants. These new townspeople found themselves in competition with Jews who were well established in their professions and prominent in the business and cultural life of Budapest. Moreover, they were all living in a truncated Hungary with fewer opportunities. In reaction to this competition, a *numerus clausus* (quota) was instituted, limiting the number of Jews admitted to universities to their percentage of the total population.

The Holocaust demolished the Jewish community. For the first four and one-half years of the war, Jews were relatively untouched, protected by Hungarian governments that resisted German pressures for The "Final Solution"—deportation to the east. This changed in 1944 when Germany occupied Hungary. Deportations began in earnest, and almost half a million Jews from the countryside were deported. Those who survived were mostly residents of Budapest. Of the 750,000 Jews in Hungary on the eve of the German occupation, only 150,000 survived the war, many of them through the heroic efforts of Swedish diplomat Raoul Wallenberg.

Today, there are some 100,000 Jews in Hungary, almost all of them in Budapest, the largest surviving Jewish community in Eastern Europe. Anti-Semitism, unfortunately, has also survived and remains a regrettable aspect of Hungarian life.

The American Connection

The first American connection with Hungary appears to have been the soldier adventurer, Captain John Smith, who fought with the Hungarians against the Turks in 1600, eight years before he came to Virginia's Jamestown Colony.

But Smith brought no Hungarians to Jamestown, as he did Poles; and there were few Hungarians in the United States until the middle of the nineteenth century when, following the failed liberal revolution of 1848, some 4,000 refugees arrived. The so-called "forty-niners" were mostly educated political refugees of the gentry class.

At the outbreak of the Civil War there were still little more than 4,000 Hungarians (including women and children) in the United States.[15] Of this number, some 800 served the Union cause, where their past military experience and sympathy for the North were recognized and rewarded with officer commissions. Hungarians in the Union armies included two major generals, five brigadier generals, fifteen colonels and lieutenant colonels, thirteen majors, twelve captains, and some four dozen lieutenants. No other immigrant group proportionately provided as many top officers as Hungarians.

The next wave of immigration came between 1880 and 1914 as part of the exodus from Europe caused by the industrial revolution. Mostly of peasant origin, these Hungarians sought to escape the grinding poverty of their native villages and to find their fortunes in the New World. They settled mainly in cities such as Cleveland, Pittsburgh, Bridgeport, Detroit, and Chicago where they found employment as workers in industry and mining.

Since 1918, most Hungarian immigrants to the United States have been members of the political and technical intelligentsia who were to play leading roles in the scientific, cultural, and academic life of the United States. They came in three waves following cataclysmic events which were devastating for a great state with a thousand-year history, and when Hungary was again on the losing side. The first wave came when Greater Hungary was dismembered after World War I, and some 3.5 million Magyars—one third of the Hungarian nation at that time—found themselves living in neighboring states where they feared becoming second-class citizens. The second wave came after the end of World War II when the truncated remnant of Hungary was occupied by the Soviet Army and, by 1948, had become a Soviet satellite. And in 1956, after savage suppression of the Hungarian Revolution by the Soviets, a third and larger wave of Hungarians found refuge in the United States and Canada.

The number of Hungarians living in the diaspora is difficult to determine because of the question, "Who is a Hungarian?" Hungarians say that some five million Hungarians are scattered throughout the world, about half the number of those who live today in Hungary. An estimated 1.5 million are in the United States.

---

[1] Claudio Magris, *Danube*, trans. Patrick Creagh (New York: Farrar Straus Giroux, 1989), 242.

[2] Arthur J. Patterson, *The Magyars: Their Country and Institutions* (London: Smith Elder, 1869), vol. 1, 166.

[3] Ibid., vol. 2, 66.

[4] John Lukacs, *Budapest 1900: A Historical Portrait of a City and Its Culture* (New York: Grove Weidenfeld, 1988), 111.

[5] Magris, *Danube*, 256.

[6] The crown was removed to the United States at the close of World War II and was returned to Hungary only in 1978, largely due to the efforts of U.S. Ambassador Philip M. Kaiser. On exhibit at Budapest's National Museum, it should not be missed by visitors.

[7] Gyula Illyes, quoted by Edmund Wilson in *Europe without Baedeker*, rev. ed. (New York: Farrar Straus Giroux, 1966), 431.

[8] Wilson, *Europe without Baedeker*, 426.

[9] Lukacs, *Budapest 1900*, 110n.

[10] Antal Szerb, in Lukacs, *Budapest 1900*, 109.

[11] Patterson, vol. 2, 179-80.

[12] Marian Burros, "To Budapest mit Schlag," *New York Times Magazine* (16 August 1992): 24.

[13] *New York Times*, 6 June 1994.

[14] Burros, *New York Times*, 27 May 1992.

[15] For data on Hungarians in the United States I am indebted to Steven Bela Vardy and Agnes Huszar Vardy, *The Austro-Hungarian Mind: At Home and Abroad* (Boulder: East European Monographs, 1989).

5

Romanians and Moldovans

...this is Romania. Nothing can be ruled out entirely.

—a *Le Monde* correspondent

Romania, it is said, is like all other East European countries, only more so. Larger in territory than the states previously discussed, with a population of 23 million, and rich in natural resources, Romania is nevertheless the second poorest country in the region (after Albania) and one of the longest suffering. Though it is said that nations get the governments they deserve, the Romanians have gotten worse than they merit.

Speaking a Latin language and claiming descent from the Romans, Romanians are unique in Eastern Europe and have a strong sense of their uniqueness. That distinction, however, has given them an exaggerated perception of their political and cultural importance and a craving for special attention.

Prior to World War II, Romanians were culturally close to the French and had a reputation for sophistication. Bucharest, with its broad avenues, sidewalk cafes, elegant women, and Latin lifestyle was known as the Paris of the East. Romanians went abroad to France for study, and French was the language of the elite.

But the war and its aftermath separated Romanians from their "French connection," and today they lament their isolation from a Europe they once had felt very much a part of. Dealing with Romanians is a challenge, and the first step is to understand their special nature. With their Romance language and Latin personality, Romanians have always been an anomaly in the Balkans. Their land has been a meeting place of empires—Ottoman Turk, Austro-Hungarian, and Russian—and Romanians have had to use their wits to survive as a nation. As Flora Lewis writes, Romania "...has always had to squeeze by on wit and cunning, on ducking when possible and bowing when necessary, on evasion and negotiation."[1]

Romanian uniqueness becomes most striking in comparison with Hungarians. "The differences between the atmosphere, people, and habits of Bucharest and Budapest," writes historian John Lukacs, "were not only immeasurably greater than those between Budapest and Vienna; it is almost as if the differences were larger than those of two neighboring nations; it is the difference of two civilizations."[2]

Romanians and Hungarians do indeed represent two different cultures, if not civilizations. Adversaries for centuries, they fear and mistrust each other and are on opposite sides of many issues.

At the center of Romanian-Hungarian discord is Transylvania, where the mixed Romanian and Hungarian populace has been a source of contention for almost 200 years. The vast majority of Transylvanians are ethnic Romanians, but the territory was ruled by Hungary for some 700 years before it was awarded to Romania in 1920 as part of the World War I settlement.

The Hungarian state has existed for almost a thousand years, for much of that time as a bastion of Western Christianity in its struggle with Islam. Romania also has a long history but its independence as a state dates only from 1878. Romanians, moreover, are mostly Orthodox, and for much of its history Romania was part of the Ottoman Empire.

Hungary may have chosen the losing side in its wars but it has usually been constant in the choices it made, even when they have led to disastrous results. Romania has been more flexible and has not hesitated to change sides whenever it was in its interest to do so. Unlike some of its neighbors, Romania was unable to make a gradual transition from its communist past. It had no Solidarity movement as in Poland and no market economy experiments as in Hungary. Unlike some East European states, there was no private ownership of small businesses and few peasant-owned farms. Unlike Russia, Romania had no perestroika reforms and no glasnost debates to facilitate a dialogue between rulers and the ruled. Dissidents were few and isolated, and the opposition was ruthlessly silenced. In Romania, totalitarian rule ended abruptly and violently, and the country now faces a total restructuring of its politics and economics in a society driven by distrust, dissembling, and doubt.

A Nation of Poets

> Every Romanian is a born poet.
>
> —Romanian proverb

The key to a people, writes Andrei Codrescu, is their sensibility and national character, not the facts that often turn out to be fabrications.[3] Codrescu, a Romanian-born American poet and commentator for National Public Radio, writes of a basic psychocultural difference between Romanians and Americans, manifested in how their media seek to elicit facts for news coverage.

"The polite, even delicate Romanian," writes Codrescu, "elicited information obliquely, through reminiscence, wit, and inference...[while the] American was direct, rude, quick to get to the heart of it" (104).

The Romanian does not understand, explains Codrescu, that the reason an American's questions can be so direct is that he is not offended if told that the information sought is none of his business. For a Romanian, telling off an impertinent questioner is the right thing to do. But for a Romanian it is also rude not to answer a direct question, so he prefers to be polite and lie rather than honestly tell his questioner to get lost.

The question-and-answer approach, moreover, is alien to Romanians (and most other East Europeans), who prefer to answer questions indirectly and with long and complex answers. Romanians will want to tell the whole story but without giving a straight answer. This should not necessarily arouse suspicions because evasion is a Balkan tradition exacerbated by forty-five years of communism when giving straight answers was not the wisest thing to do.

Romanians are anxious to please foreign visitors. Ask for directions on a Romanian street and you are likely to get an answer ten minutes long. But in their efforts to please, Romanians will often twist the truth and tell a visitor what they believe he or she wants to hear. "Yes, it will be done on time" or "It will be ready in two days," when it is likely to take much longer. Such overoptimistic responses should not be seen as malicious but rather as attempts to please. But they do make it difficult to get down to reality and ascertain the truth.

Dealing with people is a Romanian art, and *bun simt* (good sense or decency) connotes sensibility and delicacy in interpersonal relations and how to behave in embarrassing situations. The style of discourse is personal, and before discussing business Romanians will want to drink, reminisce, and talk politics. "Getting to know you"—establishing a good personal relationship—is an important prelude to doing business.

Information transfer presents problems. Because of their sophistication and competence, Romanians are insulted and turned off by patronizing foreigners who talk down to them and tell them what to do. A tactic used by one trainer is to open his workshops by telling his Romanian audiences that he will give them his experiences, which they are free to adapt to Romanian conditions or to reject. Then, in a play to pride, he adds his hope that something of what he will relate will enable them, in turn, to train people of other countries. Like many Mediterranean people, Romanians, when conversing, gesticulate, stand very close, and do not hesitate to make physical contact. An affectionate people, there is much touching among strangers and hugging and kissing among friends, and in a nation of poets, there is a national tendency to exaggerate.

Romanians and Americans also differ in their attitudes toward time. Romanians have a more relaxed attitude, as in Mediterranean and other East European countries. A meeting scheduled for 10:00 A.M. may not start until 10:30 or 11:00 A.M., and someone invited to a home for 8:00 P.M. will not be expected until some time later. The punctuality of the West, as a consequence, is a concept poorly understood. But when Romanians work with a foreigner who is punctual and come to understand that time is money, they can easily enough adapt to the importance that other people attach to time.

Romanians, however, do find time for each other, for family and the close networks of friends they have developed from childhood, schools, and shared experiences. For close friends there is always plenty of time for sitting around and talking. One American has described his dinners with Romanian friends as replete with some of the most charming moments he has ever experienced. Another American, a career diplomat who has served in many parts of the world, says that the friendships he made in Romania have lasted longer than those of any other country he has lived in.

Americans can be accepted into such Romanian groups and will be treated as equals, but they should be aware that such friendships are made for life and require nurturing. Remember name days, send greeting cards on holidays, invite them to family social affairs, and share their joys and sorrows.

When they have precise goals, Romanians can be hard workers; but, as one Romania veteran points out, they would rather discuss than do. Life is to be enjoyed when it can be, preferably through conversation, food, drink, and the company of the opposite sex. To celebrate a good crop, a peasant is likely to visit the local tavern and rejoice in his good fortune with drink, food, and revelry. There is also an attitude best described by the Spanish saying, *que sera, sera.* Events should be allowed to happen, since people have little ability to change them.

Their sense of humor is irrepressible, and Romanians will joke about the most serious things. During the communist era, Romania was known for its *bancuri* (political jokes), a form of free expression that could not be controlled by the regime. Visitors to Romania should have some jokes of their own ready to tell.

The gaiety of Romanians, however, can be deceiving. A very sophisticated and capable people, they have produced many great mathematicians, scientists, and writers. Despite the poverty, visitors should not delude themselves into thinking that they are dealing with a third-world country.

Audacious Mavericks

> For years the Rumanians [sic]* were regarded as supine; and yet, in recent time, they have shown an enviable spirit of audacity.
> —C. L. Sulzberger, *A Long Row of Candles*

The mavericks of Eastern Europe, Romanians are spontaneous and unpredictable, a Latin island in a sea of Slavs and Magyars. In 1989, they were the only nation in Eastern Eu-

---

* Until recently, the *New York Times* used an older spelling, Rumania. C. L. Sulzberger was for many years the *Times* senior foreign correspondent.

rope to overthrow their communist regime with gunfire, bloodshed, and the execution of its despised leaders, Nicolae and Elena Ceausescu. A glance back at history will help to explain the roots of Romanian differences from their neighbors. The earliest known inhabitants of Romania were the ancient Dacians, a Thracian people. When the Romans conquered Transylvania and Oltenia in A.D. 106, they named it Dacia, colonized it for the next 150 years, and administered it as an eastern outpost of their far-flung empire.

When the Romans withdrew in A.D. 271, they left behind a mixed Dacian-Roman culture, a Romance language, and an island of Latinity surrounded by barbarians. That territory, however, fell to invasions from the east and faded from history for the next thousand years. It was not until 1300 that it reappeared as the principalities of Wallachia and Moldavia.

For the next five centuries Wallachia and Moldavia were buffeted between the imperial ambitions of the Ottoman Turks, Austria-Hungary, and Russia. Little more than a despised people in their own land, Romanians were subject to the whims of more powerful nations. In the early sixteenth century, their rulers acknowledged Turkish overlordship, and the principalities of Wallachia and Moldavia, though never occupied in force by the Turks, became part of their empire. Only in the eighteenth century, as the Ottoman Turks began their retreat from Europe, did a Romanian national awakening begin which culminated in its recognition as an independent state in 1878.

World War I began with Romania courted by both sides. In 1916, having secured all the concessions it could, Romania joined the Allies, declared war on Austria-Hungary, and attempted to invade Transylvania, only to suffer defeat and occupation by German and Austro-Hungarian armies. Peace was made, and Romania withdrew from the war. In 1918, however, only two weeks after Austria-Hungary collapsed and one day before Germany surrendered, Romania again declared war on the Central Powers, just in time to obtain its share of the victors' spoils, which included Transylvania and other lands inhabited by Romanians. Romania more than doubled in size, and for the first time in modern history a majority of all Romanian-speakers (along with several minorities) were united in *Romania Mare*, Greater Romania. In World War II, Romania managed to fight first on one side and then on the other, and to emerge from the war reunited with Transylvania but occupied by Soviet armies. A communist government was imposed, and for the next forty-five years Romanians lived (with the possible exception of Albania) under the most repressive regime in Eastern Europe. After 1960, however, while continuing its Stalinist policy at home, Romania defied Moscow by pursuing an independent policy abroad.

During the Middle East Six-Day War, Romania was the only communist country not to break relations with Israel. Moreover, it allowed most of its remaining Jews to emigrate to Israel, as well as its Germans to West Germany, albeit at a head price of from $5,000 to $10,000. Jews and Germans became Romania's largest export commodity and hard-currency earner.

In 1939, there were 800,000 Jews in Romania. Some 400,000 were killed during the war, deported by Nazis to death camps from Hungarian-occupied northern Transylvania in the west or victims of pogroms in Romania's recently acquired territories in the east. Romania was allied with Germany, yet in 1943, after the war had turned against Germany, Romania defied Berlin and refused to send to death camps its remaining Jews, and 400,000 of them survived.[4] Most of the survivors emigrated after the war, and today, according to government statistics, 9,000 Jews remain in Romania although unofficial informed sources put the number as high as 20,000 or more. Half of them live in Bucharest, and most are well over the age of sixty-five.

Romania, in 1967, again defied Moscow when it established relations with West Germany and played the role of go-between in talks between Israel and the Arabs, and between the United States and China. In 1968, in its most blatant defiance of Moscow, Romania refused to join its Warsaw Pact allies in the invasion of Czechoslovakia and condemned the action. It also condemned the Soviet invasion of Afghanistan in 1979 and refused to join the Soviet-sponsored boycott of the 1984 Olympic Games.

Such maverick behavior, executed with daring and skill, allowed the Romanians a measure of maneuverability between East and West. It also gave them the pleasure of being able to tweak the nose of their traditional adversary, the Russian bear.

Romania's defiance, as well as its spontaneity and unpredictability, annoyed its neighbors immeasurably. As one Soviet diplomat said to an American in the late 1950s, shortly after Romania had begun to improve relations with the United States, "Now *you* can have the pleasure of dealing with them."

Negotiations

> If the art of survival is—as it probably must be—central to the politics of small nations, then the Romanians may be counted among the greatest practitioners of that art. At the cost of much suffering and a good deal of social corruption, they have, over centuries, managed to preserve both their national pride and their rich culture in a difficult and often hostile environment.
>
> —Istvan Deak, "Survivors"

Romanians are skilled diplomats, as demonstrated by their survival in a sea of Slavs and Magyars. They also have a well-deserved reputation as hard bargainers, and the inhabitants of Oltenia, the region to the west of Bucharest, are known as the hardest bargainers of them all.

My first experience with Romanian negotiating style was in the 1960s during negotiation of a U.S.-Romanian cultural agreement. Fulbright funds for student exchange with Romania were modest, and U.S. negotiators were under instructions to agree to an exchange of only "between three and four" Romanian and U.S. students each year.

Our Romanian negotiating partner used an entire two-hour session to seek an increase, however small, in the number of exchange students. He opened with a proposal for ten students, and when the U.S. side countered with "three to four," he used various formulations in an attempt to raise the number. He first repeated his proposal for "ten" but then retreated, in turn, to "up to ten," "between six and ten," and "four to six," until we finally agreed on "at least four." After the meeting, with obvious satisfaction in having achieved a very modest victory, he confided with pride that he was an Oltenian.

Americans are advised to establish parameters at the start of their negotiations, make clear what they can and cannot do, and maintain that position throughout the discussions. When Romanians understand that a position will not be changed, they will be ready to reach agreement. But despite their reputation for hard bargaining, Romanians are also willing to take more risks than many of their neighbors, a heritage of Byzantine and Turkish trading traditions of the East.

American directness may appear aggressive to Romanians, who are indirect, nonconfrontational, and prefer to talk around issues rather than address them directly. Americans, therefore, should try to elicit information indirectly, in the Romanian manner. Don't ask questions that will embarrass them, and don't come on too strong.

As in virtually any other country, deals should not be done on a handshake alone but spelled out in a document duly signed by both parties. When negotiations have been concluded and agreement reached, it should not be considered a done deal until signed and approved by higher-ups, a process that may result in changes in the agreed-upon terms if someone "up there" does not like it. To avoid future misunder-standings, all details should be delineated, especially who pays for what and how much.

After an agreement or contract is signed, the American signatory should insist that it be observed to the letter. This will ensure that the agreement, as well as the American signatory, is taken seriously and will not be taken advantage of in the future. And don't relax until things start to go exactly as specified in the agreement. If not, complain loudly and quickly.

Doing business in Romania can be frustrating. The commercial infrastructure has deteriorated to a greater extent than elsewhere in Eastern Europe, and it may prove difficult to arrange bank transfers and access to *valuta* (hard currency). To avoid disappointment, foreign business executives should keep their expectations modest.

In business deals, be wary of whom you deal with. Romanians with capital resources may have a shady past, and a certain amount of cheating can be expected. According to *New York Times* correspondent Jane Perlez, "Western investors in Romania say they find former *Securitate* (secret police) officers turned businessmen the most reliable, if not the most likeable partners."[5] One long-time Romania watcher advises, "Maintain a spirit of adventurous tolerance but be careful and watch out for *smecherie* (trickery or scams)."

In meetings with foreigners, Romanians seem to be always looking over their shoulders to see who is listening. If other Romanians are present, they will be circumspect and careful about what they say. Rather than express their own views, they are more likely to tell a visitor what they believe he or she wants to hear. To learn their true views, try to meet them on a one-to-one basis. But be sure to budget sufficient time, because when no others are present they will go on and on and tell you more than you really want to know.

Take your time and enjoy the game. Don't put all your cards on the table, but keep a few in reserve to be used when needed. And don't accept as the truth everything you are told. Romania may be the hardest row to hoe in Eastern Europe but the situation is improving.

Is Romania's future as bleak as its past? Western business executives, economists, and American diplomats respond in the negative. Legal reforms provide a fully competitive framework for foreign business and investment, land reform, and Western banking regulation. Major U.S. corporations have established productive and profitable operations there, and U.S. energy companies are working to modernize Romania's oil and gas fields. A body of law has been established creating genuine political freedom and European standards for a free market economy. And the press is free, to the point of anarchy.

Implementation of these laws has been slow but steady, and in the view of most U.S. officials, it is virtually irreversible.

The Bureaucracy

Thieves nowadays are not in the forests but in the offices.
—Romanian proverb

Negotiations are not limited to diplomats and business executives. Every foreign visitor who has to deal with the Romanian bureaucracy will have to do some negotiating.

The Romanian bureaucracy, it is said, is 50 percent Ottoman and 50 percent Habsburg and combines the worst features of both. Officials are passive rather than active, conforming and dissembling rather than initiating. The stamps, seals, and signatures required for documents slow things down. Creativity is wanting because change might lead to loss of a job. Romanians are an imaginative people but during forty-five years of communism they were discouraged from independent thought. Whatever reserves of creativity exist today seem to be used only to meet the personal needs of family and friends.

Minor clerks are omnipotent but not always omnipresent; and they don't always show up on time, or at all. Decision making is arbitrary, based more on whim than wherefore, and often after presentation of a small "token of appreciation." Appointments made are not always kept (high-level officials excepted), nor are promises. Exact information on what is required to conduct a transaction which requires government approval is difficult to obtain, and the information received may change from day to day depending on the official who gives it. Visitors are told *Nici o problema* (no problem) but should expect that there will indeed be a problem. Decisions are bucked from office to office with the excuse, *Nu este problema mea* (It's not my problem). Everything takes time. What to do? Visitors have no choice but to adapt to the Romanian time schedule and to be patient with the long lines they must stand in. If unsuccessful with one official, try another. "Take a deep breath," advises one American veteran observer of Romania, "and keep your cool. Getting angry does not help. Everything eventually gets done but takes time."

To get things done expeditiously it is best to have a Romanian friend or assistant to run interference for you. For each task, a Romanian will know whom to call, with whom to put in a good word, and how to handle the question of *baksheesh.*

The practice of baksheesh, the Turkish (and Romanian) word for tipping, endures but in Romania it has become an art. Gratuities of one kind or another open doors and smooth the way through the bureaucracy. In the communist era, a pack or carton of American cigarettes (Kent 100s preferred), discreetly placed on an official's desk, was likely to produce the desired result. Saul Bellow, in his novel *The Dean's December,* based on his own experiences in Bucharest, describes how an American visitor never went anywhere without a few cartons of Kents.[6] Today, Kents are still the preferred brand, and a pack will help a police officer to overlook a traffic violation. Romanians, however, will expect more than Western cigarettes, which now can be easily purchased although the cost is high.

Gift giving is a part of the culture, and while acceptance implies indebtedness to the gift giver, it is insulting to refuse one. Gifts need not be expensive but should be items that Romanians might not have access to at the time, such as those available in duty-free shops. The value of the gift should depend on the nature of the favor being given, and gifts for spouses or children will also fill the bill. Be sure to have them wrapped.

Baksheesh is often arranged through a middleman who will arrange a meeting with the intended recipient. The gratuity is not seen by Romanians as a bribe but rather as recognition of the status of the recipient and appreciation for what he has done to make the deal possible.

There is, of course, a fine line between a gift and a bribe. Gift giving is an Eastern tradition between friends, acquaintances, and those doing business. The tribute that local Romanian princes paid to the Turks was actually called a *cadou* (gift), and gifts given today by businesspeople will be considered a cadou, a sign of respect, rather than a bribe.

Hospitality

> The one with the food is obliged to invite...
> —Romanian proverb

Hospitality is a Romanian tradition, and it is overwhelming. Once in a Romanian home, guests will be invited to stay for lunch or dinner, and the host will spend his last *leu* to prepare a good table, including many items you know he cannot afford. And if you like garlic, you'll love the food.

Guests can expect to experience what Codrescu calls the Romanian art of "aggressive hospitality,"

> ...when your host offers you everything in the house and you must fight not to take it. The object, for the guest, is to leave

the house with as few things as possible, while the host considers his victory great if he can succeed in standing naked on the frozen earth while waving goodbye to you, dressed in his clothes, bent to the ground with his possessions."[7]

Making a quick exit from a Romanian home is not an easy matter, and hosts will delay the departure as long as possible. Brian Hall, an American who bicycled through the Balkans, describes how he came upon a wedding in a small Romanian village. Although Hall was a complete stranger and spoke no Romanian, he was led to the dinner table and plied with food and drink for several hours before he was able to make his escape.[8]

Guests will be plied with tsuica, the Romanian slivovitz or plum brandy and the popular drink of choice. Tsuica may not be to every American's taste and can cause a terrific hangover when drunk to excess. Easier to handle are the good wines that Romania produces. In offices, guests will be offered tea or thick Turkish-style coffee.

Prospective visitors are advised to learn something about Romanian culture and to bring it up in their conversations. Do some reading on renowned Romanians such as sculptor Constantine Brancusi, composer George Enescu, and playwright Eugene Ionesco. Show interest in the Romanian language, history, and natural beauties of the country. To be avoided, however, until you know someone well, are questions about personal life and family.

Corruption

The fish grows rotten from the head.

—Romanian proverb

Historian Robert Lee Wolff relates how the Romanian police once jailed a newly arrived foreign correspondent because he had attempted to change money legally at a bank rather than on the black market. He must, the police concluded, have discovered some new racket and they wanted to keep him in custody until they could figure out what it was.[9]

Practices that Americans will see as corruption are a fact of life and have been endemic in Romania since it became a part of the Ottoman Empire in the early sixteenth century and was ruled by local princes or Phanariot Greeks serving as agents of the sultan. Named after the district of Constantinople where they originated, the Phanariots filled many of the Romanian princely positions, which they purchased at a price, in competition with others, for periods of one or two years.

During their time in office, the Phanariots sought to maximize the return on their investment. Their corrupt practices included excessive taxation, smuggling, the sale of offices, speculation in foreign currency, and otherwise milking Romania of its riches. The entire nation suffered.

"The national experience under Ottoman and Phanariot domination," wrote Wolff, "could not help but determine the character of future Rumanian social, political, economic, and cultural development" (63). It also produced a small group of privileged at one end of the social scale and millions of poverty-stricken peasants at the other, with almost nothing Romanian in between (36). And it encouraged a tradition of corruption, nepotism, and bribery that continues today.

In 1993, a Romanian government report on corruption by high officials confirmed charges of influence peddling and abuse of office. As a result of the investigation, 49,301 cases of financial irregularities in state-owned businesses were forwarded to the state prosecutor. The report, however, absolved government officials of corruption. But as Peter Maass reported in the *Washington Post*, "...in a Balkan country where intrigue is a beloved national pastime, the lack of evidence is being interpreted as a sure sign that official corruption must be far greater than previously thought."[10]

Romania has been called a country of brown envelopes, a reference to the envelopes used to pass bribes. The extent of the bribery was confirmed by Gheorghe Florica, a retired Romanian army general who headed a special anticorruption unit in the Ministry of Finance before being abruptly dismissed along with most members of his senior staff. "You can't get anything done without giving bribes," said Florica. "Without bribes, nothing will help solve your problems."[11]

In regard to bribes, it is worth bearing in mind that Romanian traditions are more Italian than Swiss, and exchanges of "financial favors" and "recognition of contributions" are well established in the business culture.

What should an American do when solicited for a bribe (as distinct from a gratuity) in order to "solve problems?" A payoff is not mandatory but it will certainly smooth the way. Many foreign businesspeople take the easy way and make the payoff, since they are financially able to do so. Supply, however, creates demand for more payoffs.

The advice of longtime Romania watchers is to make clear that you cannot agree to a payoff. Bribery raises the price of doing business for all foreign businesspeople, and it does Romanian society no good. Moreover, once a bribe is given, additional bribes will be expected in future dealings, and the price will rise each time. Moreover, it's against U.S. law.

The Language

La langue roumaine represente la continuation de la langue latine....
—François Monmarche, *Roumanie, Les Guides Bleus*

Americans report no difficulty communicating with Romanians. The younger generation speaks English or is studying it. Older educated people are more likely to speak French. And the Romanian language itself is much easier for a Westerner to learn than Hungarian or any of the Slavic tongues.

Romanian is a Romance language, and Americans who already know French, Italian, Spanish, or Portuguese will not find it difficult, although the pronunciation will sound strange at first. Also strange is the placement of definite articles at the end of nouns so that "the radio" becomes *radioul*. Family names, often ending with "escu" or "eanu," may also sound strange but are easy to explain. Ionescu, for example, simply means "son of John," while Olteanu, a place-name, indicates "from Oltenia."

Grammar and vocabulary are of Latin origin, albeit with an admixture of Turkish, Greek, and Slavic words. As a Romanian proverb says, "Our language is one great salad." In the nineteenth century, when French cultural influence became dominant and the vocabulary was modernized, French became the source of many new words.

The French connection is frequently cited by Romanians, who will refer to Bucharest's Latin ambiance. The French connection, however, affected mainly the educated elite, a small upper layer of society; peasants, the vast majority of the people, were largely unaffected.

A keen sense of the absurd is characteristic of the Romanian language and view of the world. Romanians can see something irrational and absurd in almost everything. The absurd, writes Codrescu, in its political, social, and cultural modes has been a fact of life in Romania since its rule by the Turks.[12]

Eugene Ionesco is known as the father of the theater of the absurd which, according to Codrescu, is "...a literary genre that is the father of vampirism because it sucks conventional meanings out of things until they are rendered ridiculous and sad." Codrescu calls Ionesco "the thinking man's dracula" (178). Ionesco (originally Ionescu) is the renowned Romanian-born playwright who wrote in both French and Romanian. Dracula, of course, is the fictitious vampire of Bram Stoker's novel, based partially on the real-life fifteenth-century Romanian prince Vlad Dracula who ruled in Wallachia where he was known as Vlad Tepes (The Impaler) because of his mass impalement of his enemies.

Blame the Foreigner

There is no bitterer fruit than foreigners in one's land.

—Romanian proverb

Americans can expect a warm welcome in Romania and will be told that they have been awaited for forty-five years, a reference to the time spent under a brutal communist regime. As elsewhere in Eastern Europe, America is a dreamland, a land of comforts and conveniences, and Americans a special people deserving special attention. In a land of scarcity, visitors from a land of abundance are most welcome but will find that their wealth and resources are overestimated.

Recently, however, some cynicism has appeared regarding Americans. Romanians expected more from the United States and are disappointed in the amount of assistance they have received. Americans may also be surprised to learn that they are blamed, along with other Westerners, for having abandoned Romania to the Russians. Romanians even speak of a "Yalta/Malta sellout," a reference to the alleged sacrifice of Eastern Europe by Roosevelt to Stalin at Yalta in 1945, and a suspected sellout by Bush to Gorbachev at their Malta summit in 1989.

One American visitor reports being told by a Romanian that the Persian Gulf War of 1991 was instigated by Russia to keep the Romanian communists in power by diverting American attention from Romania and Bulgaria, two states that at the time still had prominent ex-communists in their governments.

Like most East Europeans, Romanians have a tendency to blame others for their troubles at home, only more so. "Foreigners do not understand us," they claim. That may well be true but history gives Romanians good cause to be suspicious of foreigners, since many of their travails have indeed resulted from the actions of others. Blame, however, is also freely assigned to Romanian citizens who are of Hungarian, Gypsy, or Jewish origin. Conspiracies are seen everywhere. When discussing other persons, Romanians will often whisper, "But you can't trust him," a remark perhaps understandable for a people who have lived under lock and key for so many years and learned not to trust anyone beyond family and close friends. Such suspicions, however, can be disconcerting for a foreign visitor who is trying to get something done and finds her- or himself slowly becoming suspicious of others. Moreover, such suspicions may not be justified, because some Romanians have been known to cast aspersion on others in order to build their own credibility and make themselves indispensable to the visitor.

Romanians also tend to tell foreigners what they believe the foreigners want to hear, a practice that makes it difficult to ascertain the truth. Romanian energies often seem to be directed to manipulating foreigners in a Machiavellian manner rather than taking action on their own to resolve issues.

Blame the Minorities

> After the "revolutions," establishing blame was an obsession all across the bloc, perhaps least marked in Hungary and particularly virulent in Romania...
> —Katherine Verdery, *Nationalism and National Sentiment in Postsocialist Romania*

Romania is the most ethnically diverse state in Eastern Europe. Citizens a visitor meets may not be ethnic Romanians but rather one of the country's numerous minorities. Numbering at least 17-18 percent of the population, the minorities have been traditional scapegoats for the country's troubles.

Hungarians are the largest, numbering some two million and concentrated in regions of Transylvania. Next are the Gypsies, another two million. Another large group are the Szeklers, linguistically and culturally Hungarian, who have lived in their remote bend of the Carpathian Mountains for almost one thousand years. Of the Jews, another traditional scapegoat, not many remain, as earlier noted. Among the many other minorities are Germans, Greeks, Turks, and Ruthenians (Ukrainians). Romania's minorities have traditionally been seen as a source of domestic instability. People who differ in ethnicity, language, and religion have been regarded as outsiders in a part of Europe where shifting borders have confused citizenship and nationality and where minorities have rarely been accepted as full-fledged citizens. In Romania today, they are once more targets for ultranationalists who blame them for the country's ills. The ultranationalists, however, won less than 5 percent of the vote in Romania's 1992 elections which were certified by foreign observers and the U.S. Department of State as "free and fair."

Blame Ceausescu?

There does not perhaps exist a people labouring under a greater degree of oppression from the effect of despotic power, and more heavily burdened with impositions and taxes than the peasants of Wallachia and Moldavia, nor any who would bear half their weight with the same patience and resignation.

—W. Wilkinson, *An Account of the Principalities of Moldavia and Wallachia*

For most of their history Romanians have been harshly ruled, as noted by British Consul W. Wilkinson in 1820. And, as mentioned earlier, Romania has been known for the ease with which it has changed sides in the international political arena. These changes may have benefited the Romanian state, but they exacted heavy sacrifices from the people who were compelled to shed their blood, first for one side and then for the other, according to the whims of their rulers. Folk sayings abound about the dangerous stranger and the sinister foreigner. This is understandable when one considers the damage done to Romania by successive waves of invaders and foreign rulers as well as by her geographic location in a part of Europe where rival empires clashed. Romania's most recent suffering, however, was at the hands of one of her own, Nicolae Ceausescu, a native son of peasant origin.

Ceausescu ruled Romania for twenty-four years until his execution in 1989. For many years he enjoyed broad public support resulting from his skilled exploitation of Romanian nationalism. Although nationalism was used for Ceausescu's own purposes, most Romanians welcomed the attention they received as the maverick in the Soviet bloc. In 1971, however, on his return from a visit to China, Ceausescu launched a cultural revolution of his own. Phased in over a period of years, nationalism was exalted, ideological purity was rigidly enforced, and frequent changes of government and party officials deterred development of domestic opposition.

To eliminate the foreign debt, the export of agricultural produce was given priority. Food shortages ensued in a country which had been known as the breadbasket of the Balkans. Drastic energy-saving measures were introduced, and heat and light were rationed. Abortion was prohibited and modern forms of birth control were unavailable. The result was food rationing, cold and dimly lit homes, pauperization of the people, and orphanages filled with abandoned children, many of them infected with AIDS caused by blood transfusions given in the belief that new blood would improve their health. But the blood was unscreened, the needles were unsterilized, and many infants were infected with AIDS. Romania became one of the poorest nations in Europe, and its people repressed and depressed.

To add insult to injury, Ceausescu began a massive reconstruction intended to modernize the country by replacing vestiges of its agricultural past with symbols of its industrial present. Churches and historic sites were demolished and replaced with massive buildings and construction projects. Villages were razed. Ceausescu's own palace in Bucharest, incomplete at his death, was to have been three times the size of Versailles and larger than the Pentagon.

To ensure his control, Ceausescu expanded the role of the dreaded Securitate until it permeated every aspect of Romanian society. Talking with foreigners was downright dangerous. To survive, Romanians chose to inform on each other. According to a former head of the Securitate who defected to the West, there were ten million "bugs" in a nation of twenty-three million people, almost one listening device for every two Romanians. Typewriters had to be registered with the police so that dissident writings could be traced. Isolated from the rest of the world, Romanians, despite foreign radio broadcasts, were poorly informed about what was happening abroad and became even more self-centered. The police-state regime, moreover, created an atmosphere of distrust and suspicion that prevails today.

The despised dictator is now dead but the post-Ceausescu government is run by former communists. The dreaded secret police has lost much of its clout but phones are still bugged, the populace is distrustful and apathetic, and the truth is difficult to discern. Gone, however, is the element of fear. Romanians have no fear of contact with foreigners, as long as no political or economic crimes are being committed.

"In the Bucharest newspapers," wrote William McPherson of the *Washington Post*, "it is virtually impossible to distinguish the news from rumors, manipulations, diversions and lies, many of them coming from the Rumors Directorate [sic] of the secret police."[13]

Are Romania's troubles due solely to Ceausescu? Polish writer Ryszard Kapuscinski urges us to examine the context of Ceausescu's rule:

Romania is situated in that part of Europe which was inhabited by peasant masses, ruled for centuries by sovereign lords, landlords, clan leaders, and autocrats. They held the power of life and death over their underlings. Being themselves the law, they were above the law. They were all-powerful and went unpunished. From ancient times these people were the objects of a blind and slavish worship. Ceauscscu belongs to this very tradition, fits into it, and is its product.[14]

Moldovans

Moldova has not always had the same borders; sometimes expanded, sometimes contracted, they followed the prosperity and impoverishment of the country itself.

—Dimitrie Cantemir, *Descriptio Moldaviae*, 1715

Moldova is a small, agriculturally rich land, the size of Belgium. Its misfortune in history has been its strategic location in a corner of Europe where three great empires have confronted each other over the centuries—Ottoman, Russian, and Austrian. Moldova's fortunes and farms have continually shifted between one or another of its more powerful neighbors.

A majority of its people are ethnic Romanians, speak the Romanian language, and show Romanian cultural values. Moldova, however, for more than forty-five years in our time was a part of the Soviet Union, which maintained the fiction that the Moldovans were distinct from the Moldavians of Romania just across the Prut River and spoke a different language.[†]

[†] *Moldova*, the Romanian form, is used here to refer to today's Republic of Moldova on the east bank of the Prut River. *Moldavia*, the Latin and English form, is used for land on the west bank, today a province of Romania. The two regions together constitute most of historic Moldavia (or Moldova, as you prefer).

The Soviet claim has been described by the *New York Times* as "one of the great cultural hoaxes of the 20th century."[15] That "hoax," however, was used to create, in 1940, a Moldavian Soviet Socialist Republic on the east bank of the Prut River, based on the Soviet claim that the Moldovans were not Romanians. The Soviet objective was to strengthen its claim to an agriculturally rich and strategic piece of real estate which provides access to the Danube River near where it begins to meander through its delta to the Black Sea.

But the language spoken in Chisinau (pronounced "Kishinow"), on the Moldovan side of the Prut River, is the same as that spoken in Iasi (pronounced "Yash"), on the Romanian side, and a Moldovan can just as easily converse with a resident of the Banat in the far southwest of Romania.

The Prut River is the Republic of Moldova's western boundary, separating it from the Romanian province of Moldavia. Together, the lands on both banks of the river constitute most of historic Moldavia. Rivers, however, make poor boundaries because the people who live on both banks usually speak the same language, share the same culture and religion, and even have familial ties. As Moldovans remind us, Mihai Eminescu, Romania's national poet and creator of the Romanian language's modern form, was himself a Moldavian. Through most of the nineteenth century, Moldova alternated between Turkish, Russian, and Romanian rule and during the twentieth, between Russian and Romanian. Its history since 1812 has epitomized the intrigue and instability resulting from territorial transfers between the great powers, transfers that were frequent during the nineteenth and twentieth centuries, as Moldova was tossed back and forth like a shuttlecock in a game of badminton.

Most of today's Moldova was annexed by the Russian Empire in 1812 from the Romanian principality of Moldavia, under Ottoman rule at the time and known as Bessarabia. Following Russia's defeat in the Crimean War, the southern part of Bessarabia was returned to Romania; and after Turkey's defeat in 1878, the territory was returned to Russia. In 1918, it once more reverted to Romania where it remained until 1940, when the Soviet Union regained it under the infamous Molotov-Ribbentrop Pact, only to lose it to Romania again in 1941 when Germany, Romania's ally, invaded the Soviet Union. In 1944, a victorious Soviet army once more reclaimed the territory for the Soviet Union.

Bessarabia's original inhabitants were mostly ethnic Romanians, but from 1812, during the years of Russian control, there were large influxes of Russians and Ukrainians in attempts to Russify the territory. As a consequence, Moldova today is inhabited by a number of nations of varying ethnicity and language—Romanians, Russians, Ukrainians, Jews, Gagauz (a Christianized Turkic people), and Bulgarians. Ethnic Romanians always have been, and still are, in the majority.

Slavicization resumed after World War II when ethnic Romanians were exiled en masse to Siberia and replaced by an additional million Russians and Ukrainians. The Moldavian Orthodox Church, formerly under the Romanian patriarch, was placed under the jurisdiction of the patriarch of Moscow, and the Cyrillic alphabet replaced the Latin. The rich land and mild climate provided the Soviet Union with choice vegetables, fruits, and wines; and the territory was used by the Soviets as a training ground for up-and-coming communist officials, among them Leonid Brezhnev. The Soviet claim that the Moldovans were a separate ethnic group, speaking a language distinct from Romanian, was never accepted by Romanian or Western scholars.

When Moscow's control began to loosen in 1989, the Moldovan Communist Party conceded that the Romanian and Moldovan languages are indeed identical, and Moldova in 1990 reverted back to the Latin script. In a referendum one year later, 80 percent of the population voted for independence. Moldova adopted the Romanian tricolor flag, albeit with its own emblem, as well as the Romanian national anthem.

Reunification did not follow, however, contrary to expectations in Romania and the West. Enthusiasm for reunion declined after December 1991 when a new government came to power in Moldova and adopted a policy described as "one nation, two Romanian states." The Romanian tricolor was retained but not the Romanian anthem. Several sound considerations were behind this policy change. As a predominantly rural region, Moldovans feared that in a highly centralized Romania they would be treated as second-class citizens. The markets for Moldova's produce, moreover, are in the former Soviet Union, as well as its sources of raw materials and fuel. Also putting a brake on reunification was the political and social disorder within Romania, evident to Moldovan TV viewers. All in all, Moldovans decided to concentrate on nation building, at least for the foreseeable future.

In Romania, enthusiasm for reunion also faded as Romanians came to realize that inheriting Moldova's potential border disputes with its neighbors to the east was not in Romania's best interests, and absorbing Moldova's minorities would aggravate Romania's own minority problems.

Some 65 percent of Moldova's 4.3 million population is Romanian-speaking. Ukrainians number another 14 percent; Russians, 13 percent; Gagauz, 3.5 percent; and Bulgarians, 2 percent. The Russian and Ukrainian communities, however, are concentrated along the Nistru River (Dniester, to Russians) where they number 60 percent of the population.

In 1992, Moldova's Russians and Ukrainians, fearing Romanianization and eventual union with Romania, and spurred on and supported by Moscow, established a breakaway "Transdniester Republic" on the east bank of the Nistru River in a region known to Moldovans as Transnistria. This was a territory Stalin had taken from Ukraine in 1924 and named the Moldavian Autonomous Soviet Socialist Republic. When the Romanians and Germans took Transnistria in 1941, it was given to Romania to administer, together with a large piece of Ukraine, which it did until 1944 when the territory was reclaimed by the advancing Soviet army. After 1944, six of Transnistria's nine districts were reunited with Moldova (up to the Prut River) as the Moldavian Soviet Socialist Republic. The remaining three districts were given to Ukraine.

The Transnistrian insurgents, in 1992, were supported by troops of the Russian Fourteenth Army stationed there, and in the hostilities of June-July 1992, five hundred lives were lost before a cease-fire was negotiated. In the Moldovan areas along the Nistru River that the insurgents control, they have closed down the Moldovan media, reimposed the Cyrillic script, resurrected the discredited Soviet theory of a "Moldovan language" separate from Romanian, established their own government and courts, and consider themselves autonomous.

After the many transfers of their territory between Russia and Romania, it is no great surprise that Moldovans do not yet have a strong national identity. Society has been heavily Russified and Sovietized, and Moldova is experiencing many of the problems of a new nation.

Political union with Romania, once believed to be a priority, has been replaced by a policy of fostering cultural relations. The cease-fire of 1992 is holding, but Transnistria promises to become the most recent in a long series of festering territorial disputes that have plagued Moldova in the past.

Meanwhile, the Republic of Moldova is concerned with issues of higher priority—nation building and economic development. Recognized by more than a hundred countries, it is a member of the United Nations and the Organization for Security and Cooperation in Europe and has been receiving economic assistance from international agencies and individual countries. It also has membership in the Commonwealth of Independent States (CIS), the Moscow-led organization of former Soviet republics, which its parliament ratified in March 1994. But as an indication of where Moldova's interests lie, it has announced that it will adhere to the economic structures of the CIS but not its military and political aspects.

One thing is certain, however—Moldovans and Romanians are ethnically and linguistically the same people.

The American Connection

Romanian emigration to the United States was never large. Mass emigration began only at the beginning of the twentieth century, and the number of Americans of Romanian descent today is an estimated 300,000. The early immigrants, mostly of peasant origin, settled in the industrial cities of the east and midwest but their descendants are now widely dispersed throughout the United States. More recent immigrants, fleeing political persecution, have been mainly urban professionals.

There is, however, a Romanian connection that goes back to the early colonial years. It is Captain John Smith again, the famed soldier adventurer of our schoolbooks, who fought with the Romanians against the Turks before coming to seek his fortune in the American Colonies.

And, during the Civil War, George Pomutz, a Romanian immigrant, joined the 15th Iowa Regiment at the start of the war and ended the war as its commanding officer. The 15th Iowans were called by General Sherman "the pearl" of his army. Promoted to brigadier general at the end of the war, Pomutz represented the United States in St. Petersburg, Russia, as consul and later consul general, 1866-78.

From 1881 to 1900 most immigrants from Romania were Jews, many of them from Bessarabia, and by 1929 some 50,000 had arrived in the United States. After 1900, emigration of ethnic Romanians increased because of the shortage of arable land at home, and 121,000 arrived in the United States between 1900 and 1920. Some of them hoped to save up enough money to return home and buy farmland, but most ended up in the big cities of New York, Chicago, Philadelphia, Cleveland, and Pittsburgh and did not return to their native villages. After 1945, another wave of Romanians began to arrive—intellectuals and political dissidents fleeing from a communist Romania.

Prominent Americans of Romanian origin include George Palade, 1974 Nobel laureate in medicine and biology; Mircea Eliade, University of Chicago historian of religion and mythology; John Houseman, producer, actor, and director; writer Norman Manea, a Guggenheim and MacArthur Fellow; Andrei Serban, theater director and Columbia University professor; and conductors Sergiu Comissiona and Ionel Perlea.

---

[1] Flora Lewis, *Europe*, 489.

[2] John Lukacs, *Budapest 1900*, 75.

[3] Andrei Codrescu, *The Hole in the Flag* (New York: Avon Books, 1991), 92.

[4] Istvan Deak, "Survivors."

[5] Jane Perlez, in the *New York Times*, 30 November 1993.

[6] Saul Bellow, *The Dean's December* (New York: Harper and Row, 1982).

[7] Codrescu, *Hole in the Flag*, 180.

[8] Brian Hall, *Stealing from a Deep Place* (New York: Noonday Press, Farrar, Straus, Giroux, 1988), 40-45.

[9] Robert Lee Wolff, *The Balkans in Our Time* (Cambridge: Harvard Univ. Press, 1956), 36.

[10] Peter Maass, *Washington Post*, 3 November 1993.

[11] Ibid.

[12] Codrescu, *Hole in the Flag*, 178.

[13] William McPherson, *Washington Post*, 13 September 1992.

[14] Ryszard Kapuscinski, in foreword to Edward Behr, *Kiss the Hand You Cannot Bite*, xiii.

[15] *New York Times*, 25 February 1989.

6

Bulgarians

In an area where romanticism and mysticism render rational conversation almost impossible, these hard-headed utilitarians are welcome and refreshing.
—Misha Glenny, *The Rebirth of History*

Bulgarians are a down-to-earth people. Adjectives describing them read like the traditional virtues valued by Americans—industrious, thrifty, orderly, sober, quiet, persistent, steady, and determined. Proud of their work ethic, they are more practical and better organizers than their Balkan neighbors and, writes Flora Lewis, "Neither were they attracted by what they saw as the mysticism and romanticism of the Russians and other Slavs."[1]

In making changes from communism, the slow-moving, cautious, and pragmatic Bulgarians have taken their time. While Poles, Czechs, and Hungarians were making a rapid transition from central planning to a market economy, Bulgarians waited two years and went through two nationwide elections before voting the old communist regime out of power in 1991, quietly and without bloodshed. The *Washington Post* described the Bulgarian transition as "shock therapy in slow motion."[2] Unlike its neighbors, Bulgaria's transition has been without civic or ethnic strife. The country is described as one of the least combustible in Eastern Europe. Although it has a more than thousand-year history and a rich culture, the Bulgarian nation is little known to Americans. Some call Bulgaria the best-kept secret in Eastern Europe. First-time visitors will be in for a pleasant surprise.

The People

> The Bulgarian will hunt the hare in an oxcart, and catch him.
>
> —Bulgarian proverb

The oxcart proverb, wrote historian Robert Lee Wolff, will be quite vivid to anyone who has seen the typical Balkan oxcart, "...a lumbering creaking rig, drawn by a docile hulking beast and moving at a snail's pace down the road.... Hardy, thrifty, strenuous, silent people, often dour...[the Bulgarians] were persistent and steady...."[3]

The methodical Bulgarians set goals and work slowly and deliberately to achieve them; and, once they have taken a position, they are hard to budge and not likely to compromise.

With good reason, Bulgarians have been called a Slavic people with a Mediterranean manner. Their cities are crossed by broad boulevards lined with sidewalk cafes where people sit and sip their coffee and soft drinks under umbrellas emblazoned with Marlboro, Coke, and Pepsi logos. They get very close when conversing and show their emotions by facial expressions, arm gestures, raised voices, and furrowed brows. As in many southern countries, pedestrians stroll the city streets, seemingly in no hurry to get anywhere. In crowds there is no pushing and shoving, as in Russia. Fisticuffs and brawls are seldom seen, and, in contrast to some other Slavic nations, there is little public drunkenness.

But Bulgarians do like their *rakiya* (fruit brandy), and Peace Corps volunteers report having to devise strategies to avoid drinking when in the company of Bulgarian friends. Rakiya, along with coffee, will be served at morning meetings in government offices, and visitors should be aware that each time their glasses are emptied, they will be promptly refilled. Visitors should not make the mistake of calling the coffee Turkish. In Bulgaria, it's known as *Bulgarian* coffee although, like the Turkish, it is brewed with sugar, drunk in small cups, taken without milk, and is very strong.

Somewhat reserved at first meeting, Bulgarians are a friendly people and will open up once the ice is broken. Some people, however, find them reticent, with a tendency to hedge their opinions and difficult to get information from.

A bit perplexing is their habit of nodding the head up and down for no and shaking it from side to side for yes. A legacy of the Turks, this takes some time getting used to. Today it can be doubly troubling because some Bulgarians, seeking to accommodate Westerners, are now nodding their heads in the Western fashion. A visitor may have to ask Bulgarians whether they are signaling in the Bulgarian or Western mode. To avoid confusing Bulgarians, Americans should not move their heads when saying yes or no.

A polite people, Bulgarians are reluctant to take the initiative to make the acquaintance of foreign visitors, preferring to have an intermediary introduce them. After meeting a foreigner, they will make requests in an indirect rather than direct manner. The refreshingly modest and frank Bulgarians, moreover, show none of the unctuousness toward foreigners encountered in some other Balkan countries.

But Bulgarians also manifest the small-village mentality so common in the Balkans. They lived under Ottoman rule for five hundred years, longer than any of the other Balkan nations, and were geographically closer to Byzantium. To compound the Ottoman and Byzantine influences, for forty-five years they lived under a Russian brand of communism that had its own Byzantine aspects. These experiences have made them obstinate and stubborn, cynical about each other, and suspicious of others. Prone to conspiratorial thinking, they are not satisfied with straight answers when a circuitous Byzantine response will do.

Bulgarian destiny, they believe, is controlled by outside sinister forces (read Great Powers) over whom they have no influence. Because of their history of being on the losing side so often, of being the anvil instead of the hammer, they can be fatalistic, accepting without complaint whatever happens. They can also be negative—"We can't do that" or "It won't work here" are common responses to proposals for new initiatives. Former Prime Minister Filip Dimitrov, a psychotherapist as well as a lawyer, has described his people as having a passive feeling of total helplessness.[4]

That sense of helplessness and negative self-image can lead to fear of criticism, feelings of depression, and a national inferiority complex. A common question put to newly arrived visitors is, "What did you think of when you first heard of Bulgaria?"

Bulgarians want to succeed, but they tend to believe that success is always beyond their grasp. An American with psychiatric experience who has worked in Bulgaria suggests that Americans should encourage their Bulgarian friends to take the initiative, maximize their strengths, and stress their considerable abilities. With such encouragement, she adds—given only after a good personal relationship has been established—Bulgarians can and do succeed.

Despite low expectations, tolerance for things going wrong, and belief that the future will bring little change, Bulgaria is remarkably stable despite political and economic dislocations. This is all the more remarkable considering its location in a part of Europe that is not known for stability.

With no hereditary aristocracy and no barriers to social mobility, Bulgaria in modern times has been a relatively egalitarian society. The few large landowners fled to Turkey after Bulgaria's liberation in 1878, and peasants owned their own land until the communist collectivization, in contrast to

most other East European countries. Even after collectivization, peasants retained their private plots, which they farmed
as entrepreneurs.

The business of old Bulgaria was agriculture, and in 1945
some 83 percent of the population were either peasants or
their descendants. They may have been poor but nobody
starved. Today, only 17 percent of the population is engaged
in agriculture, but the vast majority of other citizens are only
one or two generations removed from their ancestral villages.
This gives Bulgaria the atmosphere of an agricultural society,
with homespun virtues, a sense of loyalty to family and friends,
and a strong attachment to the land. Many city dwellers
return to work their family plots on weekends, and almost
everyone seems to have a weekend cottage in the countryside. One American says that Bulgarians remind him of Iowans (and, he adds, Hungarians, of New Yorkers).

Pride in local regions is strong, and the first question asked
when two Bulgarians meet is "Where are you from?" The
"from" refers to a particular region of Bulgaria, of which there
are five, each with its own dialect. Bulgarians, who enjoy
their humor, are fond of telling jokes about each other which
describe their regional characteristics.

The people of Sofia and environs, for example, known as
the *Shop*, are noted for their hardheadedness. "How do you
cook the head of a Shop?" asks one joke. "Very simple. You
cut off his head, place it in a cauldron of boiling water, cover
with a big boulder, and cook until the boulder becomes ten-
der."

The people of Gabrovo, by contrast, have a reputation for
being thrifty; and their sister city, in fact, is Aberdeen, Scot-
land. "Why do Gabrovans cut off the tails of their cats?" the
jokester asks. "So they can save fuel when they open the door
in winter to let them out."

Education is valued and seen as a panacea for life's ills. In
1939, literacy for both males and females was higher than in
any other Balkan state. Today, it is an estimated 98 percent,

one of the highest in the world, and the educated elite comprises a substantial segment of society.

An inventive people, Bulgarians approach things with intellectual curiosity. They have a reputation for being computer software whizzes, and many of the early viruses that infected computers around the world, such as the "Black Avenger," were of Bulgarian origin.

Music and opera are important; and Bulgaria, for its size, has produced a remarkable number of world-class singers, such as Boris Christoff, Nikolai Giauroff, Gena Dimitrova, and Anna Tomova-Sintow, to name a few. Legend has it that Orpheus, the god of music, was born in Thracian Bulgaria. (Herbert von Karajan believed that the mix of Bulgars, Slavs, and Thracians resulted in an unusual facial physiognomy that produced great singers.)

Belief in mysticism and the occult sciences is another Bulgarian bent. Visitors will be tested spiritually as well as professionally. They may be asked under which sign of the zodiac they were born, judged by their horoscopes, and treated accordingly. Know your horoscope, and be prepared to talk about it.

Face-to-Face

Poverty is the mother of invention.

—Bulgarian proverb

A nonconfrontational people, Bulgarians tend to avoid conflict. They do not advertise themselves and, unlike some other East Europeans, they are neither extremists nor do they wear their nationality on their sleeves. Their moderate and middle-of-the-road positions make them tolerant of foreigners and easy to work with. Eva Hoffman writes of "...the ease with which everything is settled and done, without fuss or anticipatory anxiety,"[5] and "...that health of personality... with that lack of self-consciousness and self-contortion and self-doubt (385)."

Visitors will know with whom they are dealing. Things are expected to evolve slowly, and over time. Bulgarian demands are minimal—a home, a family, and work.

"We're from the East, things are done differently here," is a comment frequently heard by foreign visitors. Americans will encounter situations never seen at home and will have to be flexible. "Be flexible" is, in fact, the advice most often given by old-time visitors to Bulgaria. When a Bulgarian official does not give the satisfaction sought, don't despair. Smile, listen carefully, plead ignorance and helplessness as a newcomer, repeat your request diplomatically as many times as necessary, keep smiling, and don't give up. Try to become the official's ally rather than adversary.

Newcomers to Bulgaria report how difficult it can be to get things done at first. Bulgarians want to help. They can promise much but may not produce what they promise. One newly arrived American student, for example, inquired about the Bulgarian language lessons she was supposed to receive as part of her scholarship.

"It will be done," was the reply to her repeated requests. But it was not done, and no lessons were arranged. Such a Bulgarian response, or lack of response, should not be seen as malicious. Rather, their way of handling a difficult or embarrassing situation is to tell the visitor what they believe she wants to hear at that particular moment—in this case that lessons would be arranged.

To make the best of such situations, be patient and resourceful. Try other approaches and other people, either higher up or lower down on the pecking order. And bear in mind that most things are done on the basis of personal contacts and favors. Bulgarians who go out of their way to help a visitor will expect something in return, not necessarily at the same time but certainly at some time in the future. Similarly, a small favor or gift for a Bulgarian will result in a return favor later on.

There may come a time, though, when patience does not

pay off, advises a Bulgarian official who deals with visiting Americans. At some point, she said, Americans may have to lose their cool and be firm if they want to get something done. Each visitor, she added, will have to decide for him- or herself when that point is reached and how tough to talk. Bulgarians initially play their cards close to the chest and are reluctant to show their feelings. Their peasant ancestry and centuries of being dominated by outside forces have made them circuitous and sly rather than frank and open. But once a good personal relationship has been established, they open up and are ready to do business.

Social encounters usually involve food and drink. When invited to a Bulgarian home, guests should bring flowers or another small gift. In restaurants and cafes Bulgarians will pick up the tab for foreign guests, and protestations to the contrary will be to no avail. If the guest is determined to pay, that should be made clear before ordering.

Bulgarian produce is known throughout Eastern Europe for its quality and taste. Thanks to an industrious peasantry, mild climate, and rich earth in a part of Europe that is mostly mountainous, Bulgaria was known as the truck garden of the communist bloc. For generations there have been communities of Bulgarian gardeners in Austria, Hungary, and the Czech lands. As C. L. Sulzberger wrote, "The Bulgars are Europe's best gardeners, earnest, hard-working and endowed with the green thumb...."[6] Among their better-known produce are vegetables, fruit, tobacco, wine, and the exclusive attar of roses oil, an ingredient in costly perfumes. Bulgarian tomatoes and peaches, with their unusually rich flavor, are, as the *Guide Michelin* might say, worth a detour.

Most Americans by now will have been exposed to a Bulgarian bacillus that is sweeping the world. Called *Lactobacillus bulgaricus*, it is a vital ingredient of yogurt, a staple of the Bulgarian diet. Bulgarians, moreover, claim that the quality of the yogurt explains their longevity and the large number of Bulgarian centenarians. Yogurt devotees will agree.

Similarities with Middle East culture have been noticed by Americans who have served in the Arabic world and Bulgaria. Shoes are removed when entering homes, banquettes are arranged around the walls of rooms, carpets are hung on walls, jewelry appears Eastern, and food has a Middle East flavor. And for those who must negotiate with them, Bulgarians can talk around an issue before coming to a conclusion which seems to have nothing to do with what they had previously been discussing.

Business with Bulgars

> Listen much, speak little.
>
> —Bulgarian proverb

Negotiation with Bulgars has its peculiarities. Decisions are made in a step-by-step process, which may seem perfectly normal, but before proceeding to the next step Bulgarians will want to reconfirm the previous step. Decisions that require approval by a government body may also require consensus, which can be a complex and lengthy procedure when dealing with city councils that may have as many as sixty or seventy members. When a decision is finally made, it may be reversed a week or two later, and the U.S. negotiators find that they must start the negotiating process all over again, and with the same official. Something may have changed to cause the reversal—governmental elections, different personnel, new regulations, or cost increases. Such changes can be frequent in a society in transition.

Similarly, an initial turndown may also be reversed and should not be accepted as final. Start all over again, return to your original proposal, and repeat all your arguments. Patience may pay off.

Bulgaria has been a crossroads of civilizations, and there is a long tradition of trading. Crusaders from Western Europe passed through Bulgaria on their way to the Holy Land, and

Ottoman Turks came in the opposite direction in their conquest of Southeast Europe. With its Danube River estuary and warm-water ports on the Black Sea, Bulgaria has been called "Europe's Back Door." That door, however, often seems to be blocked by the Bulgarian bureaucracy.

The bureaucracy will try the patience of visitors. One American authority on Bulgaria has described it as bureaucracy to the nth degree. Documents need stamps, seals, and signatures, which slow things down. Officials take their responsibilities seriously, with an "I'm in charge" attitude. Higher authority is respected. Cautious by nature, officials tend to avoid risk and responsibility by referring decisions to a higher level and seeking safety in formality and structure; and because Bulgaria is now in a transition stage, the natural caution of officials is compounded by uncertainty as to what is right and what is wrong. Different responses to the same inquiry will be given by different officials, and one is never sure which is the correct answer.

A tradition of arbitrary decision making by government officials has now become accepted as the norm. Bribery is not uncommon, and some officials may ask for a percentage cut on deals they must approve—old habits of the communist (and Turkish) rule die slowly. On a more positive note, younger people in their twenties and thirties, less inhibited by past practices, are likely to be more effective in getting things done.

The first step in any negotiation, in Bulgaria as elsewhere in Eastern Europe, is to establish a good relationship with your partner. Business is best done after they have sized you up and know who you are, but that may take time and require several face-to-face meetings, including some in a social setting. Faxes and letters will not do the job, nor will phone calls. The only alternative is a personal visit, and that is best done over a dinner table with food and wine.

Bulgarian produce has already been mentioned but wines are also good, cheap, and plentiful. "Rakiya" is the generic term for the fruit brandy they drink, the most common being *grozdova*, made from grapes, and home brews are popular. One does not drink without a toast. *Nazdrave* is "to your health." For teetotalers Bulgaria is famous for herbal teas.

Before doing business, Bulgarians will want to talk about personal relations, family, friends, and troubles. Once a friendly relationship has been established, business deals can be done.

Friendships, however, may bring consequences. At some point in a business relationship, hard reality will surface and difficult decisions will have to be made, at times to the disappointment of the Bulgarian partner who will exclaim, "But we are friends!"

As representatives of a small country, Bulgarians don't try to dominate bilateral discussions, although they do expect to be treated as equals. They don't like to appear negative, and proposals which they find unacceptable will rarely be turned down directly but rather put off or sidetracked. As a consequence, it is not always easy to know where they stand on an issue. But firmness in negotiating partners is respected, and negotiators should stand their ground when important issues are discussed. When discussing price or bottom line, Bulgarians are likely to take a roundabout approach that will test a visitor's patience and diplomacy.

"Hire more Bulgarian women," is the advice given by one American who represents a U.S. private voluntary organization in Sofia. Women are more receptive to new ideas, he claims, and have more perseverance and patience than Bulgarian men, who prefer to sit around, smoke, and talk, and may be more difficult to deal with. Women, moreover, are not trapped in the "old boy" network and are more flexible. Bulgarian women are emancipated and articulate, active in all professions, but seldom seen in high-paying jobs.

Business prospects are believed to be good in Bulgaria. With few Westerners there, the competition is not so great as in other East European countries. And you get more bang for your buck in Bulgaria.

Looking Back at Bulgaria

> The desire to achieve the standards of Western Europe, or in more general terms to modernize their society along the lines pioneered by Western civilization, has been the chief motivating force in the history of modern Bulgaria.
> —Cyril E. Black, "Bulgaria in Historical Perspective"

Bulgaria is often mentioned last in Eastern Europe, the "forgotten" Bulgaria, yet it boasts a long and glorious history. In the thirteenth century, its ancient capital Veliko Turnovo rivaled Byzantium in splendor.

Visitors to Bulgaria will do well to know something about its history, of which Bulgarians are justifiably proud. The subject will surely come up in conversations.

Bulgaria is both a new and old country. The new country dates from 1878 when Bulgaria was liberated by Russia from Ottoman Turkish rule. The old country dates from the founding of the First Bulgarian Kingdom in 681, which fell to Byzantium in 1019, and a Second Kingdom founded in 1185, which fell to the Ottoman Turks in 1396. Between the fall of the Second Kingdom and the rebirth of Bulgaria in the nineteenth century, there were five centuries of Turkish rule which cut Bulgaria off from commercial and cultural contacts with the rest of Europe.

The glories of the First and Second Kingdoms, the trials of Byzantine and Turkish rule, and the liberation by Russia shaped not only the history and politics of modern Bulgaria but also the character of today's Bulgarians and their attitude toward their Greek, Turkish, Russian, and Balkan neighbors.

The name Bulgaria derives from the Bulgars, Turkic warrior nomads from Central Asia who entered the Balkans around the middle of the seventh century and allied themselves with the indigenous Slavs in opposition to Byzantium. Within two hundred years the Bulgars were absorbed by the agrarian Slavs, culturally and linguistically, and all that remains of them is their name.

The Slav-Bulgar state became Christian in 864, choosing Orthodoxy over Catholicism, and Byzantium over Rome. Its two most famous figures are the brothers and saints Cyril and Methodius, who in 855 invented the Glagolithic alphabet (the predecessor of Cyrillic), translated church books into Slavic, and worked as missionaries in Moravia. After their deaths there, Moravia's Frankish clergy opted for the Latin script and expelled the missionaries' followers, some of whom were given refuge in Bulgaria where they continued their work.

From the followers of Cyril and Methodius came the written language of Old Bulgaria, also known as Old Church Slavonic, which replaced Greek in Bulgarian churches. Old Church Slavonic also became the language of Russian Orthodoxy and contributed to the development of literary Russian. Moreover, the Old Church language also influenced the evolution of other Slavic written languages and cultures that evolved in Eastern Europe. On the work of Cyril and Methodius and their disciples rests the Bulgarian claim that their land is the birthplace of Slavic culture.

Cyrillic script is used today in Bulgaria, Macedonia, Serbia, Montenegro, Bosnia, Belarus, Russia, and Ukraine. Not as daunting as it first looks, Cyrillic is composed of thirty letters, some from the Greek and Latin alphabets, and others invented to represent special Slavic sounds. Unlike English, Cyrillic is self-pronouncing. If you can read it, you can pronounce it.

Under Tsar Simeon (A.D. 893-927), in a period known as its Golden Age, Bulgaria extended from the Aegean Sea in the south to the Carpathian Mountains in the north and to the Adriatic in the west, encompassing most of Serbia, Albania, and southern Macedonia. With these territorial conquests came an expansion of trade and the development of literature and the arts and crafts. Bulgaria vied with Byzantium in its brilliance.

Bulgarians take immense pride in these achievements. But

its rise and expansion led to rivalry and conflict with the Byzantine empire, and later with Serbia, Romania, and Greece—and to territorial disputes that continue today. The rivalry with Greece has continued into modern times, centered on competing claims to Macedonia and Thrace. Conflict with Greece and Serbia over the Turkish province of Macedonia began only a few years after Bulgaria gained autonomy in 1878 (a prelude to full independence in 1908). Bulgarian liberation had come as a result of Russia's victory over Turkey in the bitter war of 1877-78. The Treaty of San Stefano, imposed by a victorious Russia, awarded Macedonia and a good part of Thrace (today's northern Greece) to Bulgaria. But only four months later those lands were taken away by the Treaty of Berlin at the insistence of England, which was one of Russia's principal rivals at the time.

Thus began "the Macedonian Question" which, in the following seventy years, led Bulgaria to four bitter wars in failed efforts to regain Macedonia and parts of Thrace. These were the Balkan Wars of 1912 and 1913, which together constituted a prelude to World War I and World War II. In all four wars, Bulgaria was on the losing side.

The Macedonian Question has parallels with the Bosnian question of our time, as historian Hans Kohn correctly foresaw. "The same position which Bosnia occupied in the struggle of the related yet hostile neighbors, the Croats and the Serbs," wrote Kohn in 1953, "Macedonia occupied in relation to the Serbs and Bulgars, neighborly people of the same faith and of an almost identical cultural background."[7]

Russia and Bulgaria have long had a special relationship. Both peoples are Slavs and Orthodox, and, as earlier noted, Bulgaria is considered the birthplace of Slavic culture. Even more important, Bulgarians have not forgotten their liberation by Russia from the Turks in 1878 after a war in which Russia lost more than 200,000 soldiers. A monument to Russian losses in that war, the Aleksandr Nevsky Church, stands today in downtown Sofia.

Despite her affinity with Russia, Bulgaria was allied with Germany during the two world wars but only because a German victory would have ensured Bulgaria's recovery of Macedonia. Although Bulgaria refused to declare war on the Soviet Union in World War II, she was occupied by Soviet troops in 1944 and became a Soviet satellite. Because of Bulgaria's basic affinity with Russia, as well as its slavish adherence to Soviet policy during the years of communist rule, many in the West make the mistake of assuming that Bulgarians are not much different from Russians.

One U.S. diplomat, who had served in Moscow before being posted to Sofia during the communist era, has spoken of his surprise on learning how much difference there really was. The Bulgarian officials he dealt with were more polite, friendly, and hospitable than the Russians he had dealt with in Moscow. The coffee served in Bulgarian offices was also much better and stronger. As representatives of a small country, he added, Bulgarians found it difficult to say no to a U.S. request. And when they lied—as diplomats at times must do—they did so in a charming way, making wild promises that were never fulfilled.

Minorities

A good guy, but a Turk.

—Bulgarian proverb

One out of five Bulgarians is likely to be a member of a minority, and Bulgaria has not been immune to minority problems. According to 1992 census figures, of the 8.5 million people who live in a land the size of Ohio, 9.7 percent are Turks and 3.4 percent are Gypsies. The Muslim population, 12.7 percent, includes both ethnic Turks and Bulgarians who converted to Islam during Turkish rule. The latter are commonly called Pomaks, a term some of them regard as derogatory while others do not. Both Muslims and Gypsies claim that their numbers are greatly underestimated.

Under the communists, several campaigns for assimilation were mounted against Turks, Pomaks, and Gypsies. During 1984-89, a particularly brutal campaign was waged against the Turks during which they were compelled to change their names, use of the Turkish language was forbidden, and ethnic Turkish customs were prohibited. In the postcommunist years, a Turkish party has been represented in the parliament and has provided a swing vote which has made and unmade governments formed by larger parties. To understand the historic reasons for Bulgarian animosity toward Turks, one should read the national novel, *Under the Yoke*, by Ivan Vazov, which describes the harsh life of the Bulgarian people under Turkish rule.

Jews have lived in Bulgaria since ancient times, and in the fourteenth century Bulgaria had a Jewish queen, Sara, whose son, Tsar Ivan Shishman, is a national hero for having led the last resistance to the Ottoman conquest. The numbers of Jews increased after 1492 when many found refuge in Bulgaria after their expulsion from Spain. Jews prospered in Bulgaria but prior to World War II they numbered only 50,000. Although Bulgaria was allied with Nazi Germany during the war, it resisted German pressures to surrender its native Jews for transport to extermination camps (although it did turn over Jews in the territories it had occupied in the early days of the war). The Bulgarian Jewish community survived the war almost intact and was allowed to emigrate to Israel by the postwar communist government. Today, some 2,000-3,000 Jews remain in Bulgaria, many of them prominent in academia, the arts, and journalism. Sofia's Central Synagogue, now being restored, seats 1,200 and is the largest Sephardic synagogue in Europe.

The American Connection

The United States does not loom large in Bulgarian history. Immigration has been low, and contact with Americans limited. Few Bulgarians can claim an American friend or acquaintance. Even fewer have traveled to the United States, and in 1993 only one in ten had studied English in school. One American, however, *is* known to all Bulgarians. He is Januarius Aloysius MacGahan, the Ohio farm boy who became a war correspondent and covered the Turkish atrocities in Bulgaria in 1876 for the *Daily News* of London and the *New York Herald*. His reporting greatly influenced Western public opinion, and the resulting political reaction led to the Russo-Turkish War of 1876 in which Russia defeated Turkey and liberated Bulgaria. MacGahan's photo is prominently displayed in a pantheon of Bulgarian heros in Sofia's National Museum, and a monument to him stands outside his hometown, Lexington, Ohio. Bulgarians expect all Americans to know something about their hero MacGahan, though few do.

Despite limited American contacts, attitudes toward the United States are positive and Bulgarians are seeking contacts in all fields, especially in business, scholarship, and science.

History, however, has taught Bulgarians to distrust big powers, and in this respect the United States has an advantage because it is so distant and has not played a role in Bulgarian history. Bulgarians would hope to see the United States as a benevolent power, but their skepticism of great powers causes them to reserve judgment. While there is little anti-Americanism today, American words are no longer accepted at face value as they were immediately after 1989. In a revival of the "forgotten Bulgaria" syndrome, Bulgarians feel neglected by the West. They see their country as small and vulnerable, particularly vis-à-vis Greece and Turkey, which are members of NATO and allies of the United States.

One type of American connection sought by Bulgarians is a friend in the United States to whom they can turn when assistance is needed—to establish contact with a professional colleague in the States, obtain a scholarship or a much-needed medication, or visit the United States. Americans, however, should bear in mind the Slavic distinction between "friend" and "acquaintance." A Bulgarian friend may request, and expect, more assistance than an American may be able to provide.

Estimates of Americans of Bulgarian origin run from 150,000-250,000, most of them second and third generation. As noted above, land ownership in Bulgaria was widespread. Peasants were poor but did not starve. Nevertheless, in the late nineteenth and early twentieth centuries, there was some economic emigration from "Kingdom Bulgaria" caused by rapid population growth, the subdivision of small landholdings, and increased taxation by the newly independent state.

The main emigration to the United States—an estimated 60 percent of the total—was political and by Bulgarians from Macedonia, motivated by the rebellions and wars in that strife-ridden province. Now dispersed across the United States, they have left us a Sofia, New Mexico, and a Macedonia, Iowa. But in contrast to other East European ethnic groups, Bulgarians have not banded together in national associations, perhaps because of their suspicious nature.

Prominent Americans of Bulgarian descent include John Atanasoff, inventor of the first electronic digital computer; Frank Popoff, president of Dow Chemical; Carl Djerassi, developer of the contraceptive pill; Ted Kotcheff, film director; and Christo Yavashev, known for his massive outdoor art projects.

American missionary activity in Bulgaria has left a residue of goodwill. The traditional Protestant churches in Bulgaria have been the Methodist, Baptist, Seventh-Day Adventist, Pentecostal, and Congregational. Today, there are many more, too numerous to mention.

Robert College, opened in Constantinople in 1862, was the first of several American missionary schools established in the Ottoman Empire by Congregationalists based in Boston. Among others were the American University in Beirut and several schools in Bulgaria.

Bulgaria, at that time a Turkish province, had only two secondary schools, and their academic level was not very high. Robert College, and an associated American Girls' School which opened in the 1870s, soon achieved reputations as the best foreign language schools in Constantinople, and some 50 percent of their students were Bulgarians. After 1878, Robert graduates played an important role in the political and cultural life of the new Bulgarian state. Among its Bulgarian graduates prior to the outbreak of World War I were two prime ministers, seven cabinet ministers, four district governors, ten diplomats, and more than a hundred judges and lawyers, physicians, bankers, merchants, professors, teachers, and other public figures.[8]

Of the several American schools established by the Congregationalists in Bulgaria, the most influential was the American College of Sofia, a coeducational English-language secondary school which opened in the 1860s. In 1926, the school's direction was passed to a nonsectarian corporation and board of trustees.

Renowned for its commitment to academic excellence, physical development, social responsibility, and the personal integrity of its students, many of the American College's graduates rose to positions of leadership in Bulgarian education, government, and the professions. The school operated for more than seventy-five years until it was closed by the Bulgarian government during World War II. It reopened in 1992 on its original campus in Simeonovo on the outskirts of Sofia and will have five hundred students when its first class graduates at the end of the 1997 school year. Admission is very competitive, and for the first class 102 students were chosen from 2,700 applicants.

A new American University in Bulgaria opened in 1991 in Blagoevgrad, about sixty miles southwest of Sofia. Supported by the U.S. and Bulgarian governments as well as private funding, the university is linked to the University of Maine. Most of the faculty is American, and instruction is in English.

American connections with Bulgaria are not many but the few that have been made are strong. They provide a good basis for future cooperative activities.

---

[1] Flora Lewis, *Europe*, 501.

[2] *Washington Post*, 6 March 1992.

[3] Robert Lee Wolff, *The Balkans in Our Time*, 41.

[4] Filip Dimitrov, in an address at the Woodrow Wilson Center, Washington, D.C., 5 March 1992.

[5] Eva Hoffman, *Exit into History*, 396.

[6] C. L. Sulzberger, *A Long Row of Candles [Memoirs and Diaries, 1934-1954]* (New York: Macmillan, 1969), 62.

[7] Hans Kohn, *Pan-Slavism*, 58.

[8] Much of the information on American schools in Bulgaria was provided by the Research Project on American Educational Institutions in Bulgaria, under the direction of Dr. Petko Petkov, Department of History, Sofia University. A series of monographs is planned.

7

Land of the South Slavs

A proud people acquire a habit of resistance to foreign oppression, and by the time they have driven out their oppressors they have forgotten that agreement is a pleasure and that a society which has attained tranquillity will be able to pursue many delightful ends. There they continue to wrangle, finding abundant material in the odds and ends of injustices that are left over from the period of tyranny and need to be tied up in one way or another.

—Rebecca West, *Black Lamb and Grey Falcon*

Yugoslavia, it was said, had seven frontiers, six republics, five nations, four languages, three religions, two alphabets, and one Yugoslav (Tito). In that diverse land, the size of Wyoming, all the cultural, religious, and political frictions festering in the nations described earlier came to a head in the early 1990s and erupted in a bloodbath not seen in Europe since World War II.

As shocking as the graphic details of ethnic cleansing have been to Americans, they are not new to the Land of the South Slavs (the meaning of "Yugoslavia") where nations have lived in periods of peace punctuated by eruptions of violence. In our time, however, they have been warring with modern weaponry, and the carnage in color has come into our living rooms via TV.

The similarities in the warfare between Croats and Serbs in 1993 and during World War II were described by National Public Radio correspondent Sylvia Poggioli:

> During the Croatian war, I would stop at check points to talk to people about a shooting. I could never tell whether it happened fifty years ago or the week before. The description was exactly the same.[1]

George F. Kennan goes back further in history—eighty years, to the Balkan War of 1913—to show similarities with the warfare of 1993. Commenting on a report on the 1913 Balkan War prepared at that time for the Carnegie Endowment for International Peace, Kennan writes:

> The object of armed conflict was "the complete extermination of an alien population." Villages were not just captured; they were in large part destroyed.... Woe betided the man of military age, or the woman of "enemy" nationality, who was found alive in the conquered village. Rape was ubiquitous, sometimes murderous. Victims...were obliged to take to the roads or the mountain trails by the thousands.... Little pity was shown for the sick and wounded. Prisoners of war, if not killed outright, were sometimes driven into outdoor compounds or ramshackle buildings and left there to die of hunger and exposure.

"The similarity of all this with what is happening today," Kennan concludes, "is inescapable."[2]

An American diplomat who spent eight years in Yugoslavia has said that the more he knows about the country and its people, the less he understands. Understanding the South Slavs is not easy for Americans whose experience does not permit them to comprehend the passions that cultural and religious differences arouse in those nations, nor the sense of injustice over what their tangled history has done to them. Americans seek simple solutions to complex issues, and in their efforts they tend to oversimplify.

The American search for simple solutions results in the common complaint, "Why can't they all live together in peace as we do now?" One American who traveled through the former Yugoslavia in the early 1990s told me that he was regarded everywhere as "just another dumb American" who would never understand the passions and politics that prevail there.

Americans will have to be deft in dealing with the South Slavs. The loss of life, material destruction, and injury to pride and national honor have left them traumatized, and some of the resulting hostility will be directed at Americans in the coming years.

Partisan passions, however, have made their way to the West thanks to the charisma of the South Slavs. As Rebecca West, who traveled extensively in the Balkans in the 1930s, put it:

> English persons...of humanitarian and reformist disposition constantly went out to the Balkan peninsula to see who was in fact ill-treating whom, and being by the very nature of their perfectionist faith unable to accept the horrid hypothesis that everybody was ill-treating everybody else, all came back with a pet Balkan people established in their hearts as suffering and innocent, eternally the massacree and never the massacrer."[3]

Twenty years later, American historian Robert Lee Wolff expressed the same sentiment: "To a typical Westerner almost every individual inhabitant of the Balkan peninsula seemed charming and he [the Westerner] was quite likely to adopt the prejudices of the first group he met."[4]

The intent here is not to adopt the prejudices of this group or that, nor to condemn one nation or another but rather to

describe, as dispassionately as possible, some of the characteristics that unite and divide the peoples of the former Yugoslavia whose history is intertwined with nationalist mythologies which each nation fervently believes. Rather than taking
sides or challenging one or the other of these mythologies,
Americans should be good listeners, show respect for the
nation of their interlocutors, be sensitive to their feelings,
and maintain an evenhanded approach to conflicts that defy
easy resolution.

The Nations

> Our historical memory [in the United States] is measured in
> months; in the Balkans it goes back for centuries. Grievances
> there are older than our own nation. In the mixed salad of
> Yugoslavia every group has fought every other one, commit-
> ted atrocities, signed truces, intermarried and fought again.
> This feud didn't begin when we became aware of it.
> —Ronald Steel, in the *New York Times*

As elsewhere in the Balkans, each of the former Yugoslav
nations—Slovenes, Croats, Serbs, Montenegrins, Bosnians,
and Macedonians—is passionately preoccupied with its own
national identity to the exclusion of others. History, ethnicity, and language give grounds for claims to territories once
possessed but now lost. Each nation (Slovenes excepted)
believes that it is at the center of the world, history is on its
side, and its cause is just. Exaggeration is a cultural imperative. Beliefs are based on opinions rather than facts, and
there is little tendency to ascertain the facts before forming
an opinion. Nationalism has been a way of survival, and it is
extreme. One American with long experience in Yugoslavia,
and himself of South Slav descent, advises visitors to take all
they hear with a grain of salt and believe only half of what
they see.

Amidst the passion and rhetoric, however, it is often over-
looked that these are all the same people. They are all South

Slavs, they speak the same or similar languages, and they have many cultural characteristics in common. Dividing them has been religion and neighboring great powers that have prevented the South Slavs from making common cause with each other. Slovenia was a part of the Germano-Austrian world for more than a thousand years. Croatia too was a part of that world but also reflects the influence of Hungary and Venice, to which parts of it once belonged. Serbia has been helped by Russia in times of trouble and was allied with England, France, and the United States against Germany and Austria in two world wars. Macedonia was under Turkish rule the longest.

As we have seen earlier, the Magyar arrival in the Central Danubian Plain at the end of the ninth century split the South Slavs (the six former Yugoslav nations plus Bulgaria) from the West Slavs (Czechs, Slovaks, and Poles). Cut off from their Slav brethren to the north, the South Slavs developed their own languages, which are somewhat different from those spoken by other Slavs. Serbs, Croats, Montenegrins, and Bosnians all speak Serbo-Croatian (or Croato-Serbian, if you are a Croat). Serbian, however, is written in the Cyrillic script, and Croatian in the Latin. Slovenian is also written in the Latin script and is distantly related to Serbo-Croatian. Macedonian is somewhere between Serbo-Croatian and Bulgarian.

These languages used to be described as variants of the same language but, with the recent political differences among the nations, the differences in language are now being emphasized. Those differences, however, are not significant in terms of handicapping communication among the South Slavs.

Since the breakup of Yugoslavia, the Croats have been working to create a separate Croatian language by resurrecting old Croatian words, coining new ones, and eliminating borrowings from the Turkish and Arabic. But as pointed out by a Bosnian linguist (who himself claims that Bosnian is a separate language), if Turkish words are eliminated, no Croat or Serb will have a kidney. "The Serbs, Croats, and Muslims alike use the Turkish word for kidney," *New York Times* correspondent Chuck Sudetic explains, "and there are no synonyms. Without Turkish borrowings, there could be no conversations about cotton, steel, soap, towels, blankets, or bedsheets."[5] Like it or not, they all seem to be in bed together linguistically, covered by Turkish bedsheets and blankets.

Differences other than language have also caused divergences among the South Slavs—the split between the Western and Eastern Roman Empires; the schism between the Catholic and Orthodox Churches; the five hundred years of Ottoman rule of Serbia, Bosnia, and Macedonia; the struggle in the Balkans between Christianity and Islam; and the rivalry between the Habsburg and Ottoman Empires. These are the historic origins of today's hostilities and all of them have left fault lines that run through the Land of the South Slavs.

The religious split is the easiest to define. Slovenia and Croatia are Roman Catholic; Serbia, Montenegro, and Macedonia are mostly Orthodox; and Bosnia is a mix of the two and of Islam. But it is not that simple because in each republic there are minority communities from the other South Slav nations, and the result is a patchwork of national diversity based mainly on religious differences.

The political split results from the clash of the Austro-Hungarian and Ottoman Turk Empires. Slovenia was a part of Austria for most of its history and is very much West European. Croatia was ruled in turn by Austria and Hungary and sees itself as Central European. The other republics have more of an Eastern ambiance. Serbia and Macedonia, after conquest by the Turks, lived under the Ottomans. Bosnia again was somewhere in between; it too was conquered by the Turks but in the 1878 Balkan settlement was awarded to Austria, which ruled it as a protectorate before annexing it in 1908. Mountainous Montenegro was never conquered by the Turks.

Political boundaries, moreover, do not always coincide with national borders. The continuing tension between the Habsburg and Ottoman Empires motivated massive movements of people seeking safety and security. Communities of Serbs and Croats, known for their fighting abilities, were also moved to areas where border defenses needed bolstering, and in areas ruled by the Ottomans, many Slav communities converted to Islam. Those settlements and communities are still with us today and are the main cause of the civil war. Three million Serbs—nearly one of every three—live outside Serbia; one million Croats live outside Croatia; and more than two million Albanians live in Serbia. In Serbia, there are more than 300,000 Hungarians and 60,000 Romanians; and in Macedonia, more than 400,000 Albanians. Smaller communities of Greeks, Turks, Slovaks, and Gypsies add to the clash of cultures. A veritable Balkan tinderbox is the Serbian province of Kosovo, which is home to more than two million Albanians but fewer than 200,000 Serbs.

In physical appearance, the South Slavs do not differ significantly. Slovenes and Croats appear somewhat more Western; Serbs, Montenegrins, and Macedonians, more Eastern; and Bosnian Muslims, again somewhere in between. Blonds tend to predominate in the north, and brunets in the south, but there are exceptions everywhere. Differences that do exist are seen mainly among peasants in the countryside where national traditions have been better preserved in an agricultural society.

Agriculture, as elsewhere in the Balkans, was the major occupation until industrialization began after World War II. Today's city dwellers, still in touch with their peasant past, are likely to have a piece of land in the countryside farmed by parents or relatives. With these ties to the land, the spoken languages still have the directness and earthiness of agricultural people; the pace of life is slower, and punctuality is not pursued as it is in the West.

With the defeat of both Austria-Hungary and Turkey in

World War I, there was an unusual opportunity to establish a unitary state for the first time. Called the Kingdom of Serbs, Croats, and Slovenes, the name was changed to Yugoslavia in 1929 in an attempt to put aside the national loyalties that were dividing the kingdom. The new Yugoslavia, however, continued to be plagued by political and cultural unrest, domestic and foreign intrigue, and terrorism.

During World War II, open warfare between the German invaders and Yugoslav resisters was matched by savage fighting between Croats and Serbs, and between communist partisans and supporters of the Serbian monarchy. In the postwar period, a lid on ethnic violence was maintained by Yugoslavia's victorious communist leader, Josip Broz Tito, who sought to strike a balance between the claims of the various nations. But with Tito's death in 1980, the fragility of Yugoslavia was exposed and the nations soon reverted to their traditional squabbling.

In 1990, the young men of the various nations dribbled together on the Yugoslav national basketball team that won the world championship. Two years later they were drubbing each other in a savage war.

Contacts and Conversations

> It is the overwhelming importance of personal contacts that baffles foreigners. A kind gesture, a friendly joke, the mood of the persons involved in a transaction—these are the elements more likely to influence the outcome than an insistence on rules and regulations.
>
> —Dusko Doder, *The Yugoslavs*

As elsewhere in the Slavic world, interpersonal relations are more important than state-imposed rules and regulations. It's whom you know that counts and how you relate to that person. Gestures of thoughtfulness—smiles, favors, small gifts, shared experiences and drinks together—make for good relationships but only when repeated over time.

Conversation is also important and can run for hours without anyone getting bored or tired. Talk is a pleasure to be enjoyed. "Serbo-Croat," wrote Rebecca West, "is a language that falls very easily into verse...." In the early 1890s, adds West, a Serbian minister of finance actually introduced his budget in parliament in the form of a long poem in blank verse.[6]

Emotion triumphs over reason. "The spirit of the irrational," writes Doder, "is very much a part of the Balkan atmosphere."[7] "With the possible exception of the Slovenes," continues Doder, "Yugoslavs have great difficulties in accepting the concept of corporate morality. But when their reactions depend on their own spontaneity, they are capable of extreme acts of individual bravery, consideration, self-sacrifice, and kindness" (219).

There is a downside, however. South Slavs find it difficult to admit to anything that makes them look worse than their neighbors, and a curious illogic is often used to justify actions taken. When asked about brutalities that a nation has committed, the likely response is, "But look at what they did to us!" Each nation believes it can do whatever it wishes because the others are doing worse. There is also a reluctance to engage in self-criticism, and lying for the cause of the nation is not considered a sin. As in other Balkan nations, there is a love of conspiracy and adventure; and in a macho society, men with courage are admired and respected.

Hospitality is traditional. The welcome mat will be out for visitors, along with the customary cup of coffee or bottle of slivovitsa, the local plum brandy, or *lozovaca*, the grape brandy made from crushed fruit pits. Almost every social encounter will involve a drink and a cigarette. "Without rakiya," goes a Montenegrin saying, "there is no conversation."

Rakiya can be made from plums, pears, apricots, grapes, or other fruits, and each South Slav believes that his is the best home brew around. Don't be surprised when it is served at an early morning business meeting. One American who visited his South Slav relatives reports having to drink rakiya 'round the clock, from breakfast to supper and just before retiring for the night. Sip slowly, he advises, and never let your glass become more than half empty.

Slovenes

> Enough is better than much.
>
> —Slovene proverb

Slovenes are the easiest of the South Slavs to define. In an unusual Balkan occurrence, there is a near coincidence of borders, language, and nation.

Small, mountainous Slovenia, only half the size of Switzerland, borders Croatia, Hungary, Austria, and Italy. With its spectacular mountains and forests, lush green meadows, and clear blue lakes, it resembles Austria and the Swiss Alps. Its cleanliness and well-maintained look remind visitors of the Germanic world.

The most Western of the South Slavs, the Slovenes were conquered by Charlemagne in 778 and were a part of the Germanic world until 1918. This has made them serious, solemn, and circumspect, and more quiet, reserved, and punctual than other South Slavs. A methodical and meticulous people, Slovenes use a step-by-step approach to solve problems and are difficult to draw out in conversation. West has described them as "sensible and unexcitable."[8] But they are also industrious, and their standard of living is relatively high. As a Slovene proverb says, "For the industrious, there is a loaf behind every tree and a penny under every stone."

Physically, Slovenes are almost indistinguishable from their Austrian neighbors to the north—moderately tall, predominantly blond, with light hair and eyes. And like their Austrian neighbors, they are Catholic and use the Latin alphabet. Visitors should use English or German but not Serbo-Croatian.

Slovenia was Yugoslavia's most developed republic, with manufacturing and mining the two most important sectors of the economy. Because of their industry and talents, Slovenes have been called the Czechs of Yugoslavia. Others see them as Austrians who speak a Slavic language. Slovenian industrial production fueled the economies of the other Yugoslav republics, causing much discontent at home, although as the bankers, entrepreneurs, and middlemen of Yugoslavia, the Slovenes profited from that role. Their standard of living, they believed, was being sacrificed for the benefit of the less developed parts of the country.

Although Slovenia was the first Yugoslav republic to declare independence, it is today the least turbulent and volatile of the new South Slav states. Its people are 95 percent ethnic Slovenian and are not preoccupied with the civil war raging elsewhere in the former Yugoslavia. According to Doder, "The Slovenes in the north seem to be the only ethnic group [in the former Yugoslavia] to have overcome the psychological traumas suffered because of a humble past."[9]

With a population of only 1.9 million, Slovenia is economically viable, and independent for the first time in its history.

Croats

There is no end to political disputation in Croatia. None.
—Rebecca West, *Black Lamb and Grey Falcon*

Croats inhabit the region southeast of Slovenia and south of Hungary as well as the Adriatic coast as far south as Montenegro. Like the Slovenes, they were conquered by the Franks, and after a period of independence in the tenth and eleventh centuries they were absorbed by their northern neighbor, Hungary, in 1102. When Hungary was defeated by the Ottomans in 1526, Croatia became a part of the Habsburg monarchy. From 1867 to the end of World War I, it was again a part of Hungary.

In appearance, the five million Croats are generally taller than the Slovenes, and mostly fair. They are also more West-ern-appearing than Serbs in their dress and grooming. Men wear suits and ties and carry attaché cases. Grooming is considered important, and visitors to Croatia will be judged by the way they dress. First impressions will be lasting.

Catholic like the Slovenes, Croats speak a language almost identical with that of the Serbs but written in the Latin alphabet, hence the term Serbo-Croatian. Most professionals also speak English or German.

Croatia was used by the Habsburgs as a defensive outpost against the Ottoman Empire. Croatian loyalty was to the Habsburg emperor and the Catholic Church, not to the Magyars who scorned the Croats and tried to force the Hun-garian language on them. The Hungarians failed in this en-deavor, but some of their verbosity and exaggeration appar-ently did spill over into Croatian culture.

Like the Slovenes, Croats feel that they too financed Yu-goslavia through their industry, agriculture, and tourism. The Dalmatian coast—Dubrovnik in particular—was the main-stay of Yugoslav tourism and will be a strong foreign currency earner for Croatia when peace returns.

At the heart of the South Slav strife is the animosity between Croat and Serb. As Doder explains:

> The Croats have…an animosity toward the Serbs that seems to date back to their tribal period. Centuries of subjugation have politically emasculated the Croats' elite, who dwell in a realm of intellectual opposition rather than the practical world of power. It is this negative reflex which has given an exclusivist tone to the Croatian nationalism, especially in their relationship with the more numerous Serbs, whom they covertly fear and overtly despise as Oriental barbarians (21).

Regional diversity divides the Croats. Zagreb residents are more like urban Austrians. Dalmatians, who lived under Venetian rule for four hundred years, are also Croats but in character are more Mediterranean. Serbs predominate in the Krajina and in Slavonia, regions bordering Serbia, where they were resettled by the Habsburgs to bolster border defenses against the Turks (and where they have been in open rebellion against Croatian rule). Croats are more restrained and less inclined than Serbs to openly express personal views. Business discussions will stick to business, and in social situations politics will be discussed only after drinks and dinner. Croats appreciate visitors who understand who they are, especially their culture, arts, and sports. Americans will be expected to know the names of Croatian players in the National Basketball Association.

Like the Slovenes, Croats want to be seen as West European, not Central European or, perish the thought, East European. Croats claim that Serbian propaganda about Croatian atrocities against Serbs and Jews during World War II has given them a bad name. Nationalism, they say, was forced on them by what the Serbs have done. The world does not understand them.

Many Croats have relatives in the United States. Strong ties also exist with Western Europe—Germany and Austria in particular—where Croats have lived and worked as "guest workers." At any one time in recent years, there have been a million or more Croatian guest workers abroad, separated from their families, working and saving in order to return to their native villages and build a house or start a small business.

One final difference—urban Croats prefer espresso or cappuccino, Serbs drink Turkish coffee.

Serbs

> History has made lawyers of the Croats, soldiers and poets of the Serbs. It is an unhappy divergence.
> —Rebecca West, *Black Lamb and Grey Falcon*

Serbs are the Texans of the South Slavs. Almost everything that has been said about the other Slav nations can also be said about the ten million Serbs, only more so. They are more open, expansive, demonstrative, and with their Mediterranean temperament, more volatile and less predictable than the Croats. With their charm, good looks, and flamboyance, Serbs are also bigger than life and more fun to be with. As Edith Durham wrote in 1909, "I could not but admire that imaginative nature of the Serb, who will lead a forlorn hope and face death for an idea."[10]

Serbs have a record of standing up to great powers—the Ottoman Turks, the Habsburgs, Nazi Germany, the Soviet Union, and most recently the United States and the United Nations. Whereas the Croats want to be seen as Western, the Serbs seem to delight in thumbing their noses at the West.

Serb society is peasant-based but with a degree of class freedom and independence unknown to other peasant societies of Eastern Europe. The Serb aristocracy and gentry were all but eradicated during the Ottoman conquest, and thereafter Serb peasants were only serfs to the alien Turks. After the Turks were driven out, Serbia became a nation of independent smallholders who did not hesitate to challenge their own rulers.

An outspoken and talkative people, Serbs are willing to express themselves on a wider range of issues than are Croats. With foreign visitors, there will first be small talk over coffee or juice; the serious and frank discussions, when visitors will learn their real views, will follow over slivovitsa. Punctuality is not a virtue, and Serbs are likely to be fifteen or more minutes late for meetings.

The loquaciousness of the Serbian peasant was described by Sir Charles Eliot, an Englishman who traveled in the Balkans in the 1890s:

...as soon as he has performed the simple operations necessary to secure the existence...of his maize, his plums, and his pigs, he sits down in the village wine-shop, not so much to get drunk as to engage in endless and resultless political discussion.[11]

One hundred years later, the Serb proclivity for political palaver continues, not in the wineshop but in the *kafana* (coffeehouse). It is the best place to learn what is on their minds and what they are complaining about, as complain they will. Serbs say that their backwardness, relative to Western Europe, is due to five centuries of Turkish domination. Croats will say that Turks are backward because they dominated Serbs for so long.

Boasting is a national proclivity, and much of what Serbs say should be taken with a grain of salt. As a Serb proverb says, "You may boast to strangers but tell the truth to your own people." Pride in themselves and things Serbian is another factor that must be considered in dealing with Serbs. Serbs have an enormous national pride, and threats that are made against them will be seen as challenges that they cannot submit to, as NATO and the United States learned during the Yugoslav civil war. Serbs must be given a face-saving way out of any political impasse or they will only dig in their heels and refuse to budge from a position they have taken. They also value consistency. If you say you will do something, do it. Don't waffle and don't show weakness or indecision.

Stubborn in pursuing their own interests, Serbs see themselves as an aggrieved nation defying the world, as victims of centuries of Ottoman rule, Austro-Hungarian hostility, Croat violence in World War II, and, most recently, Western criticism of their role in the civil war. Everyone is seen as ganging up on them, and this provokes a strong response.

Serbian society, as a consequence, is very macho. Serbs may be subjugated but not beaten. Men must be brave and prepared to kill or die for Serbia if necessary. Serbian (and Montenegrin) folk heroes are the Haiduks, mountain brigands who waged perpetual guerilla warfare against the Otto-man occupiers, "...playing the endless Balkan game of cops and robbers in the mountains," as Robert Lee Wolff wrote, "and freely committing what might elsewhere have been re-garded as treachery in order to survive to fight another day."[12] In recent years, the macho Marlboro Man has dominated the Serbian media and helps to explain why Marlboros are the most popular cigarettes in Belgrade.

Serbian men walk like free men, with a swagger not seen elsewhere in Eastern Europe. They get very close when con-versing and do not hesitate to make physical contact. Attitudes toward women are those of traditional male-dominated societies. Men ooze charm and flatter women to excess. Unescorted women may be approached on streets and in cafes; and if an American woman should smile at a stranger or make eye contact, as she might at home, it will be seen as a come-on. Such approaches are not necessarily dangerous, but women should be prepared to deal with them decisively and forcefully.

While some Serb women are in positions of authority, most have a difficult time making it in this society. American women will have to prove themselves before their profes-sional credentials will be accepted. In Muslim regions, the task will be even more difficult.

Other East European nations, as we have seen, claim to have saved Europe from invaders from the East—the Poles by absorbing the force of a Tatar-Mongol invasion, and the Hungarians by resisting the Ottomans. A similar claim is made by the Serbs based on their defeat—yes, defeat—by the Ottoman Turks at Kosovo Polje (Blackbird Field) on June 28, 1389. That defeat is celebrated as a national holiday because it weakened the Turks and stalled their advance into Europe. (Americans who wonder why the Serbs celebrate a defeat should remember the Alamo.)

Kosovo marked the end of the Serbian medieval state and the start of nearly five hundred years of Ottoman rule. As

Edith Durham wrote in 1909, Kosovo is "...the fatal field on which the Turks gained the victory that established them...in Europe—the Armageddon of the Servian [sic] people."[13] And as the twentieth century comes to a close, Kosovo continues as a vital element of the Serbian mystique.

Kosovo, in southern Serbia, is the Serbian Jerusalem, regarded as the birthplace of the nation, to be protected at all costs. Today, however, Kosovo is inhabited largely by ethnic Albanians and is Serbia's major minority problem.

Serbia has a population of ten million but this includes the more than two million Albanians in the south and 300,000 Hungarians in the north. Moreover, more than one million Serbs live in Bosnia, and more than a half million in Croatia. These pockets of Serbs in various parts of the former Yugoslavia are a central issue in the current conflict and make the true borders of the Serb nation a subject of great uncertainty and sharp dispute.

The war in Bosnia against Muslim Serbs and in Croatia against Catholics is seen by Orthodox Serbs as a continuation of their just struggle against Turks and Croats that began centuries ago. Most Serbs believe that that struggle can end only when all Serbs are united in one state. In the Serbian parliamentary elections of December 1993, all parties across the political spectrum, from extreme nationalists to democrats, called for creation of a Greater Serbia. One election slogan of more radical Serbs was "All Serbs in one state, and nobody else."

By tradition, Serbs have been pro-American. In both world wars they were allied with France, the United Kingdom, and the United States. But in 1994, Serbs were blaming the United States for the hardships they were suffering after the imposition of economic sanctions against the rump Yugoslavia because of its role in the civil war. Recalling their wartime alliances with the United States, many Serbs believe that Americans have betrayed them.

Russians and Serbs have an affinity based on their common Slav and Orthodox heritage as well as their common adversaries in Germany and Austria in two world wars. In the South Slav civil war of the 1990s, it was Russia to which Serbia turned for support.

In the past, it was said that Serbs were as stubborn as the French, as romantic as the Russians, and as obsessed with nation as the Germans. But, as *Washington Post* reporter Dan Morgan added in 1994, "Right now...many Serbs think of themselves more like Israelis, surrounded by enemies, struggling to survive."[14]

Bosnians

> ...the so-called ethnic groups of Bosnia all speak the same language and have shared the same historical past. The only difference among them is religious background.
> —John V. A. Fine, "The Medieval and
> Ottoman Roots of Modern Bosnia"

Bosnia was independent until conquered by the Ottomans in the fifteenth century. After almost five centuries of Turkish rule, it came under Austrian administration in 1878 and was annexed by Austria in 1908. Bosnia and Herzegovina (the Dukedom), formerly separate, are now one.

Before the deaths and dislocations caused by the civil war, 44 percent of the population was Muslim, 31 percent was Serbian (who are Orthodox Christians), and 17 percent, Croatian (who are Catholics). Although disdainfully called "Turks" by Serbs and Croats, the majority of Bosnian Muslims are South Slavs who speak Serbo-Croatian and have been living in the Balkans as long as the Serbs and Croats. Religious heritage is the sole difference that divides the three groups.

After forty-five years of living in a secular state, the majority of Bosnian Muslims have been secularized. They take a relaxed view toward their religious heritage, which is for them a matter of culture and observing such traditions as giving their children Muslim names, practicing circumcision, eating baklava, and observing the feast marking the end of Ramadan. They enjoy their pork, savor their slivovitsa, and intermarry with Christians. In the cities, some 30 percent of the marriages are mixed, and there are people with the same family names in all three religious groups. And they consider themselves European.

Among the other South Slavs, the Turks replaced the native Slav aristocracy with Muslims. Bosnia and Herzegovina, however, were the exceptions. There, the native Slav aristocrats and gentry willingly converted to Islam and were thus able to retain their feudal privileges, social status, and large landholdings, which were worked by peasants—mostly Serbs and Croats. This caused economic and social differences in Bosnian society which continue today. Muslims, for the most part, are concentrated in the cities and are better off; Christians, both Serbs and Croats, are rural and less well-off. In many respects, the war in Bosnia is an urban-rural conflict.

Despite the prevalence of mosques and the more oriental atmosphere of some cities, the Muslims of Bosnia should not be confused with the Islamic fundamentalists of the Middle East. True, there is still a Turkish influence to be seen. While they speak Serbo-Croatian, their language has a greater infusion of Turkish words than in Serbia or Croatia. Their folk music also reflects the Turkish influence, and in Muslim villages the women wear veils and pantaloons. But in Bosnian cities, Muslims are indistinguishable from Croats and Serbs except for their names, which give them away, and on market days when villagers, in their distinctive dress, come to the cities.

Sarajevo, Bosnia's capital, was once a beautiful, cosmopolitan city peopled by Muslims, Christians, and Jews who lived together in tolerance and civility. In history it is known mainly as the scene of the assassination of Franz Ferdinand, heir to the Austrian throne, which precipitated World War I. In 1984, it was the site of the Winter Olympics but in the early 1990s, Sarajevo became a Balkan Beirut, a ruined shell of a city and a memorial to a multiculturalism that was being destroyed by a rapacious nationalism.

Montenegrins

> O smallest among peoples! rough, rock-throne
> Of Freedom! Warriors beating back the swarm
> Of Turkish Islam for five hundred years,
> Great Tzernagora! never since thine own
> Black ridges drew the cloud and brake the storm
> Has breathed a race of mightier mountaineers.
>
> —Tennyson, *Montenegro*

Montenegrins inhabit the desolate mountain area to the south of Bosnia-Herzegovina that the Ottomans were never able to conquer. When other lands of the South Slavs were under Turkish rule, Montenegro (the Venetian translation of *Crna Gora*—"Black Mountain") remained a free and independent state until it joined the new Yugoslavia after World War I.

The more than 600,000 Montenegrins are mostly Orthodox and speak a dialect that is close to Serbian. Called "Mountain Serbs" by some, they regard themselves as a separate nation closely linked to Serbia, although there have been recent calls for looser ties and even outright independence.

Montenegrins are the tallest and heaviest-set people in Europe. Those who have seen them in any numbers, wrote Harvard anthropologist Carleton S. Coon, will recall "the massiveness of their frames, the wide shoulders, deep chests, rawboned arms, large, muscular hands, and long, bony legs."[15] Most distinctive, added Coon, are the "hawk beaks" found in more than half the population.

Known for their uncompromising honesty, physical courage, reckless bravery, and macho pride, Montenegrins are reputed to be the toughest fighters of the South Slavs. They are also known for their love of freedom. As an old saying asserts, "There is no freedom outside Montenegro." The roots of Montenegrin heroism, writes Doder, lay in their oral tradition:

> Exploits of their ancestors were passed down through the generations as richly embroidered stories and legends. Their proclivity for storytelling is an integral part of the Montenegrin psyche.... [They are] born poets and soldiers, with the highlander's swagger and quick temper, and with an immense sense of pride in their family and clan traditions.... Pragmatism is an alien concept equated with cowardice.[16]

Eliot described them thus in 1900:

> The inhabitants of this strange country are the very opposite of the Servians [sic]. Instead of being all peasants they are all chiefs and princes, and have the air of a well-built, well-mannered aristocracy which is so rare in the plains.[17]

Montenegro, moreover, is home to the vendetta, the blood feuds between families, tribes, and clans resulting from crimes or insults that must be avenged to maintain one's honor. Warfare against Turks and Muslims was a way of life for more than four hundred years. As Milovan Djilas, himself a Montenegrin, observes:

> So it has always been here: one fights to achieve sacred dreams, and plunders and lays waste along the way—to live in misery, in pain and death, but in one's thoughts to travel far.... Here war was survival, a way of life, and death in battle the loveliest dream and highest duty.[18]

Macedonians

> During the 1880's there began the active rivalry among the Bulgarians, Serbs, and Greeks for the Turkish province of Macedonia.
>
> —Robert Lee Wolff, *The Balkans in Our Time*

Macedonia has been the proverbial tinderbox of the Balkans, the center of Balkan intrigue since its liberation in 1912 from Turkish rule. Serbia and Bulgaria fought over it in two Balkan wars just prior to World War I. During World War II it was occupied by Bulgaria, and in 1945 it became a republic within Yugoslavia and gained home rule for the first time. But when Yugoslav Macedonia became independent in 1992 and chose to call itself the Republic of Macedonia, its admission to the United Nations and recognition by the United States were held up by Greece, which maintained that the name Macedonia implied a claim on its own territory of Greek Macedonia. (Haven't we all eaten Macedonian salads in Greek restaurants?)

The Macedonian dispute with Greece is based in part on historic rivalry and population transfers. Historic Macedonia is a mountainous region encompassing the Republic of Macedonia, parts of Greece and Bulgaria, and the port of Salonika on the Aegean Sea. When Turkish rule ended in 1912, Greek Macedonia's population was mostly Slavic, and Greeks were in the minority. But in the 1920s, many Greek refugees from Turkey were resettled in Greek Macedonia. Some twenty years later, during the 1946-49 Greek civil war, thousands of Slav Macedonians fled or were driven from Greece to Yugoslav Macedonia, and their property and land were given to the ethnic Greeks who had been resettled from Turkey. Hence the Greek fear that the Republic of Macedonia may some day seek to reclaim territory in Greek Macedonia.

Like their fellow South Slavs, the ancestors of today's Macedonians migrated to the Balkans in the sixth and seventh centuries and settled in the Byzantine province of Macedonia, which they took as their name. Most of them now live in what was formerly the Macedonian Republic of Yugoslavia. Many others, however, live just across the borders in Bulgaria and Greece. In a part of the world where national boundaries are poorly defined, nationality and citizenship are blurred, and passions easily aroused.

The Republic of Macedonia shares borders with Albania, Greece, Bulgaria, and Serbia and has minorities from all four nations. The largest are the Albanians who, according to Macedonian officials, number 21 percent of the population of two million. Albanians, however, maintain they are more like 40 percent. Lesser minorities are Turks (4.8 percent), Gypsies (2.7 percent), Muslims (2.5 percent), and Serbs (2.2 percent).

The four neighboring nations all have historic claims to Macedonia, and it has been a continuing source of contention between them. A developing country, Macedonia is one of the poorest states in Europe—poor, but hospitable. "All Balkan peoples are known for their hospitality," writes Stoyan Pribichevich,

> ...but along with the Albanians, the Macedonians are probably the most hospitable of all. A guest is a sacred person to the folk. In Western countries, he is welcomed but is expected to conform to the rules of the house; in the Balkans, especially in Macedonia, the rules of the house are suspended to accommodate every wish of the guest.[19]

A guest, continues Pribichevich, will always be asked to stay for lunch, and it is an offense not to accept. Older people are given deferential treatment and are assisted in every way possible. At meals the elders are the first to begin eating, and they are expected to begin conversations while the others listen. People understand each other silently, without words, and visitors must not be hasty in speaking lest they err or be misunderstood.

Macedonian hospitality was experienced by the American troop of five hundred soldiers, the largest unit in a United Nations force deployed in Macedonia in 1993 as a deterrent against a possible spread of the conflicts in Bosnia and Croatia, which was the first U.S. combat unit ever to serve in the Balkans. "We run into locals a lot on patrols," said one of the American GI's. "They offer you coffee and ask you into

204

their houses. Every time you turn around you get your pockets full of walnuts. You can't say no."[20]

Despite linguistic ties to both Serbia and Bulgaria, Macedonians have managed to maintain their separate identity, although not without political cost. This was brought home years ago at a reception I attended at Washington's Kennedy Center given for a visiting Yugoslav folk dance ensemble. In attendance were the Yugoslav and Bulgarian ambassadors, both of whom happened to be of Macedonian origin. When the two ambassadors were invited to join the visiting dancers in an impromptu Macedonian *kolo*, they accepted and appeared to be enjoying themselves dancing the traditional "circle." They would not, however, allow photographs to be taken of them dancing together lest this cause political problems at home.

Macedonia's ethnic and political problems are emotionally charged. Visitors are advised to avoid getting involved in these issues, which defy logical resolution.

Bargaining in the Balkans

Who bargains much is the real buyer.

—Slovenian proverb

Trade is traditional in the South Slav lands through which run two main corridors of Europe—from the North Adriatic to the Black Sea, and from Vienna to Belgrade and the Aegean Sea. Through Croatia and Serbia, Crusaders marched on their way to and from the Holy Land, and following the Crusaders on those same routes came trading caravans between East and West. The Ottomans, during their occupation, encouraged trade and left behind a trading tradition.

Yugoslavia had more experience with the free market and Western business practices than other communist countries. Large enterprises were state-owned but they coexisted with private shops, small businesses, and family farms. The entire economy, moreover, was open to the West. In 1968, Yugoslavia became the first communist country to allow joint ventures with foreign firms. Equally important, Yugoslavia was open to the Western media, and its citizens could travel abroad more freely.

As a consequence, the South Slavs barter well and have more of an entrepreneurial spirit than most other East European nations. But after forty-five years of communism, unstable political conditions, and a vicious civil war, they have become short-term traders, more interested in a quick profit than in long-range deals. To follow up on done deals, much time and effort will be required, as well as repeated visits.

As master negotiators, South Slavs open discussions with exaggerated demands, hoping to get as much as possible for as little as possible. They take their time and are ready to drag out negotiations as long as needed to accomplish their aims. U.S. Secretary of State Warren Christopher, after meeting with Bosnian Serbs in 1993, described them as "very manipulative," a remark which Serbs will take as a compliment.[21] Lord Owen, the indefatigable British mediator in the Bosnian war, said of his negotiating partners: "They will look you straight in the face and they lie. And you know it and they know you know it. You just have to go on."[22] Milovan Djilas, the Montenegrin dissident, puts it in different terms: "Balkan leaders, they know how to make a compromise, and then break it."[23]

People are more important than laws or written agreements, and agreements are broken because there is little legal tradition. In lands where illiteracy was high, oral tradition is strong and the spoken word is more important than the written. Negotiations are conducted between people rather than institutions. Numbers are not always accurate or reliable, and falsehoods are presented as facts. Cuts, kickbacks, and bribes are a legacy of Ottoman rule; and in the transition to a market economy, it is often difficult to keep up with changes in legislation and regulations. Visitors will need a willingness to listen and be patient.

Start slowly and at the top, with the director of an institute or enterprise, and if that proves too high, work your way down the chain of command. Be aware, though, that most South Slavs believe they are more important than they really are, and they may inflate their positions. Define yourself. They will want to know who you are, your national origin, and whether you have East European connections they can relate to.

Veza (pull, or influence) gets things done through networks of family, friends, former schoolmates, and professional colleagues who do favors for each other. For those who do not have the right connections, gifts and cash payments can accomplish similar results. Payments will not be requested openly but may be hinted at and are not considered as bribes. To ensure services which a Westerner would expect to be normally available, a small gift is customarily made.

The American Connection

The first South Slavs to arrive on New World shores were Dalmatian sailors, known worldwide for their seamanship and love of adventure. Tradition has it that two members of Columbus's crew on his first American voyage were from Ragusa, the medieval name for Dubrovnik. The word "argosy" is believed to derive from Ragusa.

The first South Slav community in the New World is believed to have been settled by Croats and Slovenes on the banks of the Savannah River in Georgia in 1715. Abandoned after the Civil War, only the settlement's cemetery remains today. In the late seventeenth century, Slovenes and Croats were among the Catholic missionaries who worked among American Indians in the mid- and southwest. After 1850, Slovene and Croat colonies were established in Ohio, Illinois, Nebraska, Michigan, and Minnesota, and later in New York and California. Ohio had the most.

At the turn of the century, an estimated one million South

Slavs were a part of the great migration to the United States from the poverty-stricken villages of Eastern and Southern Europe. Most were Croats, followed by lesser numbers of Slovenes and Serbs. United States census figures for that period are not reliable because South Slavs were classified at that time by their country of origin. Croats and Slovenes were listed as Austrians or Hungarians; Serbs and Montenegrins, as Bulgarians. Moreover, the South Slavs tended to define themselves by religion—Orthodox, Catholic, or Muslim. Only since 1908 has the census recorded nationality.

Most of the new immigrants gravitated to urban centers such as Cleveland and Chicago, where they found jobs in industry. Some also settled in farming communities in Colorado and Minnesota, fishing ports in California and the Pacific Northwest, oyster communities near the mouth of the Mississippi River, and rural areas of California where they became pioneers in the cultivation of apples and grapes.

The number of Americans of Yugoslav descent is difficult to determine but the largest among them are the Croats, an estimated one million of whom live mainly in New York City, Chicago, Cleveland, and Pittsburgh.

Prominent Americans of Croatian origin include Anthony F. Lucas (Lucic), a mining engineer and geologist, who struck the first oil gusher in Texas; Rudy Perpich, three-term governor of Minnesota; and Representatives John R. Kasich (Ohio) and Joe Kolter (Pennsylvania). The most famous American of Croatian descent, however, was the renowned sculptor Ivan Mestrovic, who taught at Syracuse and Notre Dame Universities, and whose works can be seen in many American cities and art galleries.

Among the prominents of Slovenian descent are Senator Tom Harkin (Iowa); former Senator and later Governor, Frank J. Lausche (Ohio); former U.S. Representatives John Blatnick (Minnesota) and Joe Skubitz (Kansas); and the late prolific writer Louis Adamic. A Slovenian bishop, Frederick Baraga (1797-1868), worked as a missionary among the

American Indians; a trained linguist, Baraga wrote a grammar of the Chippewa language. Americans of Serbian origin include Columbia University professor Michael Pupin, known for his inventions in telephony and wireless telegraphy; Nikola Tesla, inventor of the alternating current motor and the alternating current power transmission system pioneered by Westinghouse; Governor George Voinovich (Ohio); poet and Pulitzer Prize winner Charles Simic; actors Karl Malden and John Malkovich; film director Peter Bogdanovich; basketball star Pete Maravich; and former U.S. Representative Helen Delich Bentley (Maryland).

---

[1] "An Interview with Sylvia Poggioli," *WAMU Profile* (October/November 1993): 3.

[2] George F. Kennan, "The Balkan Crisis: 1913 and 1993," in *New York Review of Books* 11, no. 13 (15 July 1993): 5.

[3] Rebecca West, *Black Lamb and Grey Falcon* (New York: Viking Press, 1941), 20.

[4] Robert Lee Wolff, *The Balkans*, 6.

[5] Chuck Sudetic, *New York Times*, 26 December 1993.

[6] West, *Black Lamb*, 1014.

[7] Dusko Doder, *The Yugoslavs* (New York: Random House, 1978), 49-50.

[8] West, *Black Lamb*, 601.

[9] Doder, *The Yugoslavs*, 205.

[10] Edith Durham, *High Albania*, reprint (Boston: Beacon Press, 1987), 275.

[11] Sir Charles Eliot, *Turkey in Europe* (London: Frank, Cass, 1965), 339.

[12] Wolff, *The Balkans*, 67.

[13] Durham, *High Albania*, 278.

[14] Dan Morgan, *Washington Post*, 19 June 1994.

[15] Carleton S. Coon, "Racial History," in *Yugoslavia*, ed. Robert J. Kerner (Berkeley: Univ. of California Press, 1949), 29.

[16] Doder, *The Yugoslavs*, 182.

[17] Eliot, *Turkey in Europe*, 347.

[18] Milovan Djilas, *Land without Justice* (New York: Harcourt, Brace, 1958), 39.

[19] Stoyan Pribichevich, *Macedonia, Its People and History* (University Park: Pennsylvania State Univ. Press, 1982), 235.

[20] *New York Times*, 11 May 1994.

[21] Warren Christopher, MacNeil/Lehrer Newshour, 11 August 1993.

[22] Lord Owen, *New York Times*, 29 December 1993.

[23] Milovan Djilas, quoted by David Binder, *New York Times*, 26 December 1993.

8

Albanians

Fierce are Albania's children, yet they lack
Not virtues, were those virtues more mature.
Where is the foe that ever saw their back?
Who can so well the toil of war endure?
Their native fastness not more secure
Than they in doubtful time of troublous need;
Their wrath how deadly! but their friendship sure,
When Gratitude or Valour bids them bleed,
Unshaken rushing on where'er their chief may lead.
    —Lord Byron, *Childe Harold's Pilgrimage*

In an Albanian poem, a Turkish pasha (high government
official) is asked by his sultan why he had sustained such high
losses fighting the Albanians. The pasha explains:

Father emperor, what can I tell you?
They keep their *besa* [word] very faithfully
They do not betray each other
and for death they do not care.[1]

Albanians have a well-deserved reputation for valor in battle,
for keeping their word, and for friendship—time-honored

211

virtues that one does not expect to find in a small country that in recent times lived under a despotic regime for forty-five years. The poorest people in Europe today, Albanians nevertheless have a strong sense of their own dignity.

Albanians, or *Shqipetare* (Sons of the Eagle, pronounced "shchep-tar-eh"), as they call themselves, are believed to be descended from the ancient Illyrians, a non-Slavic Indo-European people who appeared in the Balkan lands during the second millennium B.C. According to Roman writers, the Illyrians were a tall and well-built people, politically disunited but good fighters who quarreled with each other and waged wars against Greeks, Macedonians, and Romans. Their descendants today are still politically disunited and their reputation as an argumentative people and formidable fighters has not been diminished.

For a small nation Albanians have distinguished themselves in many ways. They provided the best warriors for Roman legions and later for Turkish armies, both of which they faithfully served as well as courageously resisted. The Albanian irregular cavalry, the *sipahis*, were among the best units in Ottoman military campaigns of the sixteenth and seventeenth centuries, and the periodic levies of Albanian Christian boys provided the Turkish janissaries with their toughest troops. As British diplomat and Balkan scholar Sir Charles Eliot wrote in 1900, "The Albanians are always ready to fight for any cause or no cause."[2]

Albanians also provided a disproportionate number of high officials in the Ottoman army and administration. They were pashas in many parts of the Ottoman Empire, and *grand viziers* (prime ministers) to Turkish sultans. Napoleon Bonaparte's mother was Albanian. Kemal Pasha, known as Ataturk, founder of the modern Turkish state, was part Albanian. Mehemet Ali, an Albanian, founded the Egyptian royal line that ended when King Farouk was deposed in 1952, and, in our time, we have Nobel laureate Mother Teresa, an ethnic Albanian from Yugoslav Macedonia.

The most celebrated Albanian, however, is George Kastrioti, known as Skanderbeg, for whom the great square in the center of Tirana, the capital, is named. A former janissary, the Christian Skanderbeg led Albanian resistance against the Turks in the fifteenth century and kept them at bay for twenty years when Ottoman armies were sweeping through Europe almost unopposed.

"A Nice and Natural People"

Ah, 'tis an excellent race, and even under old degradation,
Even under *hodja* and Turk, a nice and natural people.
—quoted by Edith Durham, in *High Albania*

Albanians are a warm people—lively and loquacious, passionate and proud. But, because of their strongly held opinions, animated way of speaking, and argumentative nature, it is difficult for them to form a consensus. To foreign visitors accustomed to more restrained behavior, they often appear to be angry.

Friendship runs deep but not the kind that Americans are accustomed to. Albanian friendships are based on mutual trust, and they take longer to develop. Once developed, however, they are solid and lasting.

Hospitality is overly generous. Albanians will bankrupt themselves to prepare a good table for their guests and make them feel at home. "Albanian etiquette," wrote Eliot, "requires that a guest should be treated as if he had the appetite of Gargantua."[3] One particular honor for a foreigner is an invitation to an Albanian home on Sunday, the day usually spent with family.

An American who had been a guest in an Albanian home several times once asked her hostess, "What do you say about us after we leave?" Without hesitation the hostess replied, "Americans do not eat enough," and after some reflection she added, "and they do not shake hands enough."

You *must* eat and you *must* shake hands with everyone you meet, each time you meet, and when you say goodbye. The hands of older or senior people are shaken first, and then the younger in descending order. When a close acquaintance is greeted, a kiss on the cheek is appropriate, within gender. People who are very close get three kisses, alternately on each cheek. Kissing between genders is less common, in public that is. Women walk arm in arm in public, as do men.

Guests are welcomed at the door with a handshake and, once inside a home and seated, there will be yet another round of handshakes and the ritual greeting, *mire se erdhet* (you are welcome here). Guests reply *mire se u gjeta* (it's a pleasure to be here). *Raki*, the local grape brandy, will be served, followed by Turkish coffee. Women may be offered a sweet liqueur. Before each drink a *gezeur* (toast) will be offered by the host, and the visitor is expected to return the toast on a subsequent round of drinks. But despite their fondness for raki, Albanians are not heavy drinkers. Drunks are rarely seen in public, perhaps because of the Muslim heritage of some 70 percent of the population.

The concept of "Dutch treat" with a foreigner is alien. Albanians will insist on paying for coffee and drinks, and protestations to the contrary will be of no avail. Edith Durham wrote of "the noble traits of the Albanian character—the duty of hospitality—the sacredness of the guest...."[4] To refuse hospitality, she added, was an outrage to the Albanian people.

The idea of privacy, as Americans understand it, does not exist in Albania (nor in many other Eastern countries not far removed from a communal lifestyle). Albanians think nothing of intruding on a meeting an American may be having with another Albanian. Peace Corps volunteers living with Albanian families have found it difficult to find a few minutes of seclusion by themselves at the end of a long day. Their Albanian hosts assume that Americans are happiest when they are in the company of the host family.

Family and friends are the essentials of a clan society from which Albania is only now emerging. Knowing the right people and having an Albanian connection gets things done. American journalist Dusko Doder, after telling Albanians that his mother was of Albanian origin, says that he was "...given instant entrance into a society that had spent decades perfecting its mistrust."[5]

Not all Americans will be able to claim an Albanian family connection, but in a nation where a clan culture is still strong, a friend of a friend is also a friend and will be welcome. It will be helpful to let Albanians know that you are a friend of someone they already know and trust. Also, as in other Balkan countries, Albanians will want to know who you are and where your ancestral roots lie.

Friendship with Albanians, however, comes with a cost in a country of scarce resources. Albanians will give their all for a true friend but will expect something in return. They will not ask for anything directly, but if an Albanian should express admiration for something, it may indicate that he or she hopes it will be presented as a gift. This is the reverse of the sentiment explained in earlier chapters, that a guest should not express admiration for an object lest the host present it as a gift.

Not scarce are rumors, which seem to drive the entire country. With clan and family ties still strong, everyone seems to know everyone else, and confidentiality should not be expected. Whatever a foreign visitor tells one Albanian will be picked up and repeated to others. As Durham wrote in 1909, "There are few places where it is harder to keep an event secret than in the mountains of Albania. News spread like wildfire."[6]

Nodding the head up and down, as in Bulgaria, indicates no; shaking it from side to side is yes. And a soft clicking of the tongue (tsk, tsk) indicates disagreement with something said. In meetings with Americans, however, there is likely to be more head shaking than tongue clicking.

Reluctant to be critical of foreigners or to voice disagreement openly, Albanians would rather give a sign of approval, whether they agree or not. Receptive to foreign advice, they are loath to question it. They will sit and listen impassively without facial expression, making it difficult to know where they really stand on an issue. This may be puzzling to Americans accustomed to being frank and open, even when doing so involves honest criticism and disagreement.

Albanians, however, do not hesitate to ask blunt questions such as, "How much do you earn?" and "What did your car (or home, or clothing) cost?" One American woman recalls being asked, "Why are you so fat," while at the same time being urged by her Albanian hosts to eat more.

Women and Men

The status of women is low, as elsewhere in the Balkans, and foreign women may be at a disadvantage. While there are few formal taboos for foreign women, they should speak loudly and forcefully in order to get attention and be taken seriously. According to some American visitors, it also helps to be demanding and aggressive at times.

More important, though, are trust and friendship. If Albanians trust a foreign woman, consider her a friend, and respect her abilities—as they did that intrepid English traveler Edith Durham—she should have no difficulty working with them.

One American woman with extensive international experience describes Albania as a most pleasant place to live, adding that she has had fewer problems as a woman in Albania than in most other less-developed countries in which she has worked. And in contrast to some other Balkan countries, she notes, in Albania there is no pinching in public.

During the communist years, women and men were equal under the law but the intent was to provide additional workers for forced industrialization. As Mimoza Pashko, wife of a founding member of the Democratic Party, points out: "Dictatorship was doubly heavy for the women, at work and at home...because the grave economic situation and the extreme poverty made the woman a slave in her house."[7] And in the workplace as well.

As in other male-dominated societies, women today seem to be doing much of the necessary work, particularly in the countryside. On collective farms, the heavy work was done with tractors, driven only by men. Today, the collective farms are gone and the tractors too, and women work the fields by hand while their husbands at home do little. One American visitor to Albania speaks of "a curious kind of national psychological illness..." which takes the form of:

> ...a mindless, passive revolt against work by much of the population, especially the men. Women, who appear to be the ultimate realists, are often seen about Tirana and out in the country, doing what must be done to keep the nation going.[8]

In their efforts to "keep the nation going," about half the law students in Tirana are women, and the new law school dean is a woman.

A "Least Studied" Language

Although it is an Indo-European language, Albanian is distinct from other languages of that group. Eliot, in 1900, described it as little known and curious:

> ...it is clearly an Aryan tongue, but it is one of the least studied languages of Europe, and its exact affinities are not easy to determine. It is full of words borrowed from Italian, Slavonic, and Greek, and often much curtailed and corrupted in the borrowing.[9]

The written language developed only in the fifteenth century, but under Turkish rule its use was forbidden for the next four centuries. It was codified in 1908 when Albanians opted for the Latin script. Although it is a "least studied" language, it is not difficult to learn and a working knowledge can be acquired after a few months of diligent study.

However curious the language, it will not be an obstacle to communication with Albanians. Italian is the most widely spoken foreign language, since it is readily accessible though Italian TV which can be received in Albania. English and French are also spoken by the elite and by educated young people; German and Russian may be useful as well.

Despite forty-five years of a highly centralized state, the Albanian language has many regional dialects, and variations still exist in the mountains of the north and among emigrés in Detroit, New York, and Boston. The main differences, however, are between the Albanian people's two main groups, the Gegs and the Tosks.

Gegs and Tosks

The more numerous Gegs of the mountainous north have traditionally led a pastoral life isolated from the outside world. Never completely conquered by the Turks, it is the Gegs who today still project the image of the tough Albanian fighter.

Gegs are more animated, verbose, and at times rowdier, especially the Kosovars who live in the Serbian province of Kosovo. Gegs speak loudly and forcefully, and to outsiders they may even appear angry—gesticulating wildly and even throwing things down on the table when talking. According to an old Albanian proverb, "If you want a hundred Italians to be quiet, shoot one. If you want a hundred Albanians to be quiet, you must shoot ninety-nine."

Vendettas in old Albania, both within tribes and between tribes, were governed by a strict code of behavior. A man who failed to carry out the required vengeance for an offense to his honor was scorned in his own community, while those who did avenge the offense were liable to be shot in return by the family of the victim. Today, the practice appears to be ending because of determined government efforts to mediate the more serious cases.

The Tosks of the southern lowlands, by contrast, were mostly peasant farmers. More gentle, shy, and diffident than the Gegs, Tosks had more contact with the Mediterranean and outside world, and from the Tosk lands at the end of the nineteenth century came the wave of emigration to other parts of Europe and the United States.

Although Gegs and Tosks speak somewhat different dialects, Albania is one of the most homogeneous countries in the Balkans, with Albanians numbering some 98 percent of the population. Up to the end of World War II, some 70 percent were Muslim, 20 percent Orthodox (mostly in the south), and 10 percent Catholic (mainly in the north). Under the communists, all religion was banned and Albania was declared to be the first atheistic state. Today, the three main religious groups have again begun to function, although they do not approach their previous strengths.

Religion, moreover, does not divide Albanians as it does the Yugoslavs. In Albania, the outside enemy has been a unifying factor, and Albanians will claim that "Albanianism is our religion." In a country where Muslims have lived for centuries side by side with Christians and a small Jewish community, a high degree of religious tolerance has been traditional.

Jews have lived since 70 A.D. in Albania, a country which has no history of anti-Semitism. During World War II, almost all of the small community of a few hundred survived, although Albania was occupied by Germany toward the end of the war. The Albanian government refused to provide the Germans with a list of Albanian Jews who were being sheltered by their Albanian neighbors, and the underground issued an order that any Albanian denying refuge to Jews would be executed for disgracing the nation. No Albanians were executed, the small Jewish community survived, and three hundred and fifty were allowed to emigrate to Israel in 1991.[10]

Albania is the only European nation with a Muslim majority. Most Muslims, however, do not strictly observe their religion. They drink alcohol and, according to one foreign resident, they would not know in which direction Mecca lies. There are some eight million Albanians throughout the world—six million in the Balkans but only 3.2 million in Albania. More than two million live in the Serbian province of Kosovo, another 400,000 in neighboring Macedonia, and lesser but still substantial numbers in Greece and Montenegro. In the United States, there may be as many as 200,000 people of Albanian descent.

Kosovo, the Serbian province bordering Albania and Montenegro, is Albania's main foreign policy problem. Some 90 percent of the Kosovars are ethnic Albanians, and Kosovo has been a source of contention between Albania and Serbia since the Middle Ages. Both Albanians and Serbs (as well as Montenegrins) are emotionally attached to Kosovo and are unwilling to recognize each other's claims.

The Painful Past

> It is difficult to write the history of a race which has spent so much time under foreign domination and whose records, as well as being difficult to find, are usually to be found in the language of these foreign invaders.
>
> —Tom Winnifrith, *Perspectives on Albania*

Positioned between Montenegro, Serbia, Macedonia, Greece, and the Adriatic Sea, little Albania has always been of interest to great powers, crossed as it was by one of the main trade routes between Europe and the Middle East—the Via Ignatia, which linked Durres on the Adriatic with Salonika on the Aegean, and Rome with Constantinople. Although it is not a seafaring nation, Albania has also been of interest to maritime powers because of its command of the narrow Strait of

Otranto at the heel of Italy where the Adriatic meets the Mediterranean.

Albania has been occupied, in turn, by Romans, Avars, Byzantines, Goths, Serbs, Bulgarians, Normans, Venetians, Ottoman Turks, Italians, and Germans. Rome alone ruled Albania for more than five hundred years. In the twelfth and thirteenth centuries, the Crusaders crossed Albania on their way to the Holy Land, and traders followed the Crusaders. In the fifteenth century, a brief twenty years of independence was enjoyed under the national hero Skanderbeg before Albania fell again, this time to the Ottoman Turks. With Turkish rule in the fifteenth century came the conversion to Islam of more than two-thirds of the people, and isolation from Europe for the next five hundred years. Under the Ottomans, Albania stagnated, and when the Turks withdrew in 1912 they left Albania in almost the same condition as they had found it.

At independence in 1912, Albania had an underdeveloped economy, a primitive agriculture, a mostly illiterate population, no urban middle class, and no experience in self-government. Its boundaries, moreover, were set by the great powers for political rather than ethnic reasons, and large Albanian minorities were left in neighboring Serbia, Macedonia, Montenegro, and Greece. By the end of the 1920s Albania had become a virtual satellite of Italy and, in 1939, Italy invaded and occupied the country.

During World War II, Albanian partisans fought against each other as well as against Germans and Italians, as in Yugoslavia. When Albania's communists emerged victorious in 1944, they were dominated for the next four years by Yugoslavia, which had plans to annex the country. Those plans, however, were thwarted in 1948 by Tito's break with Stalin, which gave Albania's communist leader Enver Hoxha (pronounced "Hod-zhah") an excuse to sever relations with Yugoslavia and transfer his alliance to the Soviet Union. But in 1961, during the Sino-Soviet dispute, Hoxha transferred his alliance to the People's Republic of China, which led the Soviet Union to break all diplomatic, political, and economic relations with Albania. History repeated itself again in 1978 when Albania broke relations with China. In all three cases, the cause of the shifting alliances was Hoxha's determination to preserve his power. The downside was that, under Hoxha, Albanians were the most isolated people in Eastern Europe and, after the Romanians, the most repressed. Estimates are that as many as one-fifth of the Albanian population was imprisoned or killed during Hoxha's rule, which was characterized by paranoia and self-imposed isolation.

Rugged and remote Albania, historically mysterious and unknown, has been approachable only since 1991 when its communist regime fell and was replaced by a freely elected democratic government.

Whatever is said about Albania must be dwarfed by its extreme poverty and dire economic straits. In 1993, an estimated 10 percent of the work force was abroad seeking work, and the unemployment rate of those who remained at home was 40 percent. The country of 3.2 million, the size of Maryland, was being sustained by foreign assistance and the remittances of the 300,000 Albanians abroad. On the positive side, by the end of 1993 the democratic government had instituted radical reforms, the private sector was burgeoning, much land had been privatized, inflation had been dramatically slowed, and the currency had been stablilized and was freely convertible. Albania was described as the most stable state in the Balkans. Moreover, Albania has the youngest population in Europe; the average age in 1987 was twenty-seven, and one-third of the population was under fifteen. Change is coming fast.

Besa

An honest man does not break his word.
—Albanian proverb

"Every society has a few basic values by which it can be characterized," writes Alexander Lopasic. "In the Albanian case one of the most important is a very clearly identified sense of honour. Honour for all Albanians is the Alpha and Omega of their way of life; it is the pivot of their very existence."[11]

The lives of Albanians, by tradition, have been guided by the customs and laws epitomized by the *Kanun* (Canon of Lek), a code of behavior bearing the name of fifteenth-century Albanian chieftain Lek Dukagjin but embodying customs dating back to antiquity. The Canon governed all aspects of Albanian life and, with others like it, it was for more than five centuries the law of the mountain regions that the Ottomans were never able to subdue. The communists tried to eliminate the Canon, but it has left its mark on the Albanians and it may still arise in interactions with them. The best and highest qualities of the Canon are represented by *besa* (word of honor, trust, faith). Whatever is promised must be done, or besa (pronounced "bes-sah") will be violated. For a proud and honorable people who prior to World War II lived in a society based on family, loyalty, and trust, a breach of besa was the worst possible transgression. Today, the word of a friend is still good, and the sense of honor important.

In old Albania, writes Dusko Doder, besa

...was not merely a moral code, which, in other societies, forms the foundation of virtue and ethics. Besa was a law that served for centuries as a regulator of daily life. It governed business transactions by individuals, by villages and clans, or even by districts. To break one's besa was not only the greatest disgrace, but also subject to the most severe punishment— execution by one's peers."[12]

Foreigners today should also observe besa although they need not expect such drastic retribution if they do not. However, a visitor caught lying will be disgraced and might as well forget about accomplishing anything in Albania.

Besa reflects the collective responsibility that an individual feels for the honor of family or clan. As Lopasic explains:

> The slightest reflection on the members of a man's family or ancestors was considered an offence against honour and could be avenged only by the shedding of blood. Honour, being so important, can be taken away from a man by spitting at him, beating or pushing him, threatening him, accusing him of a lie; by breaking into someone's house (one's house is considered sacred by the Albanians), breaking an agreed truce, or dishonoring a woman. All of these demanded restitution of honor by drastic means.... In social terms a dishonoured is as though dead: he will be seldom visited and socially avoided, while his children would have difficulty in finding marriage partners. To restore his honour he must take revenge, following the principle of injury for injury, life for life.[13]

Is besa still important today when the old clan society has been weakened by forty-five years of communism when people had to steal and lie merely to survive? Will it be encountered by visiting Americans, and will they too be held to the severe standards of besa?

Besa is still observed in some parts of Kosovo, but in Albania itself it has been eroded by the Hoxha years when lying was at times necessary for survival. Nevertheless, something of besa remains today, although Albanians may not know it by that name. They will be reluctant to enter into agreements which they may not be able to carry out, and they will not want to overcommit themselves lest they lose trust.

As Doder noted after a visit in 1990, "[M]any people were still reluctant to promise me anything, no matter how small, such as fixing a light in my hotel room, perhaps for fear of making a vow that could not be honored."[14]

Business and the Law

Democracy found Albania a country with no commercial laws. During the communist period, the word of the dreaded Enver Hoxha was law, and Hoxha ruled Albania like a Stalinist fiefdom from 1945 until his death in 1985. In a sweeping judicial reform, virtually all judges, investigators, and prosecutors of the communist regime were replaced by new and younger officials. Their experience, however, as might be expected, was limited, and while the new laws are clear, regulations for enforcing them are not.

Also lacking is experience in doing business with the West. Many of those who have opened new businesses are former members of the nomenklatura (the communist elite), and their business activities constitute their first major encounter with the modern world. Their conditioning by the communist regime means that much paperwork is required to do the simplest transaction. The result is red tape, confusion, and corruption.

New business executives, accustomed as former bureaucrats to dotting every *i* and crossing every *t*, are reluctant to give firm commitments. Foreign business executives have difficulty finding the right people to negotiate with—those with a sense of responsibility that enables them to sign agreements and contracts. Once a contract is signed, however, there is likely to be something down the road that will go wrong and require further negotiation. Moreover, the fine print in a contract is not always read nor its consequences understood, and Albanians may respond with great surprise when the terms have to be enforced.

Uncertainty about the future also handicaps the business climate. Anything can happen and usually does. Deliveries may not be made on time. New legislation changes the ground rules. But "Not to worry," as the Albanians say, since laws are often not enforced.

A legacy of deep suspicion also pervades business dealings. Foreigners in the past have brought troubles to Albania, and during the communist years Albanians learned to be suspicious of their neighbors and colleagues at work. The slightest infraction, if brought to the attention of the authorities, could result in a prison sentence.

Visitors should not be deluded by the youth of their negotiating partners. As said before, Albania has one of the youngest populations in Europe, and the young man negotiating with a foreigner may be very influential. Younger people, moreover, are the most receptive to change. They learn quickly and are the easiest to work with.

The dollar sign is paramount, and Americans are assumed to be loaded with dollars and ready to part with them. As elsewhere in the Balkans, the opening price should never be accepted. Albanians will say, "This is my bottom price, take it or leave it." "Leave it" is the advice given by old Albanian hands, and the seller will most certainly come back with a better offer.

Albanians rarely show a sense of urgency, and negotiations can be lengthy and repetitive. A representative of a U.S. volunteer agency relates how he meets with an Albanian, discusses the services to be provided by his American volunteers, negotiates a contract, signs it, and believes he has an agreement. On a second visit, he is received by another Albanian who professes to know nothing about the signed agreement, and negotiations must start again from scratch. At each stage the American is asked how much money he is prepared to provide. He politely replies, "None, only volunteer services." When the volunteers finally arrive, they are warmly greeted like old friends and royally received, but on the first working day they are asked how much money they will provide.

Driving in Albania can be hazardous. Roads are poor and are shared by cars, bicycles, donkeys, and pedestrians. The cars, moreover, are mostly old and in poor mechanical condition, traffic rules are only beginning to be enforced, and most Albanians are new to driving. Horn beeping is the rule, and drivers seem to step on the gas before braking. Passing is frequent and not always on the left. Pedestrians *do not* have the right of way, even on crosswalks, and cars will drive on the sidewalks to avoid traffic. Pedestrians must be on the alert. As one Albanian relates:

> The roads are crowded with people and there aren't any rules for the streets. People will jump out in front of you without looking so you have to use your horn a lot to warn them. Of course if you don't use your horn and you have an accident, the first thing they'll say is "Why didn't you use your horn?"[15]

Despite the lack of law and rules of the road, the private sector is booming. Family-owned restaurants and small shops are proliferating, and the service is good. Talent is emerging, and there is determination to catch up with the rest of Europe. A sure sign of the return of the old Albanian entrepreneurial spirit, the country markets, forbidden by the communists, are back. On Sundays, rural roads are jammed with vehicles and animals as peasants bring their produce for sale in a lively free market.

The American Connection

> By the end of the nineteenth century Albanians had spread all over the ramshackle Turkish empire, and further afield to places like America, another breeding-ground of nationalist fervor.
> —Tom Winnifrith, *Perspectives on Albania*

As in other Balkan lands, it was traditional for young men to leave their poverty-stricken villages and seek their fortunes in foreign lands.

"There were brief returns to the village where one was born," writes P. J. Ruches,

...to wed, beget, marry off one's offspring, bury one's parents. Finally, there would be a last, long return to savor the fruits of one's labor.... Great was the exultation of a whole village in the good fortune of a native son, but his initial departure was accompanied by tears and lamentations—as always—by the womenfolk. Later, when America opened wide its hospitable gates, these lamentations of parting included this land in their doleful threnody:

What new land abroad to us appeared?
It gathered all our handsome youths.
The brides remained with hand to breast.
Maidens weep with blackened tears.
Old women don black kerchiefs.
Go to blazes, America![16]

But the bright side of this migration, continued Ruches, more than compensated for the parting tears. "Villages that had made a livelihood at the edge of poverty became wealthy...with the hard-earned gold honestly gathered in many lands by successful sons.... Whole villages prospered in the good fortunes of one or two native sons."[17]

Early Albanian immigrants to the United States prior to World War I were typically Tosks from the predominantly Orthodox region of Korce in southern Albania. Many settled in Boston where the Albanian Autocephalous Orthodox Church was founded in 1908, independent of the Greek patriarch in Constantinople who was the titular head of the Orthodox Church in Albania. The church became a center of Albanian nationalism abroad, and its founder, Fan S. Noli, was soon to play a prominent role in Albanian politics.

Most of the immigrants were single men who hoped to earn some money in the States and return home to buy land, build a house, and wed. Many of them did indeed return home after World War I when Albania was independent, but their hopes turned to disillusionment when Muslim landowners continued in power and economic opportunities were limited. This caused a second wave of immigration in the 1920s and 1930s, but this time entire families as well as fiancées joined their men in Boston.

Noli became Albania's prime minister after a popular uprising which Albanians call the Democratic Revolution of 1924. An Orthodox bishop who had spent many years in Boston, Noli favored a Western-type democracy but he was ousted after six months by Ahmet Zogu, who became president and later King Zogu of Albania. Among Noli's many accomplishments: he earned a Harvard degree, translated Shakespeare and Poe into Albanian, and was recognized as a poet in his own right.

Two other Americans are revered by Albanians. To President Woodrow Wilson the entire nation is indebted for preventing the partition of Albania at the end of World War I. At the Paris Peace Conference, Albania's immediate neighbors—Greece, Serbia, Montenegro, and Italy—all laid claims to Albanian territory, and only Wilson's intervention prevented Albanian dismemberment. Harry Fultz, another American, founded a school in Tirana which, in the interwar period, turned out an entire generation of graduates in business and technology.

In our time, Father Rrok Mirdita was a parish priest in the Bronx in 1993 (and a U.S. citizen) when he was named archbishop of Tirana and Durres. And all Albanians know Elez Biberaj, an American of Albanian descent who was *the* Voice of America to Albania, broadcasting daily in Albanian from Washington for more than ten years, reporting the news and helping Albanians to understand the United States.

Another American connection is Geraldine Apponyi whom King Zogu married in 1938. Geraldine was a Hungarian aristocrat whose mother was American, and therein lies a tale which reads like the plot of a Balkan operetta. Best man at the royal wedding was Count Ciano, son-in-law of Italy's dictator, Benito Mussolini. When Ciano returned to Rome after the wedding, he suggested to Mussolini that Italy

230

invade Albania, which Mussolini did the following year. Zogu and Geraldine were forced to flee abroad, never to return, and Albania was annexed to Italy and lost its independence once more.

As might be expected, Albanians fear their immediate neighbors more than distant powers. Perhaps for this reason, they see the United States—which has no historical baggage to bear—as their salvation and are anxious for investments and contacts of all kinds.

Some 200,000 Americans are believed to be of Albanian descent, and there are active communities today in New England, New York, Pennsylvania, Ohio, Michigan, and Washington. They have been generous in their material and moral support of Albania.

Albanians, however, have been disappointed by the amount of government aid they have received from the United States, the leader of the anticommunist West and their lifeline to the wider world during the communist years through the broadcasts of the Voice of America. This is a disappointment American visitors will hear of.

[1] Quoted by Alexander Lopasic in *Perspectives on Albania*, ed. Tom Winnifrith (London: Macmillan Academic and Professional, 1992), 96.

[2] Sir Charles Eliot, *Turkey in Europe*, 370.

[3] Ibid., 360.

[4] Edith Durham, *High Albania*, 308.

[5] Dusko Doder, "Albania Opens the Door," *National Geographic* 182, no. 1 (July 1992): 82.

[6] Durham, *High Albania*, 97.

[7] Mimoza Pashko, in *My Albania: Ground Zero*, ed. Bob Brewer (New York: Lion of Tepelena Press, 1992), 70.

[8] Brewer, *My Albania*, 8.

[9] Eliot, *Turkey in Europe*, 379.

[10] Harvey Sarner, with Joseph and Felicita Jakoel, *The Jews of Albania* (n.p.: Brunswick Press, 1992), 8-13.

[11] Alexander Lopasic, "Cultural Values of the Albanians in the Diaspora," in Winnifrith, *Perspectives*, 90.

[12] Doder, "Albania Opens the Door," 86.

[13] Lopasic, in Winnifrith, *Perspectives*, 90-91.

[14] Doder, "Albania Opens the Door," 86.

[15] Remzi Lani, in Brewer, *My Albania*, 21.

[16] P. J. Ruches, *Albanian Historical Folksongs, 1716-1943* (Chicago: Argonaut 1967), 78. The verse has been abbreviated by the author.

[17] Ibid., 78.

9

Balts

The three Baltic peoples must be treated together, and yet they are too different from one another not to require separate attention.

—Czeslaw Milosz, "Swing Shift in the Baltics"

When Lithuania, Latvia, and Estonia regained their independence in 1991, one of their first acts was to do away with the detested Soviet symbol—the obligatory statue of Vladimir Ilich Lenin, founder of the Soviet state, standing in the town squares of their capital cities.

In Lithuania, President Vytautas Landsbergis, musicologist turned political leader, gave a fiery independence speech to a large crowd in downtown Vilnius. Whipped up by his oratory, the inflamed crowd marched forthwith to the town square and unceremoniously toppled the statue of Lenin. In Latvia, a committee formed by the government to do the job commandeered a crane and truck and, in the darkness of night, quietly hauled away *their* Lenin statue. In Estonia, the government took a similar decision to remove their statue but, on learning that the monument was larger than they had thought, contracted with a Finnish firm to do the job.

How each state chose to end its reminder of Russian rule tells us much about the Baltic peoples and how they differ from each other. Such distinctions, however, have been un-known to many Americans, including some in very high Washington positions. A senior administration official, for example, told the *New York Times* in 1989:

> I have spent my entire grownup life not knowing the differ-ence between Latvia, Lithuania, and Estonia. They were like Central African lakes to me. There was never any reason to think about them. If you had told me two years ago that I would now be drawing careful political distinctions between Estonia and Lithuania, I would never have believed it.[1]

The distinctions between Estonia and Lithuania, as well as Latvia, can be easily drawn from a brief look at the national characters of the three peoples.

Lithuanians are a feisty people—warmhearted, emotional, full of moral fervor, grandiloquent, idealistic, and impetuous. With good reason, their Catholic country has been called "Spain on the Baltic." The Lutheran Latvians are more like the North Germans who colonized them in the thirteenth century—quiet, thoughtful, disciplined, and reserved. Esto-nians, also Lutheran, are calm, deliberate, and even more reserved, much like their Finnish cousins and Swedish neigh-bors. The pragmatic Estonians want to get the job done in the most efficient manner.

As Priit J. Vesilind, an American of Estonian descent, says, "Among Balts it is said that Latvia has the best politicians, Lithuanians the best prophets, Estonians the best econo-mists."[2]

The three Baltic peoples have lived as farmers in their historic homelands for millennia but for much of that time under foreign rule by Germans, Poles, Swedes, or Russians. Lithuania joined in a union with Poland in the fourteenth century that lasted for some four hundred years until it was partitioned by its neighbors. It was not until this century, between the two world wars, that all three nations enjoyed a brief period of independence only to fall once more under Russian domination. Today, they are independent again but, after fifty years of Soviet occupation and colonization, they face major economic and political challenges as they attempt to reestablish their national identities.

Indeed, the very survival of national identities in the face of foreign rule and relentless Russification is astonishing. In this regard, their remaining Russophone residents (Russians, Belarusians, and Ukrainians) are seen as threats to the national and cultural identities of the three states.

Lithuania is best off in this regard since 80 percent of its population is ethnic Lithuanian. In Estonia, 63 percent is ethnic Estonian. And in Latvia, ethnic Latvians number only 54 percent, a bare majority over the Slavs.

With such daunting demographics, one might ask how the Baltic nations have survived and why they do not today seek strength in unity and cooperation—a logical measure, it would appear—to ensure economic and political viability.

Baltic cooperation, however, does not come easily. One public manifestation occurred on August 23, 1989, the fiftieth anniversary of the Molotov-Ribbentrop pact (which divided Eastern Europe between Nazi Germany and the Soviet Union), when some two million Balts formed a human chain across all three countries in a pro-independence protest.

Since regaining independence, each state has issued its own currency and, savoring its sovereignty, each has established immigration, border, and customs controls. But in 1993, in a hopeful sign for the future, they agreed to establish a free trade zone and to coordinate their trade and defense policies. Such cooperation, however, runs against the experience of Baltic history.

In the past, the three nations have rarely cooperated effectively, divided as they have been by language, religion, foreign rulers, and dreams of separate and independent homelands. Lithuania, moreover, had a running dispute with Poland in the interwar period over the status of the city of Vilnius, which had been annexed by Poland, a dispute in which it had no support from Latvia or Estonia.

Most of Estonia's trade is with the West. Lithuania's trade is mainly with Russia and other republics of the former Soviet Union. Latvia's trade is more evenly divided between East and West.

The politics of the three states also differ. Lithuania, in 1994, had a left-of-center government; Latvia and Estonia had right-of-center governments. Lithuania has been the slowest to reform, and its economic prospects are questionable. Estonia and Latvia have eagerly embraced reform, and their economies are reviving. The three economies, however, are competitive with each other, and there is little trade between them.

Language differences also present problems. Lithuanian and Latvian belong to the Baltic group of Indo-European languages but are quite distinct from other Indo-European tongues. Estonian is a Finno-Ugric language, related to Finnish. All three languages, however, are written in the Latin script. Lithuanian and Latvian are as similar to each other as Italian and Spanish, and are to some degree mutually comprehensible. The same cannot be said for Estonian.

Russian is a language that Latvians and Estonians prefer not to speak and sometimes pretend not to know, although it is the lingua franca they must use to communicate with each other and with Lithuanians. Visitors to Latvia and Estonia should try English first, then German, and Russian only as a last resort.

Lithuanians speak Russian without resentment. They are the least Russified of the Baltic states and regard their Russophones—some 20 percent of the population—as less of a challenge. For this reason, their citizenship law is less severe than in the other Baltic states. Any permanent resident with a job can become a citizen, without having to speak Lithuanian.

Also dividing these nations are religion and history. The Catholic Lithuanians, as we have seen, were joined with Poles for four hundred years in a union that stretched from the Baltic to the Black Sea, encompassing much of today's Poland, Lithuania, Belarus, Ukraine, and parts of western Russia. Latvians and Estonians are mostly Lutheran and linked by Protestantism to Germany and Scandinavia. Because of these religious, historic, and geographic influences, the cultures of the three peoples differ.

Lithuanians are the most open, voluble, even blustery. Latvians and Estonians are quiet and unpretentious, like their Nordic neighbors whom they resemble physically. Latvians and Estonians seek to avoid offending others. They find it difficult to say no to a request and are likely to be noncommittal by saying "We'll have to look into that."

Despite these deterrents, Baltic cooperation remains imperative. As American historian William Urban points out:

> There are two contradictory forces at work in the world. The one is for each ethnic group to seek its own identity and its own homeland; the other is to unite in larger unions. The task of all peoples, the Baltic peoples included, is to find a means of achieving both of these goals at once. Economic and political units which are no larger than a few million persons will find the future difficult. The historic experience of the Baltic peoples in cooperating with one another provides only a small foundation on which to build a larger political and economic structure; that foundation must be enlarged.[3]

German traders and missionaries arrived in Latvia and Estonia in the twelfth century. They were followed by the Germanic Knights of the Sword and the Teutonic Knights, religious-military orders that converted and colonized the two territories known at the time as Livonia. In more recent history, Latvia and Estonia were ruled first by Sweden and then by Russia. And in our time, fifty years of annexation by the Soviet Union prevented any kind of Baltic unity. All roads literally led to Moscow.

Soviet rule brought a large influx of Russian-speaking residents—government and Communist Party officials, military personnel, industrial workers, and the KGB—and the three states were Russified as well as communized. Decision making was arbitrary, without established procedures. This is changing slowly but the Soviet legacy continues. Sovietization eroded the Baltic work ethic and changed moral values. Loafing on the job and stealing from the state became common, and young people today have little respect for hard work and the property of others.

Environmental degradation also resulted from Soviet rule. The Baltic peoples have become increasingly concerned about air and water pollution and the rapid depletion of their natural resources. This has given rise to a strong environmental movement that cuts across the spectrum of political parties in all three countries and provided broad public support for the independence movement. Since independence, the environment has continued to be a major concern, related as it is to the health and survival of the three peoples.

The biggest cloud over the Baltics, however, is tobacco smoke. In Lithuania, according to World Health Organization statistics, 55 percent of men and 10 percent of women are regular smokers, and 25 percent of the men are smokers by the time they leave secondary school. Statistics for Latvia and Estonia are similar.

All three nations lack a native nobility and landed gentry. Lithuania was formerly ruled by an aristocracy that had been Polonized through intermarriage. (The Polish family name-ending *wicz* usually indicates Lithuanian origin.) In Latvia and Estonia, Germans (as well as Poles and Lithuanians) ruled, and in all three countries the indigenous populations were rural and peasant. With the political upheavals of the twentieth century, the old ruling elites were eliminated and today the national cultures of the three states are peasant-based.

To first-time visitors the Baltic states may appear Eastern or Western, depending on the direction from which the visitors are coming. Travelers from the West see the Baltic states as Eastern, similar in many respects to Eastern Europe before the collapse of communism—out of date and out of touch. Travelers from the East see them as Western, and that is the attraction to their Russophone residents who appreciate the higher standard of living and the Western ambiance they find in the Baltic states. There is yet a third category— travelers from the West, who first visit Russia and then arrive in the Baltics, see them as distinctly Western in contrast to the East they have just left.

Western traders and missionaries are today again arriving in the Baltics, and a few words of caution are in order. Corruption, inefficiency, and cynicism are the legacies of a half century of Soviet rule, and foreigners are advised not to take everything at face value. Before signing agreements, it is prudent to determine whether prospective business partners actually have legal title to the property or enterprise they claim to represent. Details of agreements should be spelled out, in particular who pays for what and whether and how profits can be repatriated. Many of today's Baltic entrepreneurs are new to business and may not appreciate the true meaning of a signed agreement. Laws on business transactions are not yet in place, and new agreements often set precedents. Beware of excessive chumminess on the part of prospective business partners and others who do not show the traditional Latvian and Estonian reserve.

Business deals are often not as they appear. For example, although they have no metals of their own, the three Baltic states in 1993 ranked among the top European exporters of metals (which came from the Russian military or other former Soviet republics). In this respect, Tallinn, in a play on words, has been called Metallinn.

Despite these caveats, there are many good business opportunities in the Baltics. The three states are becoming more investor-friendly and see themselves as gateways to trade with Russia and other republics of the former Soviet Union. The three currencies are stable and freely convertible; and the economic future, at least in Latvia and Estonia, is promising. And in contrast to most other republics of the former Soviet Union, there is political and economic stability.

The Baltic diaspora is far-flung, the result of two waves of emigration. The first, mainly from Lithuania, occurred at the end of the nineteenth century and was economic—the search by peasants for a better life in other countries. The second wave, from all three nations, came after World War II and was political—escape from Soviet rule. Today, there are large Baltic communities in Scandinavia, Canada, Australia, and the United States. And from those communities many Balts have returned to their homelands with Western expertise to help in reconstruction and the transition to democracy and a free market.

Americans are admired in all three states, in part because of family connections, but also because the United States government consistently maintained a policy of nonrecognition of their forcible incorporation into the Soviet Union. President Clinton, when he visited Riga in July 1994, became the first U.S. president to visit the Baltic states.

The dark years of Soviet occupation are gone but the dark winters of the north still remain. Some Americans find it difficult to adjust to the winter days when only a few hours of sunlight may be seen, and SAD (Seasonal Affective Disorder) is common. This is especially so in Latvia and Estonia, where the local people are reserved and not very demonstrative and where Americans will have to make a special effort to communicate. English, however, is well on its way to becoming the second language and should not present obstacles to bridging the communication gap.

Lithuanians

...impressive qualities are boldness, tenacity of purpose, and an iron will. Once a Lithuanian has resolved to embark upon a given course of action, nothing will turn him from his purpose.

—E. J. Harrison, *Lithuania: Past and Present*

Lithuanians know who they are as a people. Visitors are informed with pride that Lithuanians were the last pagans in Europe to be Christianized, the most resistant to Soviet rule, the first to claim independence from Moscow, and the first to hold free elections. The geographic center of Europe, they also boast, lies within their territory near the village of Bernotai, twenty-five kilometers (fifteen miles) north of the capital, Vilnius (known as Wilno to Poles, and Vilna to Jews).

A warm and spontaneous people, Lithuanians are easy to communicate with and flexible in their dealings with outsiders. The old Polish-Lithuanian Commonwealth was a multinational state with peoples of many different religions and ethnic backgrounds—Poles, Lithuanians, Jews, Belarusians, Ukrainians, and Russians—which may explain why Lithuanians are more comfortable with Slavs than are Latvians and Estonians.

Lithuanian culture is rich in literature and music. Singing, casual and spontaneous, is popular, both at work and at play. Noteworthy are the folk songs, *dainos*, numbering in the thousands, which hand down folk traditions from generation to generation. The music is joyous, in contrast to the sorrow and melancholy of Russian music. Poetry runs deep, and Lithuanians are experts in finding hidden meanings in speech.

Catholicism has traditionally been the religion of Lithuanians, but fifty years of communist rule and atheist propaganda have taken their toll and it is questionable whether the church can regain its former strength. The birthrate, moreover, is down and the population is declining. Between 1940 and 1958 Lithuania lost one million of its people through death, exile, or emigration.

Lithuanians are one of the tallest people in Europe, and the national sport is basketball, introduced by Lithuanian Americans in the 1930s. The country has produced several European championship teams and exports basketball players to the United States. Sarunas Marciulionis, who plays for the Golden State Warriors, is a national hero, and NBA scores top the sportscasts on evening television.

A spirited people, Lithuanians are known as the hotheads of the Balts, and the most nationalistic, romantic, and idealistic. The national coat of arms—a charging knight on a white horse—tells much about them. They were the most difficult of the Baltic peoples for the Soviet Union to handle, and the Russians learned to treat those "charging knights" with caution. Along with their resolve, however, there is also a sense of fatalism, a feeling that they are unable to shape their own lives and determine their own future. But once they have made a decision, Lithuanians are full of get-up-and-go.

The largest of the three Baltic states, Lithuania (*Lietuva* in Lithuanian) has a population of 3.7 million, of whom 80 percent are ethnic Lithuanian, and a territory somewhat larger than Switzerland. Other national groups are Russians (9 percent), Poles (7 percent), and Belarusians and Ukrainians (3 percent). Some of the Russians have lived in Lithuania for centuries but most have arrived since the end of World War II as immigrants under a calculated Soviet policy of colonization. The Poles are mostly descendants of ethnic Lithuanians who were Polonized in the nineteenth and twentieth centuries. The non-Lithuanians live mainly in the towns and cities; the countryside, as in the past, is largely Lithuanian.

Lithuanians have a long and glorious history. They have lived on the edges of other cultures—Kievan Rus, German, Russian, Polish, and Jewish—and in the Middle Ages, as earlier noted, they ruled a vast territory. In 1386, challenged by Germans, Russians, and Poles, Lithuania chose to join with Poland through a dynastic union. It also embraced Catholicism and became a part of the Western world. The Polish-

Lithuanian Commonwealth was the largest and most powerful state in Eastern Europe until it was partitioned at the end of the eighteenth century by Prussia, Russia, and Austria. In 1918, Lithuania declared independence, after revolution in Russia. But for the next two years it had to defend its independence, first against the Red Army, then against Poles who occupied the Vilnius region (and annexed it in 1922), and finally against combined German and Russian forces. Independence ended in 1940 when Lithuania was annexed to the Soviet Union. In mass deportations, thousands of families deemed hostile to the Soviet regime were exiled to remote regions of Russia. With war between Germany and the Soviet Union in 1941, Lithuania was again occupied, first by Germans and again by Soviets in 1944. Between 1947 and 1952, up to 300,000 Lithuanians were deported or imprisoned by the Soviets. Armed resistance continued in the impenetrable Lithuanian forests until 1953.

In 1990, the Lithuanian Reform Movement, Sajudis, won parliamentary elections and declared independence, the first step in the disintegration of the Soviet Union. In a national plebiscite in February 1991, 90.5 percent voted for an independent and democratic Lithuania, a move recognized by Moscow in September after the failed Moscow coup.

During the interwar period, Vilnius, today's capital, was a part of Poland and populated largely by Poles, Polonized Lithuanians, and Jews. Most of the Jews are gone now, victims of the Holocaust; and most of the Poles have emigrated to Poland, but Vilnius is still the least Lithuanian city in Lithuania. Its Old Town, with many baroque churches, has a Polish look, and of the city's 592,000 inhabitants, 55 percent are Lithuanians, and 45 percent Russians, Poles, and Belarusians. Kaunas, the capital during the interwar period, is more of a Lithuanian city.

Despite the common history with Poland, an undercurrent of tension exists today between Lithuanians and Poles. Bilateral relations are correct but cool.

Poles and Lithuanians, it is said, are two peoples divided by a common history. In their commonwealth, Lithuanians were the junior partner. The gentry was Polonized, and the towns were Polish-speaking, inhabited mostly by Poles and Jews. Lithuanian was spoken mainly by peasants who lived in rural areas.

Jews have lived in Lithuania since the twelfth century, and in the Polish-Lithuanian Commonwealth they enjoyed a tolerance that was unusual in Europe at the time. Vilnius, once known as "the Jerusalem of the North," became a thriving center of Jewish religious scholarship and culture. Today, only a few thousand remain, almost all of them in Vilnius.

Also defying extinction is the Lithuanian language, the oldest living language in Europe. Lithuanian belongs to the Baltic group of Indo-European languages and is closely related to Latvian. An archaic language, Lithuanians have been stubborn in protecting its ancient sound system and morphological peculiarities. One peculiarity is that Lithuanian (like Latvian) has few swear words so that cussing someone out has to be done in Russian.

As the most rural, agricultural, and poorest of the Baltic states, Lithuania, after independence, made initial advances in economic reform because of aggressive privatization undertaken by its first noncommunist government, led by Vytautas Landsbergis. Despite that initial progress, economic reform has been slowed by the absence of an entrepreneurial spirit among the middle class. In economic progress, Lithuania lags behind Estonia and Latvia.

Americans and Lithuanians have many family ties. Emigration to the United States was high in the nineteenth and twentieth centuries, and estimates of Lithuanian Americans run from 600,000 to one million. They settled mainly in Chicago and other industrial cities of the midwest and east, but today there are also large retirement communities in Florida and California.

In the United States, Lithuanians have produced prelates of the Catholic Church, scientists, scholars, and engineers. In the arts, they have given us actor Charles Bronson, actress Ann Jillian, and film director Robert Zemeckis; in politics, members of Congress Richard Durban, Mickey Edwards, and William Sarpalius; and in sports, world heavyweight boxing champion Jack Sharkey, quarterback Johnny Unitas, linebacker Dick Butkus, the late tennis star Vitas Gerulaitis, and the basketball player mentioned earlier.

Latvians

Hard weeks, merry holidays.

Poor in goods, rich in joys.

Know a lot, talk a little.

—Latvian proverbs

Latvians are more reserved and less spontaneous than Lithuanians. A laconic people, as their proverbs indicate, they have no wasted words. Seven centuries of Germanic rule have left them with a sober Lutheran work ethic and a Germanic appreciation of punctuality. Their attitude toward change is positive.

The landowning German Baltic barons are gone now, and Latvian ethnic pride and national spirit have returned. As one Latvian told me, "We are no longer looking down but up, and even looking around."

A proud people, Latvians are savoring their newly regained independence. Released from Russian rule, they have a euphoric feeling that for them everything is now possible. Advice by foreigners may not always be appreciated and should be given carefully.

Latvians are known as "the biggest Balts" in the sense that they are the greatest promoters, organizers, and supporters of Baltic organizations and cooperation. Riga, with its central location, is usually the site of Baltic conferences and meetings.

Latvians tend to be the most international of the three as well. Through the port of Riga they have had the greatest exposure to international contacts, and they tend to look beyond Latvia and aspire to positions in the international arena. For better or worse, Latvians also played a leading role in the Bolshevik Revolution and took leadership roles in the Soviet Union. When working for other foreign powers, they are considered to be loyal and dedicated, perhaps because of their history of serving others. They like getting involved in international affairs, even before they have solved their own problems. Politics is to be enjoyed.

As Nordics, Latvians tend to be blond, tall and stocky, with blue-grey eyes; and, like the Lithuanians, they also produce basketball champions. A rural and agricultural people, proud of their peasant origins, they have a deep attachment to the land. Most townspeople have summer homes and spend their weekends gardening in the countryside.

The population of Latvia, 2.4 million, lives in a space the size of West Virginia, but little more than half of them are ethnic Latvians. One might ask, therefore, how such a small number of people have been able to survive as a nation, surrounded and ruled, as they have been, by great powers. One answer is the devotion of Latvians to the preservation of their language and culture, which has defied all odds of survival.

Another answer, according to historian Alfred Bilmanis, is that Latvians, as a nation, became physically strong thanks to continuous pioneering and agricultural work, sobriety, and a healthy diet of meat, fish, vegetables, milk, rye bread, and honey. Personal hygiene also played a role, claims Bilmanis—each Latvian farmhouse has its *pirts* (sauna).[4]

The birthrate, however, has been declining in recent years, and mortality increasing, because of suicide, homicide, and alcohol and drug abuse. Fewer marriages are being performed, and in 1992 there were seventy-seven divorces for every hundred marriages. In the same year, moreover, abortions exceeded live births.[5]

The feminist movement has been slow in developing, as elsewhere in Eastern Europe, although, in 1940, Latvia had more women's rights than elsewhere in Europe. Latvians are individualists and, as an expression of their individualism, Latvian farmers live mostly on isolated farms, in contrast to Lithuanian farmers who live in villages. Social life is centered on family and a small circle of close friends. Latvian, an old Indo-European language, is full of subtleties. A word placed at the end of a sentence is more important than one at the beginning. How something is said is just as important as what is said. A harsh view, for example, or a personal insult, can be expressed indirectly and its real meaning may not come through in translation.

This calls for good interpreting skills, and visitors who communicate through interpreters should make sure they are getting all the nuances of the Latvian language. Those who express their nuances in epithets should bear in mind that, like Lithuanian, it is difficult to swear in Latvian. There are bawdy songs, but epithets worse than "pig" or "ass" are hard to find. Anything more salty is expressed in Russian.

The oral tradition is rich, and choral singing is the national pastime. *Dainas* (folk songs), dating back to pagan times, combine oral literature and music and are used to pass on national traditions from mother to daughter, contributing to what has been described as the "fundamental decency" of the people. Latvian (and Estonian) singing is organized and in unison, much like the Welsh.

"Hard weeks, merry holidays" aptly describes *Jani* (St. John's night, June 23), a celebration more important to Latvians than Christmas or Easter. On this old pagan observance of the longest day of the year, bonfires burn atop all of Latvia's hills as a symbol of national solidarity as well as remembrance of the pagan past. As in the past, young couples hold hands and run through the fires before frolicking in field and forest in celebration of their joyous union.

Jani is a three-day festival in Latvia when even the government shuts down. Three days are necessary, it is said, because the first day is required to brew the beer, make the food, and decorate the household; the second day, June 23, is the day to celebrate; the third day is needed to sleep and sober up. Within the country as a whole, there is a strong sense of entrepreneurship dating back to the thirteenth century, when Riga joined the Hanseatic League and established economic and cultural ties with the rest of Europe. Ethnic Latvians, however, have traditionally been farmers, soldiers, and government officials; and today most business is conducted by Russians and other Slavs.

Riga, the capital city, is German-looking but Russian-speaking. A boomtown, it is the largest and most vital city in the Baltic states. With its bustling port and financial center, Riga is rapidly becoming reoriented toward its Baltic roots. Foreign capital is returning, and there is much new construction. Riga's cathedrals, castles, and walled Old Town also make it a popular tourist attraction.

Latvia (*Latvija* in Latvian) became known to the Western world in the twelfth century through German traders and missionaries. The German military-religious order, the Knights of the Sword, founded in Riga in 1202 soon subjugated the rest of Latvia. Reorganized as the Teutonic Order, it controlled the Baltic coast from Estonia to Poland, and its knights were the predecessors of the German barons, who enserfed the Latvians and Estonians and were landowners in the two territories until the end of World War I. When the north Germans became Lutheran, so did the Latvians and Estonians, although parts of Latvia that border on Lithuania have remained Catholic.

Latvia successively came under the control of Poland and then Sweden until Peter the Great defeated the Swedes in the Great Northern War (1700-21). For the next two hundred years it was a part of the Russian Empire, and its Germanic nobility provided the Russian tsars with many of their most senior military officers and government officials, which explains why so many of the tsarist generals had Germanic names.

Latvia declared independence in November 1918 after Russia had fallen to revolution, but it took another two years of fighting before Russia recognized Latvian independence. Twenty years of independence and tranquility were followed by German and then Soviet occupation in World War II, and then Soviet annexation and communization. During the German occupation, Latvia's large Jewish population was annihilated and, during the Soviet occupation, some 175,000 Latvians were either deported or executed. Armed resistance to Soviet rule continued until 1951 but independence did not return until September 1991, after the failed Moscow coup and the breakup of the Soviet Union.

Even with independence, the major political issue today still involves Russia—Latvia's Russophone residents. For Latvians, this is an extremely sensitive issue on which the future of the Latvian nation is believed to depend. It is also an issue which foreign visitors should approach with caution.

Latvians are offended by foreign support for Russians and other Slavs who seek Latvian citizenship. Many of those Latvian residents are former Communist Party officials, KGB employees, and military officers who were part of the Soviet occupation regime that colonized and ruled the Baltics for fifty years. Americans, who tend to be liberal on matters of citizenship because of their diverse national origins, should be aware that Latvians consider the citizenship issue vital to their future, because it may determine whether a Latvian- or Russian-speaking majority will govern the country. Latvians, and other Balts, are aware, moreover, that ethnic conflict could prompt Russian intervention. As Russian President Boris Yeltsin stated in an address to the United Nations in 1994, "The main peacekeeping burden in the territory of the former Soviet Union lies upon the Russian Federation."[6]

Some 46 percent of the Latvian population is Russophone. All seven of Latvia's cities have Russian-speaking majorities and, in Riga, only one-third of the population speaks Latvian. The Russophones include Russians, Belarusians, and Ukrainians who have come to live in Latvia at various times over the past three hundred years. Old Believers, who number some 25-30 percent of the Russophones, are ethnic Russians who fled Russia to Latvia after a schism in the Russian Orthodox Church. Today they are ardently pro-Latvian and anti-Moscow. Another 25 percent of the Russophones were born in Latvia during the Soviet period. Both of these groups are bilingual, assimilable, and support Latvian independence.

The problem is with the remaining 40-50 percent of the Russophones. Many are Soviet military retirees and their families. Others are workers brought to Latvia to work in industry. The military retirees are pro-Russian, and many of them do not accept as final the collapse of the Soviet Union. Negotiations between Latvia and Russia on this issue have proven difficult, but one statistic gives hope for a long-term solution—26 percent of the marriages in Latvia today are interethnic.

The big wave of Latvian emigration to the West came in the 1950s, when many found themselves in Germany and Austria as displaced persons after World War II. Today there are some 150,000 Latvians in North America, mostly in New York, Chicago, Los Angeles, and Toronto. Their names may not be familiar to most Americans but they represent a cross-section of high achievers—business executives, attorneys, professors, and scientists. Some of them have returned to Latvia and are prominent today in public life. Among them are a number of members of parliament and three cabinet members, one of whom, Valdis Pavlovskis, a decorated U.S. military officer, is minister of defense.

Ints Silins, a career Foreign Service officer of Latvian descent, was appointed first U.S. ambassador to the new Latvian republic; and Ojars Kalnins, a former U.S. citizen, is Latvia's first ambassador to Washington. Two Latvian names that may be more familiar to Americans are hockey all-stars Arturs Irbe and Sandis Ozolins.

Estonians

> The Estonians, like the Finns, are Western by culture, and Nordic by racial characteristics. Indeed, they are the same people, separated by the Finnish Gulf.
>
> —Alfred Bilmanis, *Baltic Essays*

Estonians, like Latvians, have always considered themselves Scandinavians. Indeed, until the sixteenth century there was a land bridge that connected Estonians and Finns. But when Russian Tsar Peter the Great built his new city of St. Petersburg on the Gulf of Finland in 1703, he blocked that bridge and made it easier for Russia to conquer southeast Finland and occupy Estonia.

Estonian and Finnish both belong to the Balto-Finnic group of Finno-Ugric languages. Estonian is close to Finnish, and the two languages are more or less mutually intelligible. Like Finnish, Estonian is also distantly related to Hungarian.

Estonians are even more reserved than Latvians. (It is tempting to add "sober" but they are also heavy drinkers, and men "under the influence" are a common sight on the streets at night.) Strongly individualistic, they have a reputation for stubbornness and are proud of it. They are also known for politeness, for not wanting to offend others when they dislike something; and they pride themselves in not getting worked up about things. Unlike Russians, who are known for their emotional ups and downs, Estonians are levelheaded with no emotional extremes. Dislike is expressed in a roundabout and subtle way, and it may not be recognized by persons accustomed to speaking more directly.

Somewhat distant at first meeting, Estonians will be more open once their reserve has been broken through. Handshaking is obligatory on arrival and departure but not cheek kissing or hugging. Estonians do not take easily to affection by those they do not know well. Let them initiate the affection. Attitudes toward sex, however, as in Finland, are relaxed.

Abortion is the principal method of family planning, as elsewhere in the former Soviet Union, mainly because in Soviet Estonia abortions were free, and contraceptives prohibitively expensive. In 1992, for every hundred live births in Estonia there were 157.8 abortions. Families have an average of 0.9 children, and in 1993 there was a negative population growth of minus 3.9 per thousand, figures that give cause for concern about the future of the Estonian people.

Throughout Estonia's history women have considered themselves equal partners of men and not the male-dominated weaker sex. The Estonian language is gender neutral and makes no grammatical distinction between male and female. Estonian literature, moreover, portrays women as stronger than men. As an Estonian scholar notes, "Women feel equal in Estonia."[7]

Women have made significant advances in Estonia, as in Latvia. Today, they outnumber men in higher education, 59 to 41 percent, and while there are few women in government, they are more active in political parties. A women's studies center is planned for Estonia's Tartu University.

The industrious Estonians have the reputation of being the best businesspeople of the Baltic states, and they lead the others in economic progress. Privatization has been rapid and foreign investment high. Estonian progress in making the transition from the Soviet era to a new era was lauded by Strobe Talbott, a senior U.S. diplomat, during a visit to Tallinn in May 1993. "Yours is already a success story," said Talbott, "I would say even a political and economic miracle."[8]

Estonians have lived on the shores of the Baltic Sea since their arrival from Asia in the third millennium B.C., and their history recalls that of the Latvians—conquest by Danes and Germans, enserfment by German colonizers, further conquests by Swedes and Russians, twenty-two years of independence between the two world wars, annexation by the Soviet Union after World War II, executions, deportations, and communization, and finally independence again in 1991.

Somewhat larger than Switzerland, Estonia (*Eesti* in Estonian) is the most Western and smallest of the three Baltic states. Of its population of 1.6 million, ethnic Estonians constitute 63 percent; 37 percent are Russophones (Russians, Ukrainians, and Belarusians). Most of the Slavs live in Tallinn and in and around Narva in the industrial northeast adjacent to Russia. In the countryside, 87 percent of the population is Estonian. The ethnic Estonian population is declining, however, and now numbers less than one million. Also affecting demographics are industrial pollution, heavy smoking and drinking, and other health hazards common to Eastern Europe.

Of all the Baltic peoples, Estonians are the most vehemently anti-Russian, and it is not politically correct for visitors to speak Russian on the street. English is taught today in schools from the third grade, and of the three Baltic peoples Estonians speak it best.

"Russians and Estonians," writes an Estonian journalist, "simply have different aesthetic values and different work ethics. Russians do not share the traditional Estonian penchant for order and cleanliness. In a way, Estonians and Russians are like oil and water."[9]

Order and cleanliness will indeed be noted by visitors. Estonians line up patiently to wait for buses and trams, and in stores there is no elbowing or pushing, as in Russia. Railroad and bus stations in Tallinn are immaculate, as are public rest rooms; and Estonians are never far from their saunas.

Like their Baltic neighbors, Estonians have a natural love of singing, and folk songs are the medium for passing on to new generations the traditions and culture of the old. Indeed, the nonviolent independence movement of the three Baltic states has been called the "singing revolution," since many of its political manifestations took place at mass song festivals that combined choral singing with political speeches and attracted hundreds of choral groups and hundreds of thousands of spectators. "....[I]t is no exaggeration to say," writes Nobel laureate Czeslaw Milosz, "that they sang their way to freedom."[10]

Finns and Estonians, as earlier noted, are related, and Finland has provided many of Estonia's connections with the outside world. Estonians are able to receive and understand Finnish television, and as a consequence they were (and still are) the best informed nation of the former Soviet Union. Finland, moreover, has provided much of the assistance for Estonia's successful economic reforms.

Finns, however, have a somewhat paternalistic attitude toward Estonians, regarding them as country cousins, an attitude the Estonians do not appreciate. When asked for the difference between Finns and Estonians, a Finn told me: "We both despise the Russians but we Finns fought them fifty years ago and have not had to live under Russian communism as have the Estonians."

A proud people, Estonians are somewhat sensitive about foreign aid. As one Estonian journalist has written:

"Under the banner of humanitarian aid we have received broken computers, shoes without soles, broken toys, and, what is worse, a flood of homebrewed consultants who think that we came out of the trees just yesterday and that now we need to be taught to walk, to talk and even to use the toilet."[11]

Tourism is booming. Ferryboats ply daily between Tallinn and other Baltic ports; and Tallinn's Old Town has become a mecca for foreign visitors, mostly Finns and Swedes, who find the prices for food and the taxes on alcohol much lower than at home.

Tallinn's Old Town, high on a hill overlooking the port, is distinguished by its gothic and baroque buildings, red tile roofs, and narrow streets and walkways. An old Hanseatic League city, it has maintained its character throughout the centuries and is a popular tourist attraction, particularly during the summer season when days are long and nights short. And the beer is great.

The best-known U.S. citizen of Estonian origin today is Neeme Jarvi, conductor of the Detroit Symphony. But the preeminent architect Louis Kahn was also born in Estonia, as were Indiana University linguist Felix Oinas, University of Toronto psychologist Endel Tulveing, and University of Maryland astronomer Ernst Opik. Estonia's ambassador to Washington, Toomas Ilves, is a former U.S. citizen, as is the commanding officer of the Estonian armed forces, Major General Alexander Einseln, a retired U.S. Army colonel.

---

[1] *New York Times*, 7 December 1989.

[2] Priit J. Vesilind, "The Baltic Nations," *National Geographic* 175, no. 5 (November 1990): 23.

[3] William Urban, "Implications of the Past for the Future of the Baltic States," *Lituanus: Lithuanian Quarterly* 37, no. 4 (1991): 75.

[4] Alfred Bilmanis, *Baltic Essays* (Washington, DC: Latvian Legation, 1945), 36.

[5] *RFE/RL Research Report* 2, no. 50 (17 December 1993), 47-48.

[6] *Washington Post*, 27 September 1994.

[7] Merit Ilja, in a talk at the Woodrow Wilson Center, Washington, D.C., 23 March 1994. Much of the material on Estonian women has also been drawn from her talk.

[8] *Baltic Independent*, 21-27 May 1993.

[9] Juri Estam, *Tallinn City Paper*, no. 7 (Spring 1993).

[10] Czeslaw Milosz, "Swing Shift in the Baltics," *New York Review of Books* (4 November 1993): 12.

[11] Priit Hobemagi, *Tallinn City Paper*, no. 7 (Spring 1993).

10

Belarusians

...Belarus has only recently completed the long journey to nationhood. However, the political form which its nationhood might take—whether independence or some type of association with neighboring peoples—remains for the moment unclear.

—Jan Zaprudnik,
Belarus: A Long Road to Nationhood

Belarusians are a mild and peaceful people, very hospitable, and with no native dislike of other nationalities. An American can meet a complete stranger on the street, converse for a few minutes, and be invited home for dinner. With their dispassionate view of life, Belarusians, moreover, are not prone to political strife or turmoil. As one American said after working for a year in the capital, Miensk ("Minsk" in Russian), Belarusians need to learn how to rebel and protest a little.

Rebellion and protest, however, do not come naturally to a people who have no nationalistic fervor, surrounded as they have been throughout history by more forceful neighbors— strong-willed Lithuanians to their north, patriotic Poles to their west, and imperious Russians to their east. It has been safer to acquiesce and survive than to dissent and disappear. Moreover, despite domination by Russia for more than two centuries, the anti-Russian theme of the few Belarusian nationalists has little popular support, and there is no antagonism toward Russians, whom most Belarusians regard as brothers. The Russian language can be used without rancor, especially in the cities.

One Western scholar who has written extensively on Belarus describes it as "...a state in which national consciousness has developed more slowly than in other republics, one which has been heavily Russified, and perhaps, the state with the strongest Soviet traditions."[1]

After more than two hundred years of Russification, including seventy years of Sovietization, Belarusians resemble their Russian brothers in many ways, and at first glance people on the streets of Miensk do not appear much different from those in Moscow. They dress the same, speak Russian, have attended Russian schools, share the same culture and religion, and comport themselves much as Russians do. Moreover, in Belarus there is a nostalgia for the Soviet past and considerable sentiment for rejoining Russia in a federated state. It was under Soviet rule, they recall, that Belarus was transformed from an agricultural society peopled by peasants into a heavily industrialized state with an educated and skilled populace.*

On further acquaintance, however, a few differences do stand out. Belarusians are warmer than Russians and easier to get to know, a result of having been dominated by other nations throughout their history. Although Jews were one-fourth of the prewar population and at least half of the urban population, there is little history of anti-Semitic pogroms in Belarus, and the few that took place there are believed to

---

* For a description of the Russian character see the author's *From Nyet to Da: Understanding the Russians*, Intercultural Press, Yarmouth, ME, 1992.

have been instigated by Russians. In the old Russian Empire, Belarus was one of the safest places for Jews and other minorities.

Miensk lies almost midway between Moscow and Warsaw, and the Belarusian language has elements of both Russian and Polish. Visitors who know Russian or Polish will have little difficulty understanding Belarusian. In western parts of the country, where Roman Catholicism is more evident, there is a greater awareness of Western lifestyles.

The Chernobyl nuclear explosion and its fallout have cast a shadow over the future of Belarus and subdued national expectations. Belarusians see the 1986 catastrophe as the most recent instance of destructive foreign influence in their land. Chernobyl, moreover, just across the Belarusian border in Ukraine, has produced political fallout as well—a strong strand of genuine pacifism among the Belarusian people that facilitated their government's decision in 1994 to give up its nuclear missiles.

A New State

Belarus is a new state, sovereign now after many years of being subsumed within more powerful neighboring states. Geographically positioned between Poland, Russia, Lithuania, and Ukraine, Belarus has at times been in union with or a part of each—the medieval Kyivan Rus state, the Grand Duchy of Lithuania, the Polish-Lithuanian Commonwealth, Imperial Russia, interwar Poland, and the Soviet Union, as the fortunes of one or the other rose or fell.

Belarusians are an old people with a name that is new to the outside world, taken after the Byelorussian Soviet Socialist Republic declared its sovereignty in 1990. As Byelorussia, it had been seated as a charter member of the United Nations in 1945, together with Ukraine, at the insistence of the Soviet Union, which maintained that because of its size it deserved three seats. But like Ukraine, Byelorussia's votes in the United Nations were no different from those of the Soviet Union and it had few attributes of statehood. Indeed, Andrei Gromyko, Soviet foreign minister during much of the Cold War, was an ethnic Belarusian. So was Olga Korbut, the 1972 Soviet Olympic gymnastic champion. The new name, Belarus, is a more correct version in the Belarusian idiom.

Whether Belarus or Byelorussia, the name of the country goes back to the twelfth century, and its origins have as many explanations as its various spellings. The most common translation has been "White Russia" which, while linguistically correct, has caused Byelorussians to be confused with the White Russians who fought a bloody civil war with the Red Russians (Bolsheviks).

One of the most stable of the states that emerged from the breakup of the Soviet Union, Belarus in 1992 had a population of 10.2 million, of whom 79.4 percent were ethnic Belarusians, 11.9 percent Russians, 4.2 percent Poles, 2.4 percent Ukrainians, and 1.4 percent Jews. There were also smaller numbers of Tatars, Gypsies, Lithuanians, and Latvians.[2]

The absence of ethnic conflict between these groups, writes Radio Free Europe analyst Ustina Markus, can be explained by:

> ...Belarus's lenient legislation regarding citizenship; the majority's acceptance of Russian as the lingua franca; the government's unwillingness to force the Belarusian language and culture on the country's residents; ethnic Belarusians' own comparative lack of concern for Belarusian culture; and the fact that Belarusians residing outside the republic in neighboring countries have not been discriminated against. In addition, those traditional scapegoats of extremists, Jews and Roma [Gypsies], have not become the focus of aggression or exceptional abuse for any particular group within Belarus.[3]

Of all the former Soviet republics, Belarus is the most Russified, the most pliant in its relations with Moscow, and the slowest to implement economic and political reforms. An American who spent several months in Belarus in 1993 has described his visit there as stepping back into Russia before perestroika—a drab atmosphere, little to purchase in the stores, a subdued people with little hope for the future, few Western comforts, and a low violent crime rate (although street crime at night has been increasing).

Although now sovereign, the Russian influence in Belarus is still strong. More than 1.2 million Russians live there, and 80 percent of the officers of the Belarusian armed forces are believed to be ethnic Russians. Moreover, Belarus is economically dependent on Russia, which is its major trading partner and provides much of its raw materials and 90 percent of its energy needs.

Zbigniew Brzezinski has described Belarus as "a state that is increasingly being reintegrated under the Kremlin's control."[4] "In Belarus," Brzezinski adds, "Russian economic subsidies were translated into political subordination" (73).

In 1994, the two governments agreed to unify their monetary systems through an agreement which, if ratified, would link the Belarusian *zaichyk* (the monetary denomination, literally "rabbit") to the Russian ruble and, in effect, establish an economic union. In exchange for giving up sovereignty over its currency, Belarus would have gained access to the Russian economy and, in particular, to Russian oil and gas at below world market prices. The agreement was not ratified, however, largely because Russia had second thoughts about absorbing Belarus's higher inflation and weaker currency. Many Belarusians, however, saw the proposed monetary union as quite normal and a quick fix for their declining standard of living.

Language is not a problem. Russian is spoken in urban areas, and Belarusian in the countryside and among some of the intellectual elite in the cities, but an estimated 70 percent of the population speaks no Belarusian at all. Nevertheless, a new sense of nationalism and a revival of interest in the Belarusian language are evident. Russian is still the language of instruction in most schools, but Belarusian is supposed to become the language of common usage within ten years—an overly optimistic prediction in view of the close economic and political ties with Russia.

Chernobyl and Kurapaty (the site of Soviet massacres of Belarusians) are tragedies that have mobilized public support for the Belarusian national revival.

Some 70 percent of the radioactive fallout from Chernobyl fell on Belarusian soil. According to U.S. demographer Murray Feshbach, five years after Chernobyl there was an overall increase in cancer among the population and an incredible increase in cases of thyroid cancer among children, similar to Hiroshima which released only one-tenth the radioactivity of the Chernobyl blast. In mid-1991, in the Homiel (Gomel) region of Belarus, adds Feshbach, cases of thyroid cancer, a disease relatively rare among children, were nine times the level of April 1986.[5] Feshbach believes that the Belarusian gene pool is at hazard.

Travelers to Belarus, however, need not be apprehensive about radiation risk. According to a U.S. Department of Energy analysis, levels of background radiation and radiation in food items have decreased significantly with time and are no longer of any known medical significance. Tap-water samples also showed no detectable radiation.[6]

At Kurapaty, a forest in the suburbs of Miensk, more than five hundred mass graves were discovered in 1988 containing the bodies of up to 300,000 Belarusians executed by Soviet security police between 1937 and 1941 under Stalin's campaign to eradicate Belarusian nationalism. Kurapaty was visited by President Clinton during his 1994 stop in Miensk.

A Troubled Past

Belarusians have difficulty understanding their own history, and most of them don't know it well. There are at least four versions—Polish-Lithuanian, Russian, Soviet, and now Belarusian.

As East Slavs, Belarusians share a common cultural heritage with Russians and Ukrainians dating back to the medieval Kievan period when they were all part of a larger Slav community. Belarusian, although a distinct language today, shares roots in Old Church Slavonic with Russian and Ukrainian, and all three have a high degree of mutual intelligibility. In the fourteenth century, however, the independent principalities of ancient Belarus—Polacak, Smolensk, and Turau—were merged into the Grand Duchy of Lithuania, the vast state that extended from the Baltic to the Black Sea. Lands inhabited by Belarusian speakers reached as far north as Vilna (Vilnius), Lithuania, and beyond into today's Latvia, and south into Ukraine. The official language of the Grand Duchy was Belarusian.

In 1385, Lithuanian and Poland were united in a dynastic union that led to the creation of a Polish-Lithuanian Commonwealth in 1569. Under the Commonwealth, the Belarusian nobility and gentry were Polonized, and the religious affiliation of the peasantry, some 90 percent of the population, was changed from Orthodoxy to the Uniate faith, a church that practices the Eastern rite but acknowledges the authority of the pope of Rome. Polish became the language of landowners and officials, but the Belarusian language, Polonized to some extent, was spoken by the peasants, who were without any sense of national identity and whose way of life had not changed for centuries. The cities were populated by Jews and Polonized Belarusians.

Four centuries of union with Poland and Lithuania ended with the partitions of Poland at the end of the eighteenth century. After Russia annexed Belarus, use of the Belarusian language was banned, cultural development was halted, and the nation began a process of relentless Russification. The Uniate Church was replaced by the Russian Orthodox Church, and the name Belarus was prohibited. It was henceforth known as the Northwestern Territory (of Russia). Control of elementary schools was given to the Orthodox Church in 1864, and Russian replaced Belarusian and Polish as the language of instruction.

At the end of World War I, Belarus was partitioned once more, split by the so-called Curzon line. Western Belarus was incorporated into a reconstituted Poland, and the remainder of Belarus became a part of the Soviet Union. Polonization was resumed in the West and Russification in the East, as the sad saga of Belarus under foreign rule resumed.

Under the Soviets in the 1920s, education expanded and there was a rebirth of the Belarusian language and culture. But during the Stalinist terror of the 1930s, almost the entire Belarusian intelligentsia was liquidated as hundreds of thousands were arrested and sent to almost certain death in the Soviet gulag or to mass execution sites such as Kurapaty. Russification was intensified.

The end of World War II found Belarus in ruins. Most of her cities were almost completely destroyed—in the capital, Miensk, 74 percent of the city's housing was demolished. During the war, when Belarus was occupied for three years by Nazi Germany, the population declined by 2.2 million, including 400,000 Belarusians who were transported to Germany as workers, and almost the entire Jewish community of 800,000 which was killed in the Holocaust. In 1993, there were an estimated 150,000 Jews in Belarus, 35,000 of them in Miensk.

Under the tsars, Belarus, Lithuania, and parts of Poland and Ukraine were included in the Pale of Settlement, the region in which most Jews of the Russian Empire were required to reside. Located in Belarus were many of the *shtetls*, the largely Jewish small cities and towns from which many Jews emigrated to the United States at the turn of the century. Jews from Belarus were known as *Litvaks* (Lithuanians); those from western Ukraine were called *Galitsianers* (Galicians).

In the post-World War II years, cities were rebuilt, the economy industrialized, and education opportunities greatly expanded. Belarus became urban and educated, with a skilled work force that produced heavy trucks, agricultural machinery, consumer goods, and mining and chemical equipment, as well as Belarus's traditional agricultural products. (Five percent of the tractors sold in the United States are manufactured in Belarus.) Increased economic growth, however, was accompanied by increased Russification and a further decline in use of the Belarusian language.

Perestroika in Russia brought a renewed sense of nationalism to Belarus, fueled in part by similar developments in the neighboring Baltic states. In December 1986, as previously noted, a group of twenty-eight Belarusian intellectuals and writers addressed a public letter to Soviet leader Mikhail Gorbachev calling attention to the rising growth of national awareness and seeking support for legislation to prevent the extinction of their language.

Nevertheless, in a March 1991 national referendum, Belarusians overwhelmingly voted to preserve the Soviet Union, only five months before declaring independence. After the breakup of the Soviet Union, Belarus became a member and strong supporter of the Commonwealth of Independent States, which has its nominal capital in Miensk.

All residents received Belarusian citizenship, regardless of their ethnicity. Legislation was passed making Belarusian the official language and promoting its use in schools, but language was not made a test of citizenship.

The American Connection

As an ethnic group, Belarusians may be new to Americans but they are not newcomers to this country, and their first linkage with America may have been our ubiquitous soldier-adventurer Captain John Smith. Smith had traveled through Belarus in 1603 when it was part of the Polish-Lithuanian

Commonwealth, and the craftsmen he brought to Virginia's Jamestown Colony may, indeed, have been Belarusians. Some of the Jesuits who founded the first Catholic schools in the Maryland Colony were also believed to have a Belarusian connection, since their Maryland properties nominally belonged to Jesuits in the Belarus city of Polacak.[7] And Tadeusz Kosciuszko, hero of the American Revolutionary War, was a Belarusian before he became a Polish patriot.

Large-scale immigration of Belarusians to the United States began at the end of the nineteenth century, a result of the deteriorating economic situation in the homeland. Precise numbers are difficult to estimate because immigrants were classified by U.S. authorities according to their country of origin. For most Belarusians this meant either Russia or Poland and depended on whether they were Orthodox, Uniate, or Catholic. Most of the immigrants, moreover, came from rural areas, were illiterate, and had no national consciousness. Of those who arrived prior to World War I, an estimated 550,000-600,000 settled permanently in the United States.[8]

A second sizable wave of immigrants came to the United States as displaced persons in the late 1940s and early 1950s. Estimated at 50,000-55,000, they included former war prisoners of the Polish-German war of 1939; former *Ostarbeiters* (East workers) who had been deported to Germany as laborers during World War II; political activists who had fled Belarus before the advancing Soviet army in 1943-45; prisoners of the Soviet-German war who refused to return to the Soviet Union; former Allied soldiers who had served in the Polish army in the West; and post-World War II defectors and dissidents.

From the above figures, it appears that an estimated 550,000-650,000 Belarusians became permanent residents of the United States. They settled mainly in New Jersey, New York, Ohio, Illinois, Michigan, California, Maine, Pennsylvania, Connecticut, Delaware, and Maryland. Some 80 percent are Orthodox, and the remainder, Catholic or Uniate. Now in their second and third generations, they are one of the many typical American ethnic communities.

[1] David R. Marples, "Kurapaty: The Investigation of a Stalinist Historical Controversy," *Belarusian Review* 6, no. 1 (Spring 1994): 22.

[2] *Eastern Europe and the CIS* (London: Europa Publications, 1992), 457.

[3] Ustina Markus, "Belarus," *RFE/RL Research Report* 3, no. 16 (22 April 1994): 9.

[4] Zbigniew Brzezinski, "The Premature Partnership," *Foreign Affairs* 73, no. 2 (March/April 1994): 71.

[5] Murray Feshbach and Alfred Friendly, Jr., *Ecocide in the USSR* (New York: Basic Books, HarperCollins, 1992), 149.

[6] U.S. Dept. of State Consular Information Sheet for Belarus, no. 92-006, 7 October 1992.

[7] Vitaut Kipel, *Byelorussian Americans and Their Communities in Cleveland* (Cleveland: Cleveland State Univ., 1982), 17.

[8] The statistical data presented here are from Vitaut Kipel, "Byelorussians in the United States," *Ethnic Forum* 9, nos. 1-2 (1989): 81-88.

11

Ukrainians

The Ukrainian view of the world is characterized by an optimism founded on metaphysics and ethics. In spite of the overwhelming catastrophes that have constantly shaken the historical existence of the people to its foundations, in spite of the terrible persecutions to which the heart of the nation, its peasantry, has been exposed for centuries, hope of a better future was never dead, and indeed it arose afresh at the very time when…there were practically no prospects of improvement.
—Ivan Marchuk, *Ukraine and Its People*

When Ukraine's Oksana Baiul won the gold medal in the 1994 Olympic women's figure skating competition, besting American Nancy Kerrigan, it came as a slap in the face for the entire nation, Ukrainians say, that there was an unduly long interval before the Ukrainian national anthem was played after the gold medal had been placed on Baiul's bosom. For whatever reason, they were insulted that a tape of their national anthem was not readily available at Lillehammer.

Ukrainians are sensitive about their new independence, their place in Europe, and how others see them. An old nation but a new state, they are a proud people who want the world to acknowledge their existence, to take them seriously, to recognize them as a European nation, albeit a middle-sized one (like France, they say), and to know their blue and yellow flag and their national anthem. Above all, Ukrainians want the world to know that they are not Russians. If you know something about Russia but nothing about Ukraine, stay silent and let the Ukrainians lead the conversation. They will tell you that Ukraine is the second largest state in Europe, its population is Europe's fourth largest, and it has the second largest standing army in Europe. It also has a nuclear arsenal (which will be dismantled, however, as a consequence of Ukraine's accession to the Nuclear Nonproliferation Treaty in November 1994).

Although Ukraine has many problems, it is not a third-world country; and while there is little popular support for (or confidence in) the government, Ukrainians will proudly say "It's ours."

An Optimistic People

> The forest-steppe, with its warmer, drier climate and greater sunshine brings about a more optimistic attitude to life.
> —Oleksander Kulchytsky,
> *Ukraine: A Concise Encyclopaedia*

Ukrainians are an outgoing people, more genial than their Russian cousins and more fun to hang out with. Russians, it is said, sit, talk, drink, and brood; Ukrainians eat, drink, and sing, and their songs are mostly happy and romantic. Optimistic and undemanding, Ukrainians see the brighter side of life, and have a proverb that explains it all—"Things will sort themselves out somehow."

Kyiv (Kiev) is 375 miles to the south of Moscow and has a warmer and more moderate climate. As "southerners," Ukrainians have a more sunny disposition than Russians, and make friends more easily. When they get to know you, they have a great sense of humor, joke a lot, and laugh at their own troubles.

All this reflects the abundance of a fertile land. More than half of Ukraine's land is arable, and its rich black soil and mild climate have made it the breadbasket of Europe. Bread is a staple of life, and from time immemorial Ukrainians have been known as grain growers. Bread lovers will not be disappointed in the variety and quality, and Americans who have never tasted real bread will be in for a treat.

Attachment to the land permeates the culture of a people who have been farming for millennia. Ukrainians are close to the land and have a deep devotion to their native soil. They enjoy talking about nature and the beauties of their fertile homeland that has been fought over and subjugated by neighboring nations throughout its history.

That history, however, has several versions—Ukrainian, Polish, Russian, and Soviet. The Soviet version, moreover, was distorted by ideology, and during the Soviet years discussions on history were best avoided lest they create problems with the secret police.

Today, Ukrainians are showing a renewed interest in their history, which they are seeking to relearn. They will remind Americans that while Ukraine was absorbing the invasion of Genghis Khan's Golden Horde and the yearly incursions of other Asian nomadic tribes, it was also serving as a borderland barrier behind which Western civilization could develop and spread to the Americas.

Ukraine and Europe

...Kievan Rus was a part of Europe, Moscow long remained the negation of Europe.

—Leo Tolstoy

Ukraine's origins are in Kyivan Rus, the vast medieval state that extended from the Gulf of Finland to the Black Sea and encompassed most of today's Ukraine, Belarus, and north-central Russia. When Muscovy (Moscow) was a little-known principality deep within the remote forests of the north, Kyivan Rus was the largest political entity in Europe and a major power in the east. *Ukraine* originally meant "borderland," which it actually was to the Christian world on whose eastern frontiers it lay, a buffer between Europe and the nomadic raiders of the Eurasian steppe.

Kyivan Rus converted to Christianity in 988, and Constantinople became its link to the Mediterranean and Europe. A high degree of culture and prosperity was reached within the next century before its center, Kyiv, was subjected to raids by mounted marauders from Asia. The state gradually declined in power and was fragmented into principalities, the most important of which was Galicia-Volhynia on its western border.

The Mongol-Tatar conquest in 1240 marked the end of the Kyivan Rus state. Galicia became attached to Poland and Volhynia to Lithuania, and by 1370 Lithuania had replaced the Mongol-Tatars as ruler of much of the rest of Ukraine. In 1569, the Ukrainian lands under Lithuania became part of the Polish-Lithuanian Commonwealth. Scarcely a century later, however, in 1667, the city of Kyiv and the Ukrainian lands east of the Dnipro (Dnieper) River came under Russian rule while the western territories remained with Poland. When Poland was partitioned in the eighteenth century, its Galician lands came under Austrian rule for the next 144 years.

With the Bolshevik Revolution in 1917 and the defeat of Austria one year later, the hopes of Ukrainian nationalists for a unitary state appeared close to realization. Ukrainian republics were established in Galicia and in the east, and the two were merged in 1919. But the new republic became a battleground once more as Ukrainians, Poles, White Russians, and Bolsheviks contended for the rich land. After bloody warfare, Galicia and Volhynia were once more annexed by a reconstituted Poland; an area on the southern slope of the Carpathian Mountains was joined with the new Czechoslovakia; the territories of Bukovina and Bessarabia in the southwest became a part of Romania; and the remainder of Ukraine became a "republic" within the Soviet Union. The victorious Allies were touting "self-determination" but Ukraine, without being consulted, had been partitioned among four neighboring states.

Following World War II, the western provinces were reunited once more with the rest of Ukraine, but under Soviet rule. Forty-five years later, in 1990, Ukraine declared sovereignty and, in a 1991 referendum, more than 90 percent of the voters chose independence from Moscow. Vital economic ties with Russia were severed but the long-held dreams of Ukrainian nationalists had finally been realized, and without bloodshed or upheaval.

But the Ukrainian sense of nationalism remains fragile. Some twelve million of the fifty-two million Ukrainians are ethnic Russians, the largest minority group in Europe; and many of its ethnic Ukrainians have been so Russified that they no longer speak Ukrainian. Rather than the unitary state long envisioned, there appears to be more than one Ukraine.

Two Ukraines, or Three?

The dilemma of two Ukraines, or even three, confronts us today. One is Ukrainian-speaking; another is Russian, culturally as well as linguistically; the third is Russian-speaking but culturally Ukrainian. Because of these three Ukraines, it is difficult to generalize about Ukrainians.*

---

* For a description of the Russian character see the author's *From Nyet to Da, Understanding the Russians,* Intercultural Press, Yarmouth, ME, 1992.

Western Ukraine—the seven *okruhs* (provinces) of Lviv, Ternopil, Ivano-Frankivsk, Volyn, Rivne, Zakarpattya, and Chernivitsi—is Western in more ways than geographic. The first three okruhs were part of the Polish-Lithuanian Commonwealth for four hundred years, and under Austrian rule for another hundred forty-four years. Volyn and Rivne (Volhynia and Rovno) were also part of the Commonwealth but came under Russian rule in 1772; and between the two world wars, they were divided between Poland and the Soviet Union. Chernivitsi (Chernowitz) was acquired by Austria from the Ottomans in 1775 and remained under Austrian rule until the end of World War I, when it was awarded to Romania. Zakarpattya (Transcarpathia) was a part of Hungary for many centuries and of Czechoslovakia between the two world wars.

These western okruhs (with the exception of Volyn and Rivne) were never under tsarist rule, and were under Soviet rule for only forty-two years. Ethnically they are Ukrainian, but culturally they are more Western than the rest of Ukraine.

The most Western provinces, in a cultural and religious sense, are Lviv, Ternopil, and Ivano-Frankivsk, where the predominant church since 1596 has been the Ukrainian Greek Catholic Church, so named to distinguish it from the Roman Catholic Church. (It has also been known in the West as the Uniate Church because it practices the Byzantine rite but theologically is in union with Rome and acknowledges the primacy of the pope.) Greek Catholics in Ukraine number about five million, or 10 percent of the population.

In competition with the Greek Catholic Church in the western provinces is the Ukrainian Autocephalous Orthodox Church, an independent Orthodox church that was banned under communism but survived among emigrés abroad and dissidents at home. Both churches boast unblemished nationalist credentials, are unsullied by concessions to communism or Russians, and are contesting for followers.

As a result of the relatively benign rule of Poland and Austria, western Ukraine is distinguished by its nationalism, cultural ties to the West, and resistance to Russia. In the west, moreover, the Ukrainian language has been preserved, and the political emphasis is on building a unitary Ukrainian state. Although western Ukrainians number no more than 20 percent of Ukraine's population, they are the most vocal nationalists and have strong support among the enthusiastic and organized Ukrainian diaspora in North America and Europe.

The remainder of Ukraine, ruled by Russia for more than three hundred years and by the Soviet Union for another seventy, has been heavily Russified. There, in the mid-nineteenth century, the tsarist government banned the teaching of Ukrainian in schools, the printing of popular books in Ukrainian, and even the use of a Ukrainian translation of the Bible. The Ukrainian language, however, has been preserved in the villages though Russian is spoken in most of the cities. The predominant religion is Orthodox but, as in western Ukraine, is divided between two churches. In 1991, the Ukrainian branch of the Russian Orthodox Church proclaimed independence, a move fiercely opposed by the Russian Church, which sees Kyiv as the birthplace of Slavic Orthodoxy.

Most of Ukraine's twelve million ethnic Russians live in the heavily industrial east and south where pro-Russian sentiment is strongest and the political emphasis is on renewed ties to Russia and local autonomy within a loose Ukrainian federation. But intermarriage between Russians and Ukrainians has been high in the east, and language and nationalism are not the big issues that they are in the west.

The "third Ukraine" consists of ethnic Ukrainians who have been Russified linguistically but who still consider themselves Ukrainians. This group is more difficult to define, since it shows both Ukrainian and Russian cultural traits.

What's in a Name?

Call me what you will but make sure I get my money.

—Ukrainian proverb

Ukraine (which, you recall, means "borderland") has been known by several names during its long and turbulent history. As early as the ninth century, the territory and its people were called *Rus*. One explanation for that name—and not the only one—is that the original Rus were Varangian warrior-merchants (known in the West as Norsemen or Vikings), who in 882 gained control of Kyiv and the waterways from the Baltic to the Black Sea at about the same time that other Norsemen were exploring and conquering the Atlantic shores of Western Europe and North America. From "Rus" we have the derivation *Rusyn*, the traditional name for western Ukrainians. From "Rusyn" we have the Latin translation *Rutheni* (Ruthenians in English), a term still used in the West for Ukrainians who lived in the Austro-Hungarian Empire.

In the fourteenth century, when the rulers of Moscow began to call themselves "Princes of All the Rus" to distinguish between the various branches of the Eastern Slavs, the terms "Great Russia" (Muscovy), "White Russia" (Belarus), and "Little Russia" (Ukraine) came into common usage. By the early eighteenth century, Ukraine was officially called "Little Russia" in Russian imperial decrees. The term, however, gradually acquired a patronizing connotation and dropped into disuse at the end of the nineteenth century, although some Russians still use it today. Also passé is use of "the Ukraine," which is considered inappropriate for an independent state.

Tchaikovsky's *Little Russian Symphony* (No. 2) is neither little nor Russian but Ukrainian, based as it is on Ukrainian folk songs.

For those readers who by now have not become mired in the maze of border changes, let us now turn to the Ukrainian people and how they have been molded by their memories of the past.

The Ukrainian Psyche

The hardships experienced by the Ukrainian people since 1917 have left a deep imprint on their psyche.

—Oleksander Kulchytsky,
Ukraine: A Concise Encyclopaedia

All East European nations have experienced a traumatic twentieth century but Ukraine's trials have been particularly tragic. During World War I, much of the Eastern Front combat took place on Ukrainian soil. From 1917 to 1920 Ukrainians fought and lost a war for independence. Under Soviet rule in the 1920s, many of Ukraine's artists and writers were killed or exiled and their works banned. The brutal collectivization of agriculture, begun in 1928, was followed by a Soviet-made famine in 1933, when some six million Ukrainians starved to death in the countryside where collectivization was fiercely resisted. Also in the 1930s, Ukraine's intellectuals and most of its native communist leadership were executed in Stalin's Great Terror. Tens of thousands were exiled to Siberia.

During World War II, Ukraine was a battleground twice between German and Soviet armies as the Germans first advanced and then retreated in fierce fighting. Between these two campaigns, Ukraine bore the brutal brunt of Nazi occupation for three years during which more than three million Ukrainians perished and more than one million of Ukraine's Jews were executed in the Holocaust. After the war, more deportations and arrests followed in a Soviet campaign to suppress nationalism and dissent. Armed resistance to Soviet rule by Ukrainian insurgents lasted into the early 1950s. The psyche of Ukrainians, as Kulchytsky, an eminent Ukrainian psychologist, has pointed out, has been shaped by these shattering events, especially by the Bolshevik terror and oppression, Soviet efforts to indoctrinate the people and industrialize the economy, and the widespread resistance to communism.

It is to these traumatic experiences as well as the political subjugation and denial of their language that Kulchytsky attributes Ukrainian feelings of inferiority, tinged with a sense of injustice at the wrongs done to their country. The compensation, as he puts it, "...often takes the form of idyllic dreaming (reveries) about the coming of the reign of truth, brotherhood, and universal freedom. Ukrainian socialist and liberal political parties are full of these beliefs."[1]

Dr. Jurij Savyckyj, an American psychiatrist who has studied mental health in today's Ukraine, reports that some of the most resilient and courageous Ukrainians he has met suffer from deep-seated feelings of powerlessness and despair, stemming from years of insecurity and state terror. Savyckyj believes that their sense of victimization could inhibit democratic and societal reforms for many years to come:

> In older people...elements of Post-traumatic Stress Disorder are present in varying degrees. Many have responded by feeling helpless, apathetic, powerless and detached from events. Young people seemed especially cynical and indifferent. There was a sense that, although "free at last" from the Russian Communist yoke, each person carries a private burden they [sic] can not describe.... People casually mentioned the arbitrary execution of parents, siblings, relatives and friends as they recounted life's milestones.... We must remind ourselves that these people have lost 20 million family members within the past three generations, in a different kind of holocaust. In [U.S.] terms, this would be the loss of 60 million Americans, especially those with any form of education or business initiative.[2]

Chernobyl, with its nuclear fallout, is the most recent of Ukraine's traumas. By 1994, as many as eight thousand had died from illnesses caused by the 1986 blast and its aftermath, and that number is increasing rapidly. An area the size of Alabama has been contaminated, many thousands of inhabitants have had to be resettled, and the long-term radiation cleanup costs consume 12 percent of Ukraine's annual budget.[3] The toll on future generations is incalculable.

The traumas of the twentieth century have indeed left their mark on the Ukrainian psyche. In public—on streets and in the Metro—Ukrainians are quiet and reserved. They avoid eye contact with strangers, refrain from calling attention to themselves, and mind their own business. On meeting a foreigner, they are likely at first to be suspicious and cautious, retreating behind a protective barrier. Smiles from foreigners, especially Americans, puzzle them. Ukrainians seem to be asking, "Why do Americans always smile at us?"

All this changes, however, once Ukrainians have decided that a foreigner is worth befriending and taking into their inner circle. How to get to that second stage, and into Ukrainian homes, is the challenge.

At Home

In private…[Ukrainians] radiate warmth, humor, and legendary generosity. Rare is the visitor who doesn't leave with a few new friends, and memories of long nights spent feasting and drinking vodka around the kitchen table.
—Shailaigh Murray, in *The Prague Post*

A Ukrainian who brings a visitor home is likely to say, "Let's go see what there is to eat in the kitchen." The kitchen is the center of social life and the most important room in a Ukrainian home. The second most important room, for apartment dwellers, is the glassed-in balcony that serves as a greenhouse for vegetables and a storage place for preserves. Many city dwellers have a weekend dacha or small garden plot in the suburbs that they faithfully farm.

Hospitality and generosity have roots in the Ukrainian agricultural past. The Roman chronicler Procopius, in an account of the original Ukrainians, described them as being kind to foreigners whom they received with hospitality and accompanied for a distance when they left lest any harm befall them. More recently, the eminent Ukrainian historian Michael Hrushevsky has told us that the early Ukrainians "...liked to make merry and amuse themselves, and celebrated all occasions with songs, dances, and games."[4]

Reflecting their generous and sunny disposition, added Hrushevsky, the ancient Ukrainian law reveals "...there was no capital punishment or mutilation of the guilty, no cutting off of legs, ears, or noses, as was customary among the Byzantines and early Germans." In later times, adds Hrushevsky, when the clergy attempted to introduce corporal and capital punishments,

> ...the people refused to accept them, preferring to sentence the condemned to pay fines, to imprisonment, or at worst to be surrendered into servitude so that the culprit might repay his crimes with labor, but they would not shed blood or deprive a man of his life.... (28-29).

The tradition of Ukrainian hospitality and generosity is still alive. Americans who make friends with Ukrainians can expect invitations to homes where the unwritten rule is "everything for the guest." In addition to good food and drink, served in plentiful portions, guests should expect after-dinner entertainment—songs and games—in which they will be expected to join. Ukrainians are a musical people, known for their many folk songs, and guests should be prepared to croon an American tune or two.

Alcohol, as in other Slavic states, is a lubricant of social interaction and conversation, and guests should be prepared to drain a few drams and more. *Horilka* (vodka) is the drink of choice, as in Poland and Russia. (In fact, much of the premium "Russian" vodka sold for export was, and still may be, produced in Ukraine.) But in Ukraine, fewer people "under the influence" are seen in public, and there is less brawling associated with drinking than is the case in Russia. Visitors should be warned, though, that a bottle once opened will be drunk to the last drop and never recapped and put back on the shelf. Those who do not drink for whatever reasons should have their excuses ready.

Ukrainians, like Russians, stand close when conversing, often too close for Americans who may feel that their privacy is being invaded. They also give unsolicited advice about how you look and dress and the state of your health. Accept this advice in the spirit in which it is given—concern for your welfare.

Social life revolves around intimate groups emphasizing mutual self-help and comradeship, especially in times of need, a heritage of the peasant past when groups of people provided help to improvident neighbors. Family and friends will go to extremes to assist one another whenever help is required. Having a friend who knows someone in the right place can mean the difference between success and failure, such as gaining government approval for a petition or obtaining something in short supply. Such friendships are often based on old school ties or other shared experiences.

Despite shortages that may exist, visitors with Ukrainian friends will not go hungry or thirsty. Limited resources will be shared, and visitors presented with small gifts of homemade preserves to sweeten their lives, home brews to raise their spirits, herbal teas to ward off colds, and pickled vegetables to tickle their palates. Ukrainians will not expect anything in return for their hospitality or the gifts they give, but if given a gift, they will present one in return. "In no place in the world," related one American, "have I made loyal and long-lasting friendships so quickly as in Ukraine."

Women have a strong image in the matriarchal Ukrainian culture and are idealized in literature. Sexual roles are less strictly defined than in many other Eastern countries and, in contrast to Russians, authority in the Ukrainian home is shared by husband and wife. Historically, Ukrainian women have worked side by side with their men in the fields, and when the men were away performing military service during the growing season, the women did all the fieldwork and ran the households as well. Men's absences could be long because the draft period for the tsar's army was twenty-five years until 1861, when it was reduced to sixteen years, and in 1874 to only six years!

Today, women keep busy running households, raising children, standing in lines while shopping for food and goods, caring for their men, and working at jobs and professions. Men have the authority, though, and older men even more so; but women are recognized as the glue that holds the male-chauvinist society together.

Feminism is a nonissue. Certain professions are understood to be meant for women (such as medical doctors) and others for men, but Ukrainian women seem comfortable with such gender divisions. American women who have worked in Ukraine say that Ukrainian women put up with much less and stand up to men much more than do Russian women. Ukrainian women say there is little or no sexual harassment.

The Workplace

My house stands to the side—I don't know anything.
—Ukrainian proverb

Ukrainian priorities, as seen in work habits, are a legacy of seventy years of Sovietization which corrupted the traditional work ethic. Americans value work, time, and money and spend more of their time on job-related activities and less on personal relationships.

The American obsession with jobs and careers, however, is alien to today's Ukrainians. Why work hard if jobs show no promise of advancing careers and bring in only money which has little purchasing power? Office employees show up late for work or not at all. They take long lunches and leave work early. Breaks for *chay* (tea) are long and frequent.

More important than jobs and careers are family and friends. Personal relationships represent security against the dangers and difficulties of life, and they are long-lasting. Personal needs command time and attention, such as providing the family's food for the next few days, obtaining good medical care and hard-to-find medications for family members, and putting up a supply of preserves for the coming winter. Survival is first on everyone's priority list; and corruption, if necessary for survival, is an accepted evil.

Stealing from the state has been traditional in Ukraine (as in Russia), and under the Soviets it was intensified. Says an old Ukrainian proverb: "Those who jostle their way to the government trough know they will be able to eat their fill there."

In the workplace, Ukrainians tend to be passive, without much motivation or initiative, reacting to others instead of presenting their own views. In the past, orders came from Moscow and were followed. This has produced a people who rely on inner resources and are constantly on the defensive against the outer world which they regard as dangerous. A question will be answered with a question rather than a straight answer. Don't stick your neck out, stand to the side, like the house in the Ukrainian proverb.

Problems that develop at lower levels of an enterprise are not likely to be brought to the attention of senior management. Politics is of little interest, and political parties even less so. More important is the price of *kovbasa* (sausage), which some refer to as the Dow Jones Average of the Ukrainian economy. Information received from the mass media is mistrusted and regarded as essentially biased in support of a predetermined position.

Much of this is due to the system of education inherited from the Soviets. The university system is highly structured.

Professors lecture while students take notes but rarely ask questions. There is little or no teacher-student dialogue.

Martha Bohachevsky-Chomiak, an American historian of Ukrainian descent who has taught at Kyiv University, reports that her students there were accustomed to accept only one answer as correct and had problems with questions of interpretation. Unaccustomed to writing term papers or expressing their own views, they also had difficulty understanding the difference between polemics and debate.

Moreover, according to Bohachevsky-Chomiak, Ukrainians do not know how to debate but *do* know how to make long speeches. Attacks are frontal, without subtlety or gentle persuasion. Brevity is rare, and the simplest thoughts are often expressed in a long-winded, roundabout, and often unfocused manner. "Ukraine," she concludes, "has to move from communism into the twenty-first century, but so much of its educational system has yet to move from the nineteenth century to the twentieth."[5]

But when the educational system changes, so do student attitudes, says Oleh Havrylyshyn, a Canadian economist of Ukrainian descent who has taught at Kyiv-Mohyla Academy, a new and nontraditional institution much like an American liberal arts college. He reports that students at Kyiv-Mohyla are encouraged to argue the pros and cons of issues, participate in open discussions, express their own views, and disagree with their professors.[6]

Age is respected, and older people are disinclined to take advice from those younger, a particular disadvantage for American advisers who may be young. One American reports that she was called *divchynka* (young girl), a condescending term, by the men she was attempting to counsel. Younger Ukrainians are more open to change and more likely to accept advice.

What to do? How does an American improve the performance of Ukrainian employees on the job?

One American who has worked in Ukraine advises giving

employees more responsibilities and showing them how to develop skills that will help them advance to better jobs with increased responsibilities and higher rewards. Set an example—work as hard yourself as you would want your employees to work. Punctuality is not a Ukrainian virtue, and if you want them to be at work on time, be on time yourself and stay until closing time.

Hold staff meetings (a new concept for Ukrainians), suggests another. Go over office priorities, and ask each staffer to comment on his or her responsibilities. Teach them to keep lists of "things to do today." Show them how to prepare budgets and to estimate costs realistically. If financial incentives are provided, such as payment in dollars to permit purchases with hard currency, job performance will improve. Relate rewards to performance.

Articulate your expectations at the start, advises another American who has worked in Ukraine. Make certain that each employee knows his or her area of responsibility and that other employees know it as well and respect it. Titles are valued, and each employee should have one. Give them challenges. If they are interested in their work, they will perform.

Good personal relations, however, are the greatest asset. Ukrainians will be fiercely loyal and trusting and will work hard for people they are bonded to.

In a phenomenon that never ceases to astonish visitors, Ukrainians, after taking it easy in the workplace for long spells, are capable of intense and sustained bursts of energy to complete an assigned task. If a job has to be done, it will be.

Ukrainians and Russians

> Love, oh love, you dark-browed maidens,
> Only not the Muscovite soldier.
> For the Russians are foreign people
> Who will bring you harm.
> —Taras Shevchenko, *Catherine*

The second sensitivity of Ukrainians, after nationalism, is their relationship to Russians. The two languages are closely related (like Spanish and Portuguese or German and Dutch), the lifestyles are similar, the histories are intertwined, and they can truly be called Slavic cousins. But Ukrainians are culturally distinct from Russians, and the two peoples should not be equated. Moreover, the relationship has been that of an imperial power and its colony. The result, as Ukraine's national poet Taras Shevchenko has implied, is a love-hate relationship.

Kyiv is traditionally regarded by Russians as the "mother of all Russian cities." (Ukrainians jokingly counter that the father is not yet known.) But that mother is more gentle and has less bustle and fewer hassles than Moscow. It is, moreover, cleaner, neater, and more pleasant, with tree-lined boulevards, stately statues, and green parks. Above the Dnipro River stand gold-domed churches, baroque buildings, scholarly institutes and universities, museums, and theaters.

Khreshchatyk Boulevard, the main shopping street, is lined with chestnut trees and is a sight to see in spring. The Golden Gate of Kyiv, the formal entrance to the Old City memorialized in Mussorgsky's symphonic poem *Pictures at an Exhibition*, has been restored to its former splendor. Wealth differentiation is less visible in Kyiv than in Moscow; Ukrainians are less showy than Russians about their successes.

Ukrainian villages also differ from Russian. The Ukrainian villages are more tidy and orderly. The simplest peasant cottages are decorated on the outside with elaborate wood carvings and on the inside with colorful embroidered pillows and *kylyms* (wall hangings). Floors are spotless, and unclean shoes should be removed before entering. As a Ukrainian proverb cautions, "Don't enter another's house with dirty shoes or dirty words."

Folk art is distinguished by bright colors, ornamental design, and great attention to detail in the embroidery of women and the wood carving of men. In the countryside, common agricultural tools such as straw rakes and horse yokes are painstakingly carved with cross-hatching. Those ornamental Easter eggs that Americans know are Ukrainian, not Russian. In contrast to Russians, Ukrainians are not seekers of great-power status and have no need to impress others. Behavior is marked by moderation and caution. Patriots and nationalists have a "live and let live" outlook but no "God-given mission" that Russians seem to have as protectors of other Slavs and Orthodoxy. Rather, Ukrainians see themselves as a mid-level European power to be included in all European organizations. Relatively few Ukrainians, however, have traveled abroad, and they are less knowledgeable than Russians about the outside world.

Ukrainians also have a reputation for being more sensitive and gracious than Russians. The warm Ukrainian *sertse* (heart) is often contrasted with the troubled Russian *dusha* (soul). The great Russian writer Gogol was Ukrainian, and his stories of Ukraine are lighter and have more color than his Petersburg stories.

One explanation for Ukrainian sensitivity has been provided by M. P. Drahomanov, a Ukrainian historian and political activist of the nineteenth century. Russians and Ukrainians, he wrote, have a basic difference in understanding the word *Boh* (God). For Russians, wrote Drahomanov, religion contains elements of fear and awe. Ukrainians, in describing their God, will use such terms as "merciful" and "kind."[7] Moreover, as Hrushevsky has told us, in pagan times when the original Ukrainians worshipped several gods, each of their gods was called *boh*, which means "good" or "weal" and bestower of welfare.[8]

The culture of Ukrainians has also been shaped by their historic form of agricultural production. In Ukraine, the traditional agricultural unit was the *hromada*, a loose and voluntary association of peasants, and later the *khutir* (homestead), a privately owned farm. Moreover, much of southern Ukraine, after its recovery from the Turks, was settled and farmed by free men. The Russian agricultural unit, by contrast, was the *obshchina*, a commune in which peasants lived in small villages and farmed communal land together. To survive in their harsher, northern climate, Russians became more collectivist and more submissive to authority.

Ukrainians, with more favorable climatic conditions and the freedom of the open steppe, were less ready to submit to authority. They became more individualistic and developed an ethic of hard work, since, in their warmer climate, they were able to work the year round in agriculture. They respected private property and were economical and cautious about using their financial assets. These traits typify the *kurkuls* (*kulaks* in Russian), the more successful and wealthy peasants, as they were called before the Soviet collectivization of agriculture.

Ukraine was also less influenced by Asia than was Russia. The Mongol-Tatars ruled Russia for some two hundred years, intermarried with Russians, and left a lasting Tatar legacy in the development of Russian social life and governmental institutions. Ukrainians were under Mongol rule for a much shorter period of time and were less influenced by them. Serfdom, moreover, was imposed in Ukraine in the middle of the eighteenth century, much later than in Russia, and for a relatively short time, less than one hundred years.

And Ukrainians are not puzzled by that great Russian question, "Are we Asian or European?" For Ukrainians, especially in the western part of the country, the question does not exist. They have always known that they are European.

Russians, however, have not reconciled themselves to Ukraine's independence. Boris Yeltsin, in January 1994, described Russia's position in relation to other members of the Commonwealth of Independent States as "first among equals"; and Russian Foreign Minister Andrei Kozyrev, in summer 1993, called Ukraine "a mythical state." Zbigniew Brzezinski writes of "...the widespread feeling in Moscow that Ukrainian independence is an abnormality as well as a threat to Russia's standing as a global power."[9]

Economics, however, may determine history, even after the collapse of communism. In early 1994, the CIA forecast that if current economic trends continue, a significant minority of Ukraine's population will favor unification with Russia and thereby divide Ukraine along ethnic and geographic lines. Russian speakers in the east, said the study, will seek to rejoin Russia; Ukrainian speakers in the west will want to remain independent.[10]

Despite their divergences, there is little likelihood of violence between Ukrainians and Russians. They are two Slavic, mostly Orthodox people, whose leaders are successfully negotiating and defusing the issues that divide them. If the two countries can resolve their economic problems, they should be able to coexist peacefully.

Who Is a Ukrainian?

> A political nation is now being formed in Ukraine, and...the distinction between ethnic and political identity does not make much sense.
> —Roman Szporluk, "The Ukrainian Identity Today"

You don't have to speak Ukrainian to be a Ukrainian. Prior to independence in 1991, Ukrainian was a symbol of nationalism but Russian was the language of government, industry, science, and education. Since independence, Ukrainian has become the official language of government but not all Ukrainians can speak it, and it is no longer the symbol of nationalism it once was.

Ukrainian, Russian, and Belarusian, as members of the East Slavic group of Indo-European languages, all have common roots in the language of the medieval Kyivan state. Although today they are three distinct languages, they have a high degree of mutual intelligibility despite differences in pronunciation, vocabulary, and orthography, a result of political and religious changes over the years. The most obvious

Ukrainian difference from Russian is that *g* in Ukrainian is pronounced as *h*. Ukrainian also has fewer borrowings from Old Church Slavonic than modern Russian but more borrowings from West European languages by way of Polish. The spoken language has regional variations, but today's literary Ukrainian is based on the language spoken in the middle Dnipro region around Kyiv.

In Kyiv government offices, Ukrainian is spoken, although not always correctly. Russian, however, is still heard on the streets of Kyiv and in the workplace. Moreover, if you add the 22 percent of Ukrainian citizens who are ethnic Russians to the 12 percent of ethnic Ukrainians who speak Russian as their first language, you will find that at least one-third of Ukrainians are Russophone, although in many areas the Russian they speak is an amalgam of Russian and Ukrainian.

Language, however, is not always an indicator of nationality. Many Ukrainians use Russian as the language of their profession and Ukrainian as the language of social interaction. The language issue in Ukraine, writes Elehie Natalie Skoczylas, "...appears analogous to the medieval times when Latin, the language of science and philosophy, competed with Italian, the language of song and sentimentality."[11]

The closeness of the Ukrainian and Russian languages and cultures creates problems in ethnicity. Intermarriage between Ukrainians and Russians is common, and many Ukrainians are bilingual but with only passive fluency in Ukrainian. In the east, moreover, many Ukrainian children go to Russian-language schools and watch Moscow TV at home. Once beyond childhood it is difficult for them to learn to speak Ukrainian.

Russian is still the lingua franca of the region, the language Ukrainians use to talk with Russians, Balts, Moldovans, and Central Asians. English is not as widely spoken in Kyiv as in Moscow, but German is.

Half of the 25 million Russians who live outside Russia—what Russians call "the near abroad"—are in Ukraine. They are concentrated mainly in the east and south, especially in the Donbas, the industrial heart of Ukraine where half the population is non-Ukrainian. If living standards continue to deteriorate, they are a potential source of unrest.

Jews have lived in Ukraine since the founding of the Kyivan state. In the sixteenth and seventeenth centuries they were brought to Ukraine in large numbers by Polish landowners to serve as stewards of estates, artisans, merchants, petty traders, innkeepers, and rent collectors. Jews were seen by Ukrainians as agents of the Polish Catholic nobles, as aliens and infidels, and their occupations as rent collectors and estate managers for absentee landlords made them particularly resented by the local peasants. The Poles, it was said, brought Jews and Jesuits to Ukraine.

Anti-Semitism intensified after the partitions of Poland when Jews lost the protection provided by the Polish nobles. Moreover, Jews were forbidden to live in Central Russia without special permission and were forced to reside in the Pale of Settlement, Russia's newly acquired western territories that included parts of Ukraine, Poland, Belarus, and Lithuania. Prohibited from owning land, they lived mostly in small towns and villages, the shtetls, where they were the indispensable but maligned middlemen in an agricultural society composed of a small number of landowners at the top and large numbers of peasants at the bottom.

Ukrainian-Jewish relations historically have been marred by conflict and discord. This is not surprising, as Jack Nusan Porter writes,

> ...given that these two peoples have inhabited the same territory, aligned themselves with different powers, and lived in a land which has seen more than its share of famine, revolution, civil war, world war, and anarchy. Much of the problem stems from the fact that the Ukrainians have rarely been masters of their own country but continually subjugated by Poles, Russians, Austrians, and Germans.[12]

By the end of the nineteenth century some three million Jews lived in Ukraine, the highest concentration of Jews in the world. Because the Jews are traditionally an urban people, it was not surprising, as Canadian historian Orest Subtelny notes, that "...over 33 percent of the urban inhabitants of Ukraine were Jewish, and in the shtetls of the [Dnipro] Right Bank the percentage reached as high as 70-80."[13]

The Jewish question in Ukraine, therefore, can also be seen as an urban-rural problem. At the turn of the century, Kyiv was the third largest Jewish city in the world. Sholem Aleichem's Tevye stories, on which *Fiddler on the Roof* is based, were written in Kyiv, and his fictitious village of Anatevka is Ukrainian. His memory was honored by the city of Kyiv in a Sholem Aleichem memorial week celebrated in 1994.

The Holocaust and World War II decimated the Jewish community, which still numbered three million on the eve of the war. In western Ukraine, only 2 percent of the Jews survived. In Kyiv, up to 100,000 Jews, Gypsies, and Ukrainians were executed by the Germans and buried at Babi Yar, a ravine in the northwest part of the city, including 33,771 Jews (by German count) who were systematically slaughtered there during a two-day "action" in 1941. Babi Yar is commemorated in a poem by Yevgeny Yevtushenko that was set to music by Dmitri Shostakovich in his *Thirteenth Symphony*.

In 1994, an estimated 500,000 Jews remain in Ukraine, more than half of them older than forty. Some 100,000 live in Kyiv, and there are also active communities in Kharkiv, Dnipropetrovsk, and Odessa. Emigration is high, however, as well as assimilation and intermarriage with Ukrainians and Russians, and the Jewish community is dwindling.

Latent anti-Semitism still exists though, especially in rural areas and among the less educated. But despite the history of ethnic strife and the new spirit of nationalism, anti-Semitism has been condemned by the Ukrainian government and *Rukh* (the democratic opposition). Moreover, it is on the margins of social and political life and has not been marked by violence. The government has encouraged the rebirth of Ukraine's Jewish community, giving official support for Jewish newspapers, schools, and Hebrew studies in universities. According to a report of the Ukraine Bureau of the Union of Councils, a major U.S. Jewish organization:

> State anti-Semitism has receded, in no small part due to efforts of prominent Ukrainians...including [former] President Kravchuk who...has condemned anti-Semitism. However, the state anti-Semitism of the past has been absorbed by the Ukrainian "new right"—the national-radicals...[who] articulate xenophobic policies [and] advocate against ethnic Russians and Jews, whom they hold responsible for Ukraine's problems.[14]

Still, as Jewish activist Oleksander Z. Burakovsky points out, "....it's easier to be a Jew in an independent Ukraine" now that the "elder Soviet brother that oppressed many Jews, just the first in the chain, is gone." "Ukrainians," adds Burakovsky, "don't have a pathological anti-Semitism," but were manipulated by anti-Semitism "from above."[15]

Cossacks

Cossacks were not a people, they were a way of life.
—Adam Zamoyski, *The Polish Way*

Ukrainian Cossacks, according to mythologists as well as historians, were fierce fighters, frontiersmen and pioneers of the steppe, adventurers and fugitives, rebels and robbers, honorable mercenaries, a brotherhood of knights, self-governing democrats, brutal pirates, Orthodox Christian soldiers, defenders of an oppressed peasantry, heroes of Ukrainian nationalism, destroyers of the Polish-Lithuanian Commonwealth, trusted troops of Russian tsars, and, to use a modern term, freedom fighters.

Which of these descriptions is true? Probably all of them and more, but at different times.

"Cossack" derives from a Tatar-Turkish word denoting a free soldier. The Zaporozhian Cossacks (the term comes from the Ukrainian *za porohy*, "beyond the rapids") began as a brotherhood of free soldiers whose principal purpose was protection of Ukraine's southern frontier from incursions of the Crimean Tatars. From their *sich* (fortress) below the Dnipro rapids, some forty-five miles south of today's Dnipropetrovsk, Cossack cavalry raids repelled Tatar horsemen seeking to reclaim lands the Tatars regarded as their own.

Originally a breakaway group of Ukrainian peasants who had fled to the south, the Cossacks were joined by men of other nations who sought a free and adventurous existence, including, strange as it may seem, Tatars and even some Jews who had converted to Christianity.

As free men, the Cossacks chafed when Ukrainian peasants increasingly came under domination by Polish landowners in the sixteenth and seventeenth centuries and Poland consolidated its rule in Ukraine. In the seventeenth century, the Cossacks began a series of uprisings against the Poles, which eventually brought independence to Ukraine and signaled the start of Poland's decline. But Cossack *hetman* (leader) Bohdan Khmelnytsky, in a fateful decision reflecting lack of political vision, swore allegiance to the Tsar of Muscovy in 1654, and Ukrainian independence was subsequently lost. Khmelnytsky is honored today as a Ukrainian warrior-hero but his "diplomacy" delivered Ukraine to Russia for the next three hundred years and made Russia the largest state in Europe.

Further uprisings against Russian rule failed, and Ukraine was absorbed within the expanding Russian Empire. Under Empress Catherine the Great, the Cossack fortress below the Dnipro rapids was destroyed, serfdom in Ukraine was strengthened, and Russification intensified. The Cossacks became folk heroes, however, and even today they remain a symbol of Ukrainian nationalism and independence.

Crimea

Jutting into the Black Sea, the Crimean peninsula is a valuable piece of real estate and a big bone of contention between Ukraine and Russia. A prime vacation spot, with lush beaches and a Mediterranean climate, Crimea was the site of the 1945 Yalta conference between Roosevelt, Churchill, and Stalin. It is also the home base of the three-hundred-vessel former Soviet Black Sea Fleet whose control has been contested by Ukraine and Russia. Crimea was given to Ukraine by Nikita Khrushchev in 1954 to mark the three-hundredth anniversary of Ukraine's union with Russia. Most Russians regret that gift now that Ukraine is independent.

The Tatars, a Turkic people, arrived in Crimea in the thirteenth and fourteenth centuries. In the fifteenth century, they founded a state, the Crimean Khanate, which lasted until Russia annexed the peninsula in 1783. During the eighteenth century the peninsula was colonized by Russians, but Tatars continued to maintain their national culture despite Russian efforts at assimilation. With the fall of tsarist Russia, the Tatars were able to reestablish temporarily their own state, but in 1920 it came under Bolshevik control.

During World War II, the Tatars were suspected by Stalin of being German sympathizers and were exiled to Central Asia. In 1967, the charges were withdrawn by the Soviet government, the Tatars were rehabilitated and, in 1987, they began to return to their ancestral homeland in large numbers.

Today, however, 70 percent of Crimea's population of 2.7 million is ethnic Russian and only 10 percent is Tatar; and Crimea is the only Ukrainian okruh with a Russian majority. Plebiscites in 1993 and 1994 produced victories for the Russians and raised fears that they might move to rejoin Russia.

Crimea's importance lies not in the territory itself but rather in its role as a symbol of Ukraine's sovereignty. If Ukraine should yield to Russia on Crimea, it fears similar concessions may have to be made on potential territorial disputes with Poland, Slovakia, Hungary, and Romania.

"Biznes," Ukrainian Style

> Ukraine has two vast resources—the richness of its land and
> the education of its people. It must harness those resources to
> solve its own problems. How does an American, perceived as
> a rich outsider, make that point?
> —Randall R. Rader, "Memoirs of Ukraine"

Ukraine was on an emotional high after achieving independence in 1991. Rich in farmland, coal, and mineral deposits,
it had both agriculture and heavy industry, Black Sea ports,
proximity to Western Europe, an educated and skilled work
force, and a developed infrastructure of scholarly and scientific institutions. With its important contributions to Soviet
economic, scientific, and military power, it accounted for 18
percent of Soviet economic output and had the potential to
be a strong and viable state.

Three years later, however, production had plummeted,
inflation had skyrocketed, foreign reserves were negligible,
living standards had fallen by half, foreign investment was
down, the currency was nearly worthless, and there was no
new constitution. Fields were rich with wheat but there were
lines for bread in the cities, and there was no clear political
mandate for reform.

Laws were enforced at times, and at other times not. There
was little confidence in the judiciary, no effective banking
system, and no system for judicial review of contractual obligations. Huge industrial behemoths were being kept alive
by state subsidies. Privatization had slowed, and most enterprises still belonged to the state, run by former communists
who had no incentive to institute reforms or earn profits as
long as the subsidies continued. Managers who had made
their careers in Moscow were poorly informed about the rest
of the world and how to do business there. Energy was imported from Russia at close to world market prices but fuel
was being guzzled without regard to cost.

Corruption and bribery were rampant, and the mafia was

ubiquitous in both government and the private sector. Every transaction with a foreigner seemed to involve a kickback for some intermediary. "It is impossible to do business in Ukraine legally and make a profit," says Walter Kish, Seagram Company's manager in Kyiv.[16]

Payoffs were the rule rather than the exception, as explained by an American who was distributing humanitarian aid. To clear her ship containers through customs she would send an employee to the port armed with dollars. The first person to be paid off was the old woman who controlled access to the customs building. Payments were then made to other customs employees up the line until all the necessary clearances had been obtained and the containers with the much needed humanitarian aid were released.

Biznes, moreover, has a bad connotation, a holdover from the Soviet period when socialism was good and capitalism was bad. Many Ukrainians still believe that if they actually reach agreement with a Western businessperson, then it is the Westerner who has gotten the better of the deal and it should be renegotiated.

For officials, time is not money, and everything takes longer. The Soviet system did not encourage speedy decisions, and today some refer to "a mentality of delay," since it is safer to say no and avoid responsibility. Detailed information is difficult to obtain, and instructions are not always accurate. Business cannot be done over the phone but requires a face-to-face meeting.

"In principle, it can be done." This seemingly optimistic expression is often given in response to a visitor who asks if something is possible. But a gap exists between theoretical principle and realistic practice, and caution is advised.

A similar gap exists in language—what Ukrainians say and what they actually mean. One American, who speaks fluent Ukrainian, recalls her experiences interviewing Ukrainian organizations about placements for American volunteers. The Ukrainians, she reports, would talk about their work but provide few details. Branch offices were claimed in several cities but the cities were not named. Further probing revealed that offices were foreseen in those cities but were not yet open. When asked about a work plan, the Ukrainians would state what they hoped to do in the future rather than what they were actually doing. When asked how many staffers they had, they would reply "many" but give no numbers. An organization with an impressive front office would have nothing to back it up. Annual budgets were said to exist but none were shown. In such meetings, there appeared to be no common language although the interviews were conducted in Ukrainian. Words simply did not have the same meaning.

Such unfounded claims should not be seen as attempts to deceive. Rather, the Ukrainians were stating what they hoped to achieve in the future rather than what they were doing in the present. To get the facts, one should ask them specific questions, such as how many employees they now have full-time, how many projects have been completed, how much office space they have, and whether they can send a fax to the United States. A copy of the operating budget should be requested, as well as the sources of funding.

There is also a tendency to tell foreign visitors what Ukrainians believe they want to hear. Many visitors have come away from a three-hour dinner with prospective Ukrainian partners believing that they had an agreement. Only later did they learn that there was in fact no agreement—there were still questions the Ukrainians wanted answered, or they may have reconsidered the entire deal or wanted a better price.

Beware of Potemkin villages—the staging of something to impress gullible visitors. The original Potemkin villages were named after a favorite of Russian Empress Catherine the Great, who, according to legend, constructed false village facades along the Empress's travel routes to show how well her people were living. The practice continues today, and visitors should try to get behind the facades.

High government officials are accessible but don't like to

make appointments and be pinned down too far ahead of time. On the other hand, it is easy to get an appointment a few days in advance, or even on the same day as requested. If good personal rapport with the official can be maintained, access will be assured and deals can be done. (The difficulty in making advance appointments is a holdover from the Soviet era, when officials preferred to keep their future calendars clear so they would be immediately available when summoned by a higher-up.)

Find people you can trust and who trust you, advises another frequent visitor to Ukraine. Cooperate first on a trial basis, and expand your efforts as trust is built. Friendship in business is much more important than in the United States where "friends are friends but business is business." Ukrainians will expect their friendships to extend to their business relationships as well, with the obligations and trust that friendships require.

As Thomas M. Claflin, a Boston-based venture-capital investor in Ukraine, advises:

> Don't go to Ukraine with more money than you can afford to lose, and don't depend on their legal process or their accounting. If you bring a lawyer, you can forget it. Business there depends on personal relationships and mutual trust.[17]

Claflin advises foreign investors to understand the risks involved before taking them. He invests only in small, privately-owned companies managed by young Ukrainians in their twenties and thirties who have demonstrated good managerial skills. Claflin looks to the future and points out that a younger generation is coming to the fore in Ukraine—in business, government, and the parliament—who are less encumbered by the past and more receptive to change. And that change, he adds, is coming peacefully.

Foreign investors are advised to go for the long term. Ukraine has a huge market of fifty-two million, good human resources, low costs, and a central location in Europe. The potential is great but there are no guarantees of success.

Western assistance and advice can play a constructive role, but advisers and volunteers should be aware that Western ideas and practices will not always be applicable in Ukraine. The new state that is evolving will reflect Ukrainian culture, history, and values.

A new state has been born. The birth was painless but the weaning was sudden and premature and the growing pains protracted. The new state now must decide what it wants to be when it matures and work toward that goal.

Negotiations

> Whether you buy or not, you can still haggle.
> —Ukrainian proverb

Other people, Ukrainians believe, do not take them seriously, especially Russians. Ukrainian sensitivity with regard to Russians may be exaggerated but it can spill over into negotiations with the West. In business and professional meetings, Ukrainians will be trying to decide, in their own minds, how negotiators on the other side of the table would be treating Russians in a similar situation.

At the start of negotiations, Ukrainians will dwell not on substance, but rather on their own place within the context of the issues under discussion. Their first priority will be to establish recognition of their role in the negotiations, and the initial pleasantries will be a part of that search for status.

Ukrainians, moreover, tend to see each negotiation as a confrontation in which one side must win and the other lose. They are only beginning to understand a "win-win" situation in which both sides gain something. Uppermost in their minds is whether they will be winners or losers and whether they will be treated as equal partners.

Americans new to Ukraine may not understand this jockeying for position nor why the Ukrainians are not following the American step-by-step, substantive approach. What to do?

Let the Ukrainians take the lead in the initial pleasantries, advise experienced negotiators. Acknowledge their status and recognize them as equal partners. Agree with them, and make them feel comfortable. Make it appear as if they have established their role. When that point has been reached, proceed to the substantive negotiations.

In contractual negotiations, Ukrainians may not understand the meaning of shared burdens and responsibilities as seen by their Western partners. Ukrainians seek shared security—one side comes to the rescue of the other if it goes under. Foreign partners should emphasize the shared responsibilities and put them down on paper—not only what each side brings to the partnership but what each is responsible for and obliged to do.

Initially, Ukrainians will try to establish some handicap or disadvantage on their side which they will later seek to trade off for a concession by the opposite side, a tactic they learned from the Russians. Try to understand their concerns and address them, but have two types of concessions of your own prepared in advance in the event they will be needed—one symbolic and the other substantive—and use them as necessary.

At the end of a meeting it is customary to sign a *protokol* (memorandum of understanding) describing what has been discussed. Westerners may question why they should sign such a statement if nothing has been agreed to formally. The protokol, however, does serve as a useful record of the discussions. It has no legal status but makes people feel good by having something to sign.

The Future

> We are not a poor country; we are a young country, and an inexperienced one.
> —Leonid Kuchma, President of Ukraine

The independence euphoria of 1991 has been moderated by the realities of economic dislocations caused by the severing of traditional trade ties following the breakup of the Soviet Union. Many Ukrainians, moreover, are nostalgic for the order and stability of life in the communist era although not for the communist system. But if the economy continues to decline, Ukrainians will likely assign failure to the political system (democracy) rather than to the economic system.

Problem analysis in Ukraine, as one American has observed, is not an exercise in exploring specifics but invariably becomes holistic, looking at all of Ukraine's problems and searching for a comprehensive political solution:

> This holistic orientation probably reflects not only the gravity of the problems, but is a legacy of the Soviet period. Under communism, all problems were the domain of political action and today this perception prevails—whether economic or social, structural or procedural—most believe that there is an overarching political solution to the problems confronting the country.[18]

In the political arena a struggle is ensuing over the nation's future direction. As one team of international consultants sees it:

> ...the struggle can be defined as a pitched battle between democratic reformers and state socialists; free marketers and state central economists; and those looking westward toward European integration and those looking perhaps nostalgically eastward toward Russia and other states formerly of the Soviet Union.[19]

Despite these dichotomies, most informed observers believe that Ukraine's prospects for creating a viable unitary state are good *if* it can institute the necessary economic reforms and reconcile its diverse regions and cultures.

Defying the dire economic data, Ukraine in 1994 was

showing no evidence of crisis. The streets of Kyiv and other cities were lined with well-stocked shops, albeit far beyond the budgets of most people. Industrial behemoths were going bankrupt, but at the local level, where government control was weakest, the privatization of small and medium-sized enterprises was proceeding. City dwellers were tending their gardens, and in the countryside farmers were replacing their modest cottages with solid brick houses. This phenomenon was attributed by Kyiv journalist Oleksander Tkachenko to the stubborn mentality of Ukrainian peasants. As he explained: "We have a tendency to go ahead and build our houses and maintain our gardens no matter what the external circumstances."[20]

Ukrainians have a history of survival which disregards such "external circumstances." Many people have one or more jobs in the "grey economy," thereby avoiding tax payments, and everyone seems to have a cousin in the countryside who helps out with food. For a people who have always suffered with a patience that has become a national characteristic, today's degree of distress is relative, and life goes on.

As Ivan Marchuk has reminded us, "...hope of a better future was never dead, and indeed, it arose afresh at the very time when...there were practically no prospects of improvement."[21]

The American Connection

Close to two million Ukrainians live in the North American diaspora—some one million in the United States and a similar number in Canada. There are also substantial numbers in Poland, Britain, Australia, and Brazil. Most are members of the Ukrainian Greek Catholic Church, and their ancestral roots are in western Ukraine.

But Ukrainians were in the United States long before the mass immigration of the late nineteenth and early twentieth centuries. They fought in the Revolutionary and Civil Wars, and—you guessed it—they may also have been among the Poles (or Belarusians) whom our widely traveled Captain John Smith brought to Virginia's Jamestown Colony in 1608. Ukrainians were also among the early settlers of the colonies established by Russians in Alaska and California, and some made careers in the local politics of California and Hawaii.

Mass migration from Ukraine to the United States followed the immigration pattern of other Slavic nations, beginning in the late 1870s, largely from the poverty-stricken villages of the Austro-Hungarian Empire. Accurate figures for the early years are difficult to determine because most of the immigrants gave their birthplace as Austria or Hungary rather than Ukraine. Few came from the Ukrainian lands under Russian rule but from those Russian lands, as well as from western Ukraine and Poland, close to one million Jews arrived on U.S. shores between 1897 and 1926. Most of the Jews were listed by immigration officials as "Russians."[22]

Early Ukrainian immigrants settled in the industrial cities of Pennsylvania, New York, New Jersey, and the midwest, where they found work in coal mines, steel mills, and factories. Those who went to Canada became farmers in the western provinces. Most came to North America for socioeconomic reasons—to earn some money and return home—and many actually made two or three crossings before reaching a final decision to remain. After World War II, more than 80,000 Ukrainians came to the United States and 30,000 to Canada as displaced persons rather than return home to a communist Ukraine.

Prominent Americans of Ukrainian descent include George B. Kistiakowsky, science adviser to President Eisenhower; Igor Sikorsky, pioneer aircraft builder; Jack Palance, actor; Paul Plishka, Metropolitan Opera baritone; Andy Warhol, artist (actually, a Carpatho-Rusyn); Representatives David Bonior (Michigan), House Majority Whip in the 103d Congress, and Maurice Hinchey (New York); and Mike Ditka, former Chicago Bears coach and erstwhile TV commentator.

Ukraine lacks experience in governing a large country, and the Ukrainian diaspora has been actively assisting the new state in initiating governmental, judicial, and economic reforms, and conducting foreign relations. In the Soviet period, when decisions were made in Moscow, the development of local initiative was not encouraged. Since independence, many talented individuals from the diaspora have returned to provide assistance and participate in the rebirth of their ancestral homeland. Since they speak fluent Ukrainian, they do not need interpreters.

Many Ukrainian officials, however, feel threatened by diaspora expertise, and there have been reports of tension and petty jealousies. Despite its large numbers, and in contrast to some other East European states, the diaspora has provided no one from its ranks to fill a high position in government or academia.

---

[1] Oleksander Kulchytsky, in *Ukraine: A Concise Encyclopaedia* vol. 2 (Toronto: Univ. of Toronto Press, 1971), 952.

[2] Jurij Savyckyj, "Investigating Psychiatric Practices in Ukraine: A Personal Account," *Ukrainian Weekly* (23 May 1993).

[3] *Washington Post*, 1 April 1994.

[4] Michael Hrushevsky, *A History of Ukraine*, ed. O. J. Frederiksen, reprint (New Haven: Yale Univ. Press, 1970), 28.

[5] Martha Bohachevsky-Chomiak, in an interview with the author, 9 February 1994.

[6] Oleh Havrylyshyn, in an interview with the author, 1 July 1994.

[7] Nadia M. Diuk, *M. P. Drahomanov and the Evolution of Ukrainian Culture and Political Theory*, unpublished Dr. Phil. thesis, Faculty of Modern History, St. Anthony's College, Oxford, 1986, 85.

[8] Hrushevsky, *History of Ukraine*, 29.

[9] Zbigniew Brzezinski, "The Premature Partnership," *Foreign Affairs* 73, no. 2 (March/April 1994): 74.

306

[10] *Washington Post*, 25 January 1994.

[11] Elehie Natalie Skoczylas, "Impressions from a TDY in Ukraine, August 7-27, 1993," an informal report submitted to the United States Information Agency, Washington, D.C.

[12] Jack Nusan Porter, "Ukrainian-Jewish Relations Yesterday and Today," *Journal of Ethnic Studies* 11, no. 4 (Winter 1984): 120.

[13] Orest Subtelny, *Ukraine: A History* 2d ed. (Toronto: Univ. of Toronto Press, 1994), 297.

[14] *UCSJ Monitor* (February 1994), 1.

[15] *New York Times*, 27 August 1992.

[16] Walter Kish, in *New York Times*, 27 January 1994.

[17] Thomas M. Claflin, in *Ukrainian Weekly*, 15 May 1994.

[18] Skoczylas, "Impressions."

[19] Larry B. Hamby et al., *Project Manifest: Analyzing Political Stability in Ukraine* (McLean, VA: Booz-Allen & Hamilton Inc., 1993).

[20] *Financial Times*, 8 August 1994.

[21] Ivan Marchuk, ed., *Ukraine and Its People* (Munich: Ukrainian Free Univ. Press, 1949), 45.

[22] Much of the material on Ukrainian immigration to the United States has been drawn from *Ukraine: A Concise Encyclopaedia* vol. 2 (Toronto: Univ. of Toronto Press, 1971), 1100-21.

Appendix A

Tracing Roots

To forget one's ancestors is to be a brook without a source, a tree without a root.

—Chinese proverb

Americans seeking to trace the roots of their East European family trees will be pleasantly surprised by the opportunities now available. Archives in Eastern Europe have opened to visitors from the West, and more records are being made available every year. Travel restrictions have ended, government officials are more cooperative, and much of the research can even be done in the West without the expense of foreign travel. Genealogy, moreover, has become a veritable cottage industry, and there are scores of books and journals to provide guidance to beginners and archival institutions to render assistance. For those who are computer literate, there are software systems to help nurture their family trees.

Let's start with names. Family names that indicate noble origin pose few problems. For such families, there are books

307

on heraldry (coats of arms), centuries-old archival records, and often detailed family histories. Be aware, though, that some families, when they took surnames in the nineteenth century or earlier, chose names that were aristocratic-sounding. A high-sounding name may not always indicate noble origin.

More difficult to trace are families of peasant or Jewish origin that were known by their patronymics (e.g., Jan son of Stefan, or Samuel ben Isaac) before taking surnames in the nineteenth century or earlier. The spelling of a family name, moreover, may have been changed in the United States, at the whim of immigration officials at the port of entry or by immigrants themselves seeking to Anglicize or Americanize their names. (When an immigration official suggested to my Polish-language teacher, Ludwik Krzyzanowski, that he change his name, the new arrival angrily retorted that a Krzyzanowski had been a Union Army general.)

Most immigrants were reluctant to talk with their children about their Old World experiences, and the records of long-deceased ancestors may be widely dispersed and difficult to find. Second- and third-generation Americans, moreover, may not have the language skills to facilitate their genealogical research. Also, the shifting borders in Eastern Europe may make it difficult to locate an ancestral town or village on a map.

The name of a town or village may be known but not the country in which it was located when an ancestor left for the States. In our time, for example, an elderly resident of Lviv (Lemberg in German, Lwów in Polish, and Lvov in Russian), without changing residence, would have lived in turn in Austria, Poland, the Soviet Union, and Ukraine. "As late as 1900," writes John Lukacs, "there were hundreds of thousands, perhaps millions, of peasants in Austria-Hungary who did not know what their nationality was."[1]

In Hungary at the turn of the century, only 52 percent of the population was ethnic Hungarian; and from 1867-1914, only three of every ten emigrants from Hungary were Magyars.

In 1900, moreover, many of the states of today's Eastern Europe simply did not exist. How to trace the Poles, Ukrainians, Balts, Czechs, Slovaks, Croats, and others who lived in those lands?

Moreover, immigrants from Eastern Europe arriving at Ellis Island at the turn of the century knew what church they worshiped at but did not always know the name of the language they spoke. In many nations, it was simply called "the local" language (e.g., *tutejszy*, in Polish or Ukrainian). Was someone from the southern slopes of the Tatra Mountains a Slovak, Hungarian, or Ruthenian? Was a resident of western Ukraine a Ukrainian, Pole, or Austrian? Was an immigrant from Poland, a state that did not exist at the turn of the century, a Russian, German, Austrian, Lithuanian, Belarusian, or Pole?

Fortunately, all of these handicaps to tracing family roots can be overcome—with persistence, patience, ingenuity, and, at times, a little luck.

How to Start

Begin the easy way, by reading. There are many good books and periodicals on genealogy these days, written in response to public demand for professional advice on tracing roots, especially in Eastern Europe now that genealogy research is possible there. The books and periodicals listed here in Appendix B, "Recommended Readings," all provide useful material, but the more recent publications are likely to be more up-to-date on Eastern Europe. Periodicals and newsletters will be the most up-to-date.

Especially strong on Eastern Europe and Russia is *Avotaynu: The International Review of Jewish Genealogy.* Although written primarily for Jewish readers, this respected quarterly publishes articles with current information useful to all persons who are searching roots in Eastern Europe. *Avotaynu's* Winter 1993 issue (vol. 9, no. 4), for example, has articles on archival access in Belarus, Hungary, Poland, Slovakia, and Ukraine.

Collect what you can from family members. Old trunks in attics often reveal much that is useful—documents, letters, and memorabilia that provide clues to family roots in America and the Old Country. Older family members can contribute oral history; interview them, and write it all down or record it before their memories become clouded with time. Other clues may be found in family legends, traditions, songs, proverbs, folk art, snatches of a foreign language, and holidays that are celebrated.

Material that may be available in the United States includes vital statistics (birth, marriage, and death certificates), church records, newspaper obituaries, city directories, wills and deeds, school records, and immigration and naturalization documents. Birth and death certificates list names of parents, which will bring you another generation closer to your roots. Other documents that can be researched locally concern court proceedings, land use, taxation, business, and medical and school records.

Join a genealogical society. There are many such societies for ethnic groups, and some have branch chapters in cities across the country. They publish newsletters, hold seminars, maintain libraries, and can help with approaches to the archives and institutions that may have information on your family roots.

Next, broaden your search to include archival material not available locally but still in the United States. This might include ship passenger arrival lists, declarations of intention and petitions of naturalization, census entries, military service records, and others. Many of these records are available at the National Archives.

National Archives

The National Archives is a virtual treasure trove of information on persons listed in U.S. government records. These include ship passenger arrival lists, census records, military service and pension files, land records, and many other documents of interest to genealogists. Preserved on microfilm, they can be accessed without cost at the National Archives Building in Washington, D.C., located on Pennsylvania Avenue, between Seventh and Ninth Streets, N.W. The mail address is National Archives and Records Administration, Washington, DC 20408.

National Archives records may also be accessed at the Regional Archives in Waltham and Pittsfield, Mass.; New York; Philadelphia; East Point, Georgia; Chicago; Kansas City, Missouri; Fort Worth; Denver; Laguna Niguel and San Bruno, Calif.; Seattle; and Anchorage. Consult a local phone book for the address. In addition, all National Archives microfilm files are available at the Mormon Family History Centers (see below).

A comprehensive guide to the National Archives' holdings and how to use them, directly or by mail, is the *Guide to Genealogical Research in the National Archives*, published by the Archives in 1985 in a revised edition, and available for $15 in softcover, $25 in hardcover. Also useful for beginners, and available without cost, are the National Archives "General Information" leaflets. Among these are *Getting Started, Beginning Your Genealogical Research in the National Archives in Washington; Aids for Genealogical Research; Using Records in the National Archives for Genealogical Research; Military Service Records in the National Archives;* and *The Regional Archives System of the National Archives.* These leaflets and others may be obtained by writing to the National Archives or one of the Regional Archives.

Passenger lists of people arriving in the United States from 1800 to 1957 are available at the Archives, and many of these lists are indexed by name. Ship passenger lists often include name, age, occupation, place of birth, place of last residence in Europe, and destination in the United States. To obtain a list, however, you must know the name of the ship and its date and port of arrival—information that many immigrants seem to remember or have recorded somewhere—as well as the full name the ancestor used when immigrating and approximate age on immigrating. If this information is not available, the ship name and information on the immigrant may be listed on two naturalization documents, the Declaration of Intention (also known as "first papers") and the Final Petition for Naturalization.

If immigration document originals cannot be located, copies can be obtained. The Regional Archives often have the federal court naturalization records, so if you know the court and the approximate date of naturalization, check with the appropriate Regional Archive first. If that doesn't work, try the Immigration and Naturalization Service, although you may have to wait up to three years for your copy. For persons naturalized on or after September 26, 1906, write to the U.S. Immigration and Naturalization Service, Washington, DC 20536, and request a copy of Form G-641, Application for Verification of Information. Prior to September 26, 1906, naturalizations were done locally at federal, state, or local courts, and it may be necessary to search court records in the area where the immigrant lived on the date of naturalization, which can be time-consuming. A good guide to naturalization search is James C. and Lila Lee Neagles's *Locating Your Immigrant Ancestors: A Guide to Naturalization Records*.

If the name of the ship and arrival date are known, you should consult the *Morton Allan Directory of European Passenger Steamship Arrivals*, a standard reference work that can be found in most large libraries. The directory lists all steamship arrivals in New York between 1890 and 1930, and in Baltimore, Boston, and Philadelphia between 1904 and 1926.

For Canadians, similar services, and more, are provided by the National Archives of Canada. The Canadian Archives has a broad mandate that authorizes collection of whatever is of national significance, from individuals and the private sector as well as government agencies. In addition to passenger lists for arrivals at Canadian ports, land patents, and census, military, and other government records, the Archives has collections on and from Canada's various ethnic groups. Especially valuable for genealogical research are the official records of the Imperial Russian Consulate General in Montreal to the year 1921, which contain information on immigrants from the lands of Imperial Russia. This collection, titled Li-Ra-Ma after three Russian consuls general, holds personal files of varying extent on some 14,000 individuals. There is also information on cross-border movements—immigrants who first arrived in either Canada or the United States and then migrated to the other country. The staff is able to help with individual requests, and the address is Genealogical Service, Manuscript Division, National Archives of Canada, 395 Wellington Street, Ottawa K1A 0N3, Ontario, Canada; (613) 995-5138.

Library of Congress

The Library of Congress in Washington, D.C. has an extensive collection of books on Russia and Eastern Europe and is a rich resource for genealogical research. Your first stop should be the Local History and Genealogy Reading Room, located on the first floor of the Jefferson (main) Building. Other "musts" to visit are the Main Reading Room and European Reading Room (Jefferson Building), the Geography and Map Reading Room (Madison Building), and, for Jewish genealogy, the Hebraic Room (Adams Building). The staff is informed and helpful but cannot do the research for you. Books may not be borrowed but there are copying machines, and the new computerized catalogue and old card catalogue are available to all. The Library Main Building is at First Street and Independence Avenue, S.E., directly across from the Capitol, and the two other buildings are adjacent.

Mormon Church Archives

Another source for ship passenger lists and much more on Eastern Europe is the Church of Jesus Christ of Latter-Day Saints (Mormon). Genealogy is important to Mormons, and in Eastern Europe they are currently working in most countries, filming census and communal records, and other items of interest to genealogists. This work may take years to complete but the filmed material is entered in the catalogue as soon as it is received. The church is unable to service telephone requests, but its archives are open to the public and may be accessed at Salt Lake City or one of the church's family history centers near your place of residence. The Mormon central agency for genealogy research is the Genealogical Society of Utah, located at 50 East North Temple Street, Salt Lake City, UT 84150. Family history centers are listed in local phone directories under Church of Jesus Christ of Latter-Day Saints.

The Mormons also have ship passenger lists from 1850 to 1934 for the port of Hamburg, a common port of debarkation for emigrés from Eastern Europe. The Hamburg lists are on microfilm in Salt Lake City and may be accessed directly or through the family history centers as described above.

Jewish holdings of the Mormon library are extensive and include census, synagogue, and communal records as well as lists of East European shtetls (towns) and countries in which they are located. Alternatively, Gary Mokotoff's and Sallyann Amdur Sack's *Where Once We Walked: A Guide to the Jewish Communities Destroyed in the Holocaust* lists more than 21,000 Jewish shtetls with their exact geographic location. Because the same town or village usually had different names and spellings in several languages—Russian, Belarusian, Ukrainian, Polish, or Yiddish—the guide also provides the alternative names and spellings. If you know the name of a town but not where it is located, these are the places to look.

Other Archival Resources

The Immigration History Research Center (IHRC) of the University of Minnesota is one of the nation's leading archival/library repositories of source material on immigration and ethnicity. Located in St. Paul, Minnesota, IHRC collects and makes available for research the records of twenty-four ethnic groups, including all of those covered in this book.

IHRC's collections include 25,000 books and pamphlets, more than 3,000 serial titles, and over 900 newspaper titles of ethnic presses in the United States and Canada from the late nineteenth century to the present. Typical collection items include personal papers of community leaders, clergymen, journalists, and educators, and records of fraternal organizations, immigrant service agencies, and publishing companies. The materials do not circulate but many items are available on interlibrary loan. The address is 826 Berry St., St. Paul, MN 55114; (612) 627-4208.

The YIVO Institute for Jewish Research in New York City has extensive materials on Eastern European Jewry, including detailed records from more than 800 *Landsmanschaftn* (societies of people from various geographic localities) as well as genealogies and family histories. Most of the material is in Yiddish, Hebrew, Polish, or Russian, and translation services are not provided. However, an English-language guide to the Landsmanschaftn Archive is available, and individuals are listed in a card catalogue. The address is 1048 Fifth Avenue, New York, NY 10028; (212) 535-6700.

The United States Holocaust Memorial Museum has rich archival materials collected in Eastern Europe, Germany, and Russia. A valuable resource for persons tracing their family histories is the museum's collection of *yizkor* (memorial) books that preserve the memory of the families and cultural life of towns destroyed in the Holocaust. The address is United States Holocaust Research Institute, United States Holocaust Memorial Museum, 100 Raoul Wallenberg Place, S.W.,

Washington, DC 20024-2150; (202) 488-6115, fax (202) 479-9726.

Israel's Yad Vashem Martyrs' and Heroes' Remembrance Authority also has the yizkor books for more than six hundred East European shtetls as well as extensive files on Holocaust victims and a duplicate file of Holocaust survivors. Mail inquiries are not possible but personal research or research by Israeli genealogists is permitted. Written requests for information on individuals may be sent to Yad Vashem, Har Hazikaron, PO Box 3477, Jerusalem, Israel.

The original file of Holocaust survivors is maintained by the International Tracing Service of the Red Cross, located in Arolsen, Germany. While its primary mission is to reunite families and supply information related to restitution and other legal claims, requests regarding family members may be submitted through your local Red Cross Chapter or by calling 1-800-848-9277. Because of the many requests and the limited staff, replies may take up to two years.

Research in Eastern Europe

For those who are able to travel to Eastern Europe, a gold mine of material is available at state and local archives, churches, and cemeteries. Despite the destruction of World War II and the shifting of borders, a surprising amount of information on family roots may be obtained by resolute researchers who have the requisite language capabilities or are willing to hire an interpreter and guide.

Before planning a trip to Eastern Europe, check to see what information may be obtained from East European embassies in Washington, D.C. For a nominal fee, these embassies will provide copies of certificates of birth, marriage, and death if the full name of the person(s) and the towns and counties in which they lived are known. Address inquiries to the Consular Section of the particular embassy.

In many countries, civil vital records were maintained by

church parishes before local governments took over the function. The year of transfer for this responsibility varies from country to country, but chances are that the older a record is, the more likely it will be found in a church parish. Church records will include data on births, baptisms, marriages, and burials.

Documents from the Russian Empire and the Soviet Union are more difficult to obtain because of the bureaucratic confusion in Russia today as well as the more widespread destruction of records there during World War II. American citizens seeking Russian documents should write to the Consular Section, American Embassy Moscow, Department of State, Washington, DC 20521, and request the information sheet and order form used to obtain copies of public records in Russia. A modest fee is charged for each application. However, the process may take up to one year, and the result of the search may be negative. For Ukraine and the Baltic states, write to the Consular Section of the appropriate U.S. embassy at the Department of State address.

Archives, both national and local, are treasure troves of information for genealogical research. In cities that were not destroyed, local archives will have birth, marriage, and death certificates. Some will also have census returns, emigration records, voting lists, and records of tax payments, land use, and military service, some of them dating from the 1700s.

For veterans of the Austrian army, the military records in Vienna may have useful information. For the period 1740-1820, the Vienna records list the names of soldiers and officers, their place of birth, age, religion, occupation, and marital status. For the period 1820-1918, the records provide enlistment orders, birth dates, and names of parents. For enlisted men, you must know the name of the regiment. Regiments were stationed throughout the Austrian Empire and recruited locally, so if you know where your ancestor lived and when he served, the name of the regiment will follow. The address is Austrian State Archives, Nottendorfergasse 2, 1030 Vienna, Austria; the telephone is 786641.

Professional genealogists can help, for a price of course, but their work can be uneven and costly. Those who come recommended by reputable institutions and journals are responsible but others may be rip-offs, and it is prudent to check first with someone you know who has used a professional. More productive results, and at much lower cost, may be had by hiring a local researcher yourself or requesting an archive to do the search and pay its fee. Dollars open doors in Eastern Europe, and a few dollars will go a long way.

In any event, try to visit your ancestral town and village. Even if you find nothing, you will have immense satisfaction knowing that you have walked the same streets your ancestors walked generations before you.

---

[1] John Lukacs, *Budapest 1900*, 127.

Appendix B

Recommended Readings

General

Ian Bremmer and Ray Taras, eds. *Nations and Politics in the Soviet Successor States.* New York: Cambridge Univ. Press, 1993.

David Crowe and John Holsti. *Gypsies in Eastern Europe.* Amonk, NY: M.E. Sharpe, 1991.

Nadia M. Diuk and Adrian Karatnycky. *New Nations Rising.* New York: John Wiley, 1993.

Eva Hoffman. *Exit into History: A Journey through the New Eastern Europe.* New York: Viking Penguin, 1993.

Dennis P. Hupchick. *Culture and History in Eastern Europe.* New York: St. Martin's Press, 1994.

Robert D. Kaplan. *Balkan Ghosts: A Journey through History.* New York: Vintage Departures, 1994.

Flora Lewis. *Europe: Road to Unity,* rev. ed. New York: Touchstone, Simon and Schuster, 1992.

Paul Robert Magocsi. *Historical Atlas of East Central Europe.* Vol. 1. Seattle: Univ. of Washington Press, 1993.

Andrew Nagorski. *The Birth of Freedom.* New York: Simon and Schuster, 1993.

Joseph Rothschild. *Return to Diversity: A Political History of East Central Europe Since World War II.* 2d ed. New York: Oxford Univ. Press, 1993.

Vladimir Tismaneanu. *Reinventing Politics: Eastern Europe from Stalin to Havel.* New York: Free Press, 1993.

Piotr S. Wandycz. *The Price of Freedom: A History of East Central Europe from the Middle Ages to the Present.* New York: Routledge, 1992.

Albania

Elez Biberaj. *Albania: A Socialist Maverick.* Boulder, CO: Westview Press, 1990.

———. "Albania's Road to Democracy." *Current History* 92, no. 577 (November 1993).

Edith Durham. *High Albania.* First published 1909. Boston: Beacon Press, 1987.

Shtjefen Gjecov, ed. *Kanuni I Leke Dukagjinit* (The Code of Leke Dukagjini). Translated by Leonard Fox. (Albanian text with parallel English translation). New York: Gjonlekaj, 1989.

Margaret Hasluck. *The Unwritten Law in Albania.* Cambridge, England: Univ. Press, 1954.

Ismail Kadare. *The General of the Dead Army,* and other novels. Franklin, NY: New Amsterdam Books.

The Balts

The Baltic States: A Reference Book. Tallinn, Riga, and Vilnius: Encyclopedia Publishers, 1991.

Anatol Lieven. *The Baltic Revolution: Estonia, Latvia, and Lithuania and the Path to Independence.* New Haven: Yale Univ. Press, 1994.

Rein Taagepera. *Estonia: Return to Independence*. Boulder, CO: Westview Press, 1993.

V. Stanley Vardys. *Lithuania: A Rebel Nation*. Boulder, CO: Westview Press, 1994.

Belarus

Nicholas P. Vakar. *Belorussia: The Making of a Nation*. Cambridge: Harvard Univ. Press, 1956.

Jan Zaprudnik. *Belarus: At a Crossroads in History*. Boulder, CO: Westview Press, 1993.

Bulgaria

R. J. Crampton. *A Short History of Modern Bulgaria*. New York: Cambridge Univ. Press, 1987.

Ivan Vazov. *Under the Yoke*. New York: Twayne, 1971.

Czechs and Slovaks

Jaroslav Hasek. *The Good Soldier Svejk*. New York: Penguin, 1983.

Josef Korbel. *Twentieth-Century Czechoslovakia: The Meaning of Its History*. New York: Columbia Univ. Press, 1977.

Eugen Steiner. *The Slovak Dilemma*. Cambridge, England: Cambridge Univ. Press, 1973.

Hungary

John Lukacs. *Budapest 1900: A Historical Portrait of a City and Its Culture*. New York: Grove Weidenfeld, 1988.

Peter F. Sugar, ed. *A History of Hungary*. Bloomington: Indiana Univ. Press, 1994.

Poland

Neal Ascherson. *The Struggles for Poland.* New York: Random House, 1987.

Norman Davies. *Heart of Europe: A Short History of Poland.* New York: Oxford Univ. Press, 1986.

Laura Klos-Sokol. *Speaking Volumes about Poles.* Warsaw, Poland: IPS Wydawnictwo, 1994.

Adam Zamoyski. *The Polish Way: A Thousand-Year History of the Poles and Their Culture.* New York: Hippocrene Books, 1994.

Romania

Andrei Codrescu. *The Hole in the Flag.* New York: Avon Books, 1991.

Vlad Georgescu. *The Romanians: A History.* Edited by Matei Calinescu, translated by Alexandra Bley-Vroman. Columbus: Ohio State Univ. Press, 1991.

Ukraine

Martha Bohachevsky-Chomiak. *Feminists Despite Themselves: Women in Ukrainian Community Life, 1884-1939.* Edmonton: Canadian Institute of Ukrainian Studies, 1988.

Michael F. Hamm. *Kiev: A Portrait, 1800-1917.* Princeton: Princeton Univ. Press, 1993.

Peter J. Potichnyj and Marc Raeff. *Ukraine and Russia.* Edmonton: Canadian Institute of Ukrainian Studies, 1992.

Orest Subtelny. *Ukraine: A History,* 2d ed. Toronto: Univ. of Toronto Press, 1994.

Yugoslavia

Ivo Banac. *The National Question in Yugoslavia.* Ithaca: Cornell Univ. Press, 1984.

Bogdan Denitch. *Ethnic Nationalism: The Tragic Death of Yugoslavia.* Minneapolis: Univ. of Minnesota Press, 1994.

Milovan Djilas. *Land without Justice.* New York: Harcourt, Brace, 1958.

Dusko Doder. *The Yugoslavs.* New York: Random House, 1978.

Alex N. Dragnich. *Serbs and Croats, The Struggle in Yugoslavia.* New York: Harcourt, Brace, Jovanovich, 1992.

Brian Hall. *The Impossible Country: A Journey through the Last Days of Yugoslavia.* Boston: David R. Godine, 1994.

Trpimir Macan and Josip Sentija. *A Short History of Croatia.* Zagreb: Most, 1992.

Noel Malcolm. *Bosnia: A Short History.* New York: New York Univ. Press, 1994.

Rebecca West. *Black Lamb and Grey Falcon: The Record of a Journey through Jugoslavia in 1937.* 2 vols. New York: Viking Penguin, 1982.

Tracing Roots

Avotaynu: The International Review of Jewish Genealogy quarterly. Teaneck, NJ: Jewish Genealogical Society.

Angus Baxter. *In Search of Your European Roots: A Complete Guide.* Baltimore: Genealogical Publishing, 1992.

Alexander Beider. *A Dictionary of Jewish Surnames from the Russian Empire.* Teaneck, NJ: Avotaynu, 1993.

Edward Reimer Brandt. *Content and Addresses of Hungarian Archives,* 2nd annotated ed. Baltimore: Genealogical Publishing, 1993.

Gilbert H. Doane and James B. Bell. *Searching for Your Ancestors: The How and Why of Genealogy,* 6th ed. Minneapolis: Univ. of Minnesota Press, 1992.

Patricia Kennedy Grimsted. *Archives and Manuscript Repositories in the USSR: Estonia, Latvia, Lithuania and Belorussia.* Princeton: Princeton Univ. Press, 1981.

324

————. *Archives and Manuscript Repositories in the USSR: Ukraine and Moldavia.* Princeton: Princeton Univ. Press, 1988.

John-Paul Himka and Frances A. Swyripa. *Sources for Researching Ukrainian Family History.* Edmonton: Canadian Institute of Ukrainian Studies, 1984.

J. Konrad. *Polish Family Research.* Munroe Falls, OH: Summit Publications, 1977.

Arthur Kurzweil. *From Generation to Generation: How to Trace Your Genealogy and Personal History.* New York: William Morrow, 1980.

Benedict Markowski. *An Annotated Guide and Topical Listing of Aids to Polish Genealogy.* Detroit: Detroit Public Library, 1984.

Gary Mokotoff and Sallyann Amdur Sack. *Where Once We Walked: A Guide to the Jewish Communities Destroyed in the Holocaust.* Teaneck, NJ: Avotaynu, 1991.

Morton Allan Directory of European Passenger Steamship Arrivals for the Years 1890 to 1930 at the Port of New York and for the Years 1904 to 1926 at the Ports of New York, Philadelphia, Boston, and Baltimore. Reprint of the 1931 ed. Baltimore: Genealogical Publishing, 1979.

James C. and Lila Lee Neagles. *Locating Your Immigrant Ancestors: A Guide to Naturalization Records.* Logan, UT: Everton Publishers, 1975.

Dan Rottenberg. *Finding Our Fathers: A Guidebook to Jewish Genealogy.* New York: Random House, 1977.

Sallyann Amdur Sack. *Guide to Jewish Genealogical Research in Israel.* Teaneck, NJ: Avotaynu, 1994.

Daniel M. Schlyter. *A Handbook of Czechoslovak Genealogical Research.* Buffalo Grove, IL: Genun Publishers, 1985.

Jared H. Suess. *Handy Guide to Hungarian Genealogical Research.* Logan, UT: Everton Publishers, 1980.

Michael Tepper. *American Passenger Arrival Records: A Guide to the Records of Immigrants Arriving at American Ports by Sail and Steam.* Updated and enlarged. Baltimore: Genealogical Publishing, 1993.

Index